Talking Blue

Talking Blue

A collection of candid interviews with
Everton heroes

by Becky Tallentire

breedon books
PUBLISHING

First published in Great Britain by
The Breedon Books Publishing Company Limited
Breedon House, 3 The Parker Centre, Derby, DE21 4SZ. 2000

ISBN 1 85983 209 1

Printed and bound by Butler & Tanner Ltd., Selwood Printing Works,
Caxton Road, Frome, Somerset.

Colour separations and jacket printing by
GreenShires Group Ltd., Leicester.

Contents

Foreword 7

Introduction and Acknowledgements 9

They Asked the Questions...

Alan Ball 28

Paul Bracewell 37

Martin Dobson 43

Andy Gray 52

Adrian Heath 69

Howard Kendall .78

Brian Labone 96

Duncan McKenzie 106

Derek Mountfield 119

Joe Parkinson 128

Graeme Sharp .133

Kevin Sheedy 141

Neville Southall 151

Gary Stevens 162

Alex Young 171

Index 184

Dedicated to my nieces,
Georgia Robyn and
Arabella Star
May you grow into
splendid and successful
women

Foreword
by Howard
Kendall

WHEN I was approached to give an interview for this book, I didn't hesitate. The concept of the supporters asking the questions was so original and exciting, if not a little nerve wracking, and reading through the resulting chapters it would seem that all the players felt the same way. It pleases me to see that their responses have all been so heartfelt and honest, and I believe this to be a measure of Becky's skill as an interviewer.

When I returned as manager for the third time, Becky was covering Everton for L!VE TV. As you can probably imagine, I've dealt with a lot of press in my time, but as a reporter, she stood out from the crowd with her relaxed and unique style. She has a great talent of putting people at their ease and I could guarantee that her questions would be searching, well researched and honest. I respected Becky on a professional level because she'd always done her homework and never failed to make me laugh.

Talking Blue is an insight into the lives and personalities of our boys in blue and an absolute 'must have' for every fan. It's lovely to think there are people all over the world who, despite their distance from Goodison Park, follow Everton Football Club with such gusto. The loyalty of Evertonians is unsurpassed and as I was invited to write this foreword, I now have a perfect opportunity to pass on a message.

Many thanks for your tremendous support over my 17 years as player and manager at Everton Football Club. Evertonians are the most loyal and dedicated fans in the land, and will always remain close to my heart.

Enjoy your book – I'm sure you will.

Introduction and Acknowledgements

IT IS with great pride and a touch of mental exhaustion that I finally draw to the close of my first book. It goes without saying that throughout this project, I've had magnificent support from a number of people and I'm delighted to take this opportunity to thank them for that.

This is in no particular order: Billy Williams, my proofreader, for your astonishing tolerance with my ignorance of statistics and commas; Paul Tollet for providing me with the finest computer software, but sadly not the ability to utilise it properly – remember TCK? Pearls in front of swine, and all that! Big Neville Southall for your help and guidance in the uncharted waters of the book-publishing world; Kenny Fogarty, Patchie, Stoo Roberts, Jon Gard and Colin Berry for never failing to make me guffaw; Michael Dunford for your tremendous encouragement and support which was deeply appreciated; Steve Allinson for supplying me with endless fags, lifts, drinks and laughs; Howard Kendall for your unswerving belief in my ability; members of the Evertonia and Bluenose mailing lists, whose astounding recall of bygone events and absurd trivia led directly to my idea for the book. Thank you for sharing your profound knowledge with me and I'm sorry for being so bossy; Perelandra Blanche and Louise Irving, for being my two dearest friends and such massive influences in my life – without you I am nothing; Anton Rippon, my publisher, for believing in me and giving me my first break; Ste Barr – Liverpool's finest – you made me forget myself; Ian Ross for allowing me to peak into your bulging contact book; John O' Kane, you know what for; Les Anderson for letting me plagiarise your title. I hope you'll agree it looks rather splendid; Mark Tallentire, my big brother, I wouldn't have known anything at all about Everton if it hadn't been for trying to make you like me; you were my hero. Lynne Hudson and Neil Bent, my lovely sponsors from One 2 One. Thank you for backing me. I told you it would be great and I knew I was right; Kenny Myers – there is no conspiracy! Mum and George, you really shouldn't still have to be looking after me but I'm so glad you do. Sorry it took me so long, Mum, I always was a bit of a slow starter.

And if you've read this far, you might also like to know that on a personal level every player between these covers was nothing short of fantastic and I'd like to thank them all for their co-operation and time. As you read through this book, you will see that some of the questions are 'curve balls' and they, like all the others, were asked as written. Not one man took offence or even raised an eyebrow; they just answered their questions in the spirit which was intended.

In return for their honesty, I feel a few ghosts have been laid to rest and we have been gifted with a rare insight into these men, not only as Royal Blue heroes, but also as people with emotions, imperfections, anxieties and feelings.

Sleep well in your beds tonight, my Bluenosed friends, for none of your idols has feet of clay.

Evertonians are born, not manufactured.
We do not choose, we are chosen.
Those who understand, need no explanation,
those who don't...don't matter.

Goodison For Everton

They Asked the Questions

Here listed in alphabetical order are the 100 and more Everton supporters who posed the questions which were answered in such forthright manner by our Blue Boys.

Stuart Ainsworth was an Evertonian from an early age thanks to his dad who, despite marrying into a rabid RS family, was determined that his sons and daughters would be raised in the true faith. Brought up in Southport but now living in Basingstoke, Stu shook the hand of Andy Gray in his local a few years ago.

Les Anderson looks like the scary bloke in the Ben Sherman advertisement. His finest day as a Blue was hitching to London for the 1984 Cup Final, getting in for a quid and then getting home on the special for nothing. His hero is The Latch and he can't stand Emlyn Hughes.

Vince Balfe from Wicklow, Ireland, has a young Blues fanatical son and now makes the pilgrimage to Goodison Park once or twice a season. His finest hour was the European Cup-winners' Cup in 1987 – sheer brilliance, he says.

Jon Berman has spent 35 years watching his beloved Everton. One of the writers of *Everton Greats – Where Are They Now?*, he is married with two daughters and spends his spare time trying to convince them that Everton are better than shopping. His favourite player ever is Alan Ball.

Colin Berry has been Blue for longer than he can remember in spite of his grandad taking him to watch Phil Thompson's testimonial. Col lives in Liverpool, works in the computer games industry and once met Neville Southall on the beach while on holiday in Llandudno.

Clive Blackmore was born in Crosby but now works in Washington DC as information officer for Worldbank. He almost bummed a fag from Johnny Morrissey in a bar one night then bottled out at the last minute, but definitely met Bob Latchford at Hightown Squash club.

Rob Bland has been an Everton fan since he was mesmerized by the mercurial skill of Duncan McKenzie on Gerald Sinstadt's *Kick-Off* in the 1970s. Seldom seen without some form of Everton attire, Rob comes from Morecambe and used to run the unofficial Everton website *Feelings Blue*.

Ian Bonnar was an Evertonian from birth, for which he is forever grateful to his father. He grew up in Formby and had to endure the Colin Harvey years at high school. A season ticket holder for many years, he had to give it up when he moved to London. Ian is now a journalist and web-developer for an American Internet company and lives in the shadow of Upton Park.

Phil Bowker is from a rugby league family and watched the 1968 FA Cup Final to see what football was all about. Because he was only eight, he thought 'Bromwich' was a stupid word, so naturally became an Everton supporter. Such logic typifies all the work he's done in the IT industry since 1979, hence the need to keep moving. He is living in Brussels this year, or at least until he gets rumbled.

Simon Bradley lives in Wirral and doesn't mind admitting that is capable of filling up when he hears the *Z-Cars* theme. He has been going to the match for over 30 years, although he missed the bulk of Saturdays in the glory years because of his own (non-glory) playing days. Simon has returned to being a season ticket holder since his eldest son has been of an age to sway arguments with The Enemy (wife).

Charlie Brewer is based in Seoul, South Korea, and runs a banking and finance IT consultancy. He was indoctrinated from an early age and could recite the Everton team with positions and main characteristic from the age of three – much to the amusement of his dad's mates.

Mike Burke is a London-based barrister and has supported Everton since his first gasp of air. His darkest day was when the forces of evil triumphed and the heavens rent – Everton 0 Liverpool 5. His finest hour was when God smiled down on this sceptred isle – Spurs 1 Everton 2 in 1985.

Simon Burke is a silver-tongued, trumpet-playing, idle layabout, occasionally earning a living as musician. Originally from Rossendale but now residing in Toxteth, Simon looks a bit like a haggard version of David O'Leary.

Dave Cairns went to his first game against LFC with his Uncle, a die-hard Red. Giddy with the sheer magic of the occasion, Dave was hypnotised by both Alan Ball's white boots and his goal – we won 1-0. And so it began. Unlucky, Uncle Terry.

David Catton moved away from his home city as an 18-year-old in 1962. Nowadays he goes back mostly to watch Everton – as he's done through thick and thin for almost 50 years. David is managing director of Sheffield University Enterprises Limited, overseeing the transfer of technology from the University's research labs into the commercial marketplace.

Ian Chaderton is originally from Bootle, living in Berkshire and working as an IT auditor. A season ticket holder in the Park End, he once presented Graeme Sharp with the Sheffield University EFC Supporters Club player of the year on the pitch before a game. His magic moment was the mass pitch invasion at Highbury when Inchy scored in the semi-final.

Paul Christopherson lives in Nottingham and works as a design engineer for packaging machinery firm. Fortunately, his first match was EFC 6 Chelsea 0 when Bob Latchford scored the fourth and sixth to achieve his 30 goals for the season. Vows were made that day, for better or for worse, and so began the addiction.

David Chow (Pronounced Daveed – the French way.) Born in Hong Kong, but currently studying building environmental engineering at UMIST. David has supported Everton since arriving in England in 1985 and is a season ticket holder in the Lower Gwladys Street. His hero is Neville Southall.

Andy Clarke is an IT consultant living in Essex with his wife and two boys. Converted to the blue faith by his Godfather who stood on the Street End in the 1950s, his first match was a 2-0 victory over Stoke City in January 1973, aged nine.

Pete Clarke moved south in 1992. He lives in Hertfordshire and works in North London as a school bursar. His first game was Everton 1 Liverpool 0 when Andy King scored.

Jim Conboy is a life long Evertonian who met his wife on the ESCLA train to Ipswich in December 1984 (we won 2-0). His worst moment was being in the boys' pen at Anfield watching them murder us 5-0 sometime in the 1960s and his most imminent project is to discover just how many Evertonians there are living in Hesketh Bank.

Iain Cooke is a computer programmer for the Bank For International Settlements in Basel, Switzerland. Born in China, he became an

Evertonian when he first visited the UK in 1976, because his older brother was a rabid RS supporter and he just wanted to annoy him. He soon realised it was his calling.

Michael W. Coville lives near New York but manages to get back once or twice a season to watch his Blueboys. His magic moment was 14 February 1953, watching Dave Hickson, with blood pouring down his face, score the winner against Man United. His most treasured possession is a framed set of old cigarette cards featuring Warney Cresswell, Joe Mercer, Cliff Britton, Tommy Lawton, Sam Chedgzoy and Dixie Dean.

Ste Daley is from Speke on Merseyside. He once spent a whole day taking photos of himself in the 'Whistling Dixie' mascot outfit, after finding an unlocked door during a pre-season.

Gary Davis is an astrophysicist and professor of physics at the University of Saskatchewan, Canada. When he adopted the Blues in 1984 he didn't realise that it would become an endurance trial of Herculean proportions. A frequent visitor to the UK and Goodison Park, his claim to fame is doing unspeakable things to Kenny Myers' hotel room.

Tommy Davis spent his honeymoon watching EFC in the 1989 Cup Final. Born and raised in Walton, he migrated to Texas in 1978 and is self employed, selling packaging products. He still gets to see his beloved Blues at least once or twice a year.

Charlie Deeney first saw the beautiful Blue light in 1962-63. Born in Derry, his arrival on Merseyside to study at Liverpool University coincided with Everton's curious and painful descent, so he selflessly migrated to Canada in 1977. During one of his infrequent return visits home, Charlie managed to squeeze in the 2-0 victory over QPR in May 1985. He lives in Ottawa and works as a sales consultant.

Michael Dudley was born in Liverpool in 1957. He first sat on a crowd barrier in the old Goodison Road ground section with his dad; a season ticket holder who has been watching Everton since he saw William Ralph score his 60th. Michael missed all the good stuff in the 1980s when he moved to the States to become a professor but is now more fanatical than ever, keeping in touch via the Internet and through regular phone calls to his good old dad.

Adrian Evans once got offered a trial for Everton as a goalkeeper but then got run over. An ex-roadie and biker, he has supported Everton since 1964, aged six. He now lives in Middlesex and works as a senior software developer.

Steve Fairclough was born and raised in Wallasey but moved to Toronto in 1982. His greatest time as a Blue was when he returned to live in the UK (for 18 months) and got to witness, first hand, the 1986-87 season. His therapist agrees that this helped rid him of the trauma of living through the 1970s. His all-time hero is Mick Lyons.

Tony Field was born to shout for the Blues and vote Labour. One of his best memories was watching the Blues at Molineux when Peter Knowles thought it would be a laugh to kick Alan Ball, but gave up the game for good after getting a serious battering, simultaneously from Brian Labone and Jimmy Gabriel.

Kenny Fogarty was born in Liverpool in 1966. He departed England in 1991 in search of work and hasn't been able to get back since. He is a systems programmer at IBM Finance Systems, living in Amsterdam in his swanky new apartment and his all-time Everton hero is Neville Southall.

Ged Fox loves Bally, Latch and Sharp and hates Rod Belfitt, Bernie Wright and Clive Thomas. He moved from Liverpool to the capitalist south in 1982 to work for an investment banking and asset management company.

Jon Gard is as mad as a tree. He looks a bit like Robin Williams and is so small he can get bottles of champagne down his pants and still walk normally. Good to go to town with, Jon supports Everton but doesn't know why.

Nicholas Gard was born in Halewood but is now residing in Washington, USA. He works as a consulting ecotoxicologist (definition provided upon request) and his biggest challenge is constantly trying to explain his Everton devotion to uncomprehending Americans. His proudest accomplishment is teaching his elder daughter to say "Everton" as one of her first words.

Keith Giles is originally from Aintree but now lives in Perth, Australia. He hasn't been back to England yet as he's a student and a bit short on money these days, but stays up till all hours watching Everton on TV and wants to know if that counts?

James Goddard has been an Evertonian for 13 years, inspired by Gary Lineker being the best striker around when he was six and impressionable. His worst moment was the 1989 Cup Final with Stuart McCall scoring twice, taking it to extra time and still losing to Liverpool. A software developer working for BT, he lives in Ipswich.

Joe Hannah already had Blue blood on joining the Merchant Navy at 16. He sailed the seven seas until he fell in love with an Australian girl, jumped ship and married her. Joe has lived in Sydney for 30 years is a grandfather of five, but his first love is still Everton.

Frank Hargreaves has a recurring nightmare in which he's holding an inflatable toffee, has his face painted blue and white and applauds a Liverpool team in a European Cup Final saying: "At least it will come to the city." He's also been wondering whether it's just him who's rapidly losing interest in an over-hyped, over-priced pastime, which always made money for those in control, but never quite so blatantly.

Kevin Hazard is a process manager for a gold mining company in Indonesia. His father is a Red but was away at sea when Kevin was smuggled to Goodison by a cousin. Learning to surf at a ridiculous age he will probably die in a helicopter accident some time in the near future.

Mike Hazard cried at half-time during the Cup Final in 1966. His claim to fame is playing for Otis Elevators alongside John O'Leary who Bobby Charlton billed as the best amateur footballer he had ever seen. Mike lives in Canada and still plays regularly despite having notched up his own half-century.

Jonne Hellgren from Tornio, northern Finland, began supporting Everton after the 1986 Cup Final. He was told to watch the game, as the team in red were supposed to be really good – he rang his mate after the match and said he preferred the blue ones. Jonne moved to Manchester in 1998 to study and finally visited Anfield to witness yet another victory for the mighty Blues Boys in the same year.

Jon Hughes is 30 odd and lives in Wirral. His first game was a 1-1 with Nottingham Forest Reserves in 1970. He cried when Duncan McKenzie was sold and wept again when Mark Pembridge was bought and would like to see Everton play in royal blue shirts again before he dies.

Wayne Hughes is a consultant-business analyst working in Paris who first started going to see Everton in the 1960s. His most treasured possession is a fully autographed picture of the 1969-70 team and he invaded the pitch when big Bob scored his 30th goal. Favourite moments include Sharp's goal at Anfield, the Watford Cup Final all the other usual culprits.

Julian Jackson is head of presentation at ESPN STAR Sports, Singapore. His prize possession should be a signed menu of the Everton team circa 1976 but he ended up swapping it for the bumper book of ghost stories. His claim to fame is that a fairly famous model once dumped him because he went home for the 1995 FA Cup Final and didn't invite her.

Steve Jensen emigrated to Australia in 1987 and lives in Wamberal, 50 miles north of Sydney. He watches every live televised game despite the time difference and can't decide who his hero is between Sharpie, Andy Gray, Reid or Brace. His most treasured possession is the photograph he had taken with Alan Ball in 1997.

Colin Jones first went to Goodison in September 1971 and thought that the 8-0 thrashing of Southampton in his third game was a sign of things to come. How wrong can one person be? Colin is a season ticket holder and lives in Mossley Hill, Liverpool.

Colm Kavannagh is a newsagent in an outer suburb of Ballykissangel. His all-time Everton hero is Mike Lyons and he once had his hair cut beside Joe Royle at the barber's in Walton Vale. His best moments were full time after that Wimbledon game and Michael Thomas bringing eternal joy to Bluenoses the world over for his dagger through Kopite hearts.

Yusuf Kay is based in Singapore and is involved in expanding the fan base via the Singapore Evertonians Supporters Club. He works as an IT assistant and is studying for an advanced diploma in computer studies.

Michael Kenrick is our colonial representative in the frontier outpost of Seattle. He escaped Thatcherism just as Everton peaked and is now chief anorak and web page wizard behind *ToffeeWeb*, the greatest independent Everton website, bar none.

Mark Kenyon was born in Liverpool in 1965. His first game was at Goodison against Stoke City in 1974. We won 2-1 and Joe Royle scored them both. He moved to Minneapolis in 1999, where, among other things, he coaches under-13 boys on how not to play 'soccer' by showing them Everton videos from the last five years.

Michael Kidd is an associate professor of law at the University of Natal, South Africa. Seriously outnumbered by both Man Utd and Liverpool supporters he was often devastated at our inability to beat them in various FA Cup Finals in the 1980s, but chuffed to bits in 1995. Mike has been to Goodison Park once, in 1997, which was a very important and emotional pilgrimage but the next time he takes the trouble to visit, he hopes that we can win.

Steve Kirkwood's great-grandfather, Danny Kirkwood, was an ever-present in Everton's first championship side in 1890-91 and Steve has been watching the Blues since 1976. He lives in Brentford, West London and is a season ticket holder.

Tony Kuss left Ireland for Australia at the turn of the Millennium and has never been heard of since.

John Lloyd was born in Liverpool into a family of Blues and watched his first game at the age of four. A regular attendee at Goodison until 1963 when he left Liverpool for vocational reasons, John is now based in Scotland having worked as an academic at the University of Stirling for a number of years.

Lyndon Lloyd was born and raised in South Africa. He lived in the UK for 15 years and migrated to San Francisco in 2000. Lyndon is an implementation designer for an e-business agency and cites dancing in the centre-circle of Goodison in the pouring rain after the 1998 escape from relegation as his most memorable day as an Evertonian.

Chris Lord has been travelling to watch Everton from Blackpool since the age of seven. His greatest moments include finally witnessing Everton win a trophy in 1995, but more importantly, seeing a Sheedy 'dead ball special' with his own eyes after he had signed for Blackpool.

Jim Lynch first went to Goodison on 3 March 1962; the day that Gordon West made his debut. A leisure management consultant originally from Bootle but exiled to Essex, Jim kept a clean sheet at Wembley Stadium in the Brent Football festival and wasn't shortlisted for the Everton chief executive vacancy in 1999.

Neil McCann regularly attended matches during the glory years of the mid-1980s and still manages to get to a few games every season in spite of living in Thailand. His greatest memory was the FA Cup win in 1984 and his darkest day was losing the League title in 1986 at the Manor Ground, Oxford.

Ciaran McConville lives in Dublin and manages to get over three or four times a year depending how good the exchange rate is. His first game was Liverpool v Everton at Anfield in 1994, paid for with his first official pay cheque.

Dominic McGough is a director of a global logistics company, was born and raised in Kirkdale within earshot of Goodison Park. He exchanged Liverpool for the south in 1984 and has followed Everton since the 1969-70 season.

Ray McNamara lives in the west of Ireland in the hometown of Kevin Sheedy's ancestors. He believes that fate has made him a Blue – in the natural course of events his Scouse cousin, who used to visit his family frequently as a child, should have turned him the other way…but the Dark Side of the Force could not break him and goals by Andy Gray and Graeme Sharp against Watford at Wembley, saved his soul. Hallelujah!

Terry McWilliams named his son after his favourite player, Alan Ball. He was born in Wallasey and emigrated to Canada in 1970. A lifelong Blue, He swears he will never forget the euphoria of the 1966 Cup Final nor the utter dejection of 1968. He now lives in Ontario but spends his winters in Florida.

Richard Marland is a 37-year-old computer programmer, raised in Maghull with Gordon West as a neighbour, but now living in Waterloo, Merseyside. Richard has held a season ticket for the Upper Gwladys Street since 1985-86 (the season he finally started work).

Sid Martin was born in Walton hospital the day after the Busby Babes perished in Munich. His grandfather was a barber to the stars and Sid's claim to fame is that Alex Young once shot him in the eye with a cap gun. He now lives in Sandwich, Kent.

George Mason started watching Everton in 1957 from his vantage point in the boys' pen and was a season ticket holder for years. He has since relocated to Clearwater, Florida, where he works as a quality assurance and product certification manager.

Roy King Miaa was born in Liverpool in 1956 and moved to Norway in 1980, ostensibly for two years. His most enduring Everton memories include the 1966 FA Cup Final, which resulted in a broken toe due to his father's celebration of Temple's winner, and the European Cup-winners' Cup, which entailed a 17-hour car trip from Norway to Rotterdam. Roy spent the game standing in the rain outside the stadium, while his mates got to see it for free having been dragged in by the Everton stewards.

Dave Morris was brought up just outside Ellesmere Port, where every random bike ride as a kid ended up with a trip past Dave Hickson's house – this part of the ride was always conducted at the speed of one of those dawdles in velodrome events before they break for home. Dave's most poignant game was a humdrum 3-1 win over Sunderland in October 1982; it was his Pa's last match and the first for his son, Roland.

Ken Myers graduated through the ranks of the Gwladys Street boys' pen before leaving for California in 1971, when his feet mysteriously stopped growing. Based in Long Beach, he gets home for at least four or five games a season; his visits always include at least one of the derby matches.

Darryl Ng has been a fan since Everton wore 'those nice royal blue jerseys' in the Charity Shield of 1986. From Singapore, his first live game was a 4-1 thrashing by Aston Villa in 1998 and he has continued to show the necessary sado-masochistic nature that all good Evertonians must have, by attending several other Everton maulings since.

Michael O'Connell is a postman but he'd rather be an artist. An Everton fan since the FA Cup Final in 1968, Michael drinks Bushmills and claims to be the only Evertonian living in Galway.

Mike Owen lives in Childwall and his first match was at 0-0 draw at home to Blackburn, on Saturday, 6 April 1963, leaving a six-year-old bitterly disappointed because we had two goals disallowed. Mike never played for Everton despite writing to Alan Ball and asking for tips. Alan replied and advised him to practise, eat lots of fruit and go to bed early. Mike still practises and eats lots of fruit but rarely goes to bed early.

Jason Palmer is a tutor at Pontypridd College. His best Everton moment was listening to the Bayern game on the radio at home; the crowd were so loud he swears he could have been there. He looks like a member of the boy band Hanson and his best ever player is Kevin Ratcliffe (because he's Welsh).

Brian Parkinson was living in Doncaster but has disappeared off the face of the Earth, perhaps travelling with Tony Kuss.

Phil Pellow spent most of the 1970s and 1980s working in London and the Middle East then returned, prodigal son like, to his native Merseyside. He now works for HM Land Registry, is founder of the Everton fanzine *Satis?*, has a bald spot and a cat called Josh.

Eddie Pepper is a Southerner, but went against his natural MU supporting instincts after listening to 'that game' against Wimbledon in 1993. His claim to fame is that by yelling from his seat in Lower Bullens at exactly the wrong moment, he is responsible for Andrei Kanchelskis' worst touch in the professional game.

Marko Poutiainen is a software engineer living in Oulu, Finland. He had affection for Everton since his teens, but not until that Wimbledon game did he realise how much the club meant to him. A pioneer of Everton Internet community, Marko started the first Everton-related website and gathered the flock for the mailing lists.

San Presland's first match was EFC v Man United in 1966 and she was shocked to see it was in colour. San won loads of money on *Who Wants to be a Millionaire?*, lives in New Brighton and once had a double-page spread in the *Football Echo* when she wrote a football simulation-prediction at their request.

Paul Preston is old enough to cite Alex Young as his hero and works as a professor of contemporary Spanish history at LSE. Paul began following Everton in 1959 and his magic moments include Derek Temple's goal in the 1966 Cup Final and Danny Cadamarteri's against Liverpool in 1997-98.

John Quinn is 51, fading fast and living discreetly in Tewkesbury. His only claim to fame was that he once man-marked Tony Kay in a Business Houses match in the 1960s, just after Kay's release from prison.

Osmo Tapio Räihälä (b.1964) is a Finnish composer living in Helsinki. His life changed dramatically on the 26th of November 1977 when he was converted to an Evertonian by Bob Latchford's hat-trick. Räihälä gets inspiration for his work from Everton, this is reflected in orchestral pieces like *Hinchcliffe Thumper – tha' bloody intermezzo* and *Barlinnie Nine*.

John Reynolds is only 34, although everyone seems to think he's an aul' fella. He fled London after the Harvey years and is now resident on top of a mountain in Ireland's highest village of Roundwood, Co Wicklow, with his wife, two dogs and four cats. He still suffers from Everton addiction.

Andy Richardson's worst moment was watching the Everton team disappear in Schipol airport and boarding what would have been his flight if only he'd arrived on time. Working in computing support at BT, Andy is a biker, lives in Hackney and always arrives at The Netley looking very windswept and interesting.

Antony Richman from Johannesburg is a bank manager. Originally hailing from Birkenhead, Ant has spent 25 years off and on in South Africa. His finest moments so far have been the 1995 Cup Final (watching on telly) and the best game he attended was the 1989 semi-final.

Dave Richman migrated to South Africa in 1974 aged 13. He's now married with two children, works as a quantity surveyor and is legendary for suffering horrendous injuries playing football with the kids. Founding member of the imaginatively titled Everton FC Supporters Club of South Africa and editor of *Gwlad Tidings*, the fanzine for EFCSCSA.

Rob Rimmer is from Aintree. His most treasured memory is almost falling from the front row of the Upper Bullens celebrating the third goal against Bayern and realising it was all over.

Stuart Everton Roberts has been a regular match-goer since 1981. His most magical moment was the 1995 FA Cup semi final v Spurs and his favourite player of all time is Kevin Sheedy. He changed his name by deed poll.

Pete Rowlands was raised in New Brighton and now lives and works in London for a medical charity. The finest game he attended was Bayern Munich at Goodison and his favourite player of all time is Neville Southall. Pete is waiting patiently for the glory days to come round again.

Mike Royden is a high school history teacher in South Wirral and author of several local history books. His magic moment was meeting Alex Young and asking if he thought it was a penalty in the 1966 Final. "No question about it," came the reply he had waited 32 years to hear. Mike's first match was against Blackpool in November 1962.

Lol Scragg was born in Liverpool but has relocated to Arbroath where he makes computer games for a living. He is (arguably) the only person to miss Sharpie's screamer at Anfield past Brucie the Clown as he was in the bloody bog at the time...

Gagandeep Sethi is studying economics in Minnesota and modelling in Minneapolis to pay for it. Originally from Twickenham, Gag fell in love with Kendall's 'dream team' of 1984.

Robert Sharratt travelled from Australia for the Coventry game just to help keep the boys in the Premier League – and it worked. He held a season ticket from 1962 until he emigrated in 1968 and he now lives in Narara. His first game was a 2-2 draw at Hillsborough.

John Shearon lived in Liverpool until 1978 sustained by the twin pillars of Catholicism and Everton FC. After stints abroad in Mexico, Peru, Germany, Spain and Holland he has finally settled down in Derbyshire. A Top Balcony season ticket holder along with his son Michael and administrator of the *Other Everton* website dedicated to our namesake in Chile, he works as a project manager for ICL.

Ari Sigurgeisson started following Everton when they visited Iceland to play Keflavik FC in the 1969-70 season. After that, his wish for years was to own a white pair of boots like a certain Mr Ball.

Martin Smith went to watch Everton in the late 1970s as a five-year-old but his first concrete memory is of Bobby Latchford's penalty in that 6-0 defeat of Chelsea. Having been a regular since the late 1980s it would appear that his attendance at the match is something of a jinx. Thankfully Martin has now relocated to New Jersey so the Blues can look forward to more success.

John Staines migrated to Australia from South Shields aged 15. Now a library technician at the University of Adelaide, John has supported Everton since his mum bought him the 'wrong' top for Christmas, in 1976.

Mark Staniford is the editor of *Speke from the Harbour* fanzine and occasional freelance journo (when pressed). The first game he went to was the 6-2 drubbing in the late 1970s at Elland Road and he's been hooked ever since. His most valued possession is the shirt that Trevor Steven wore in the 1985 FA Cup Final. Mark lives in Allerton, works in accounts, is a season ticket holder in the Paddock and married to the lovely Bernadette.

George Lee Stuart first ascended the Park End stairs to the real theatre of dreams as an awe-struck four-year-old in 1960. Now a university lecturer in Lismore Australia, his hobbies are catching up on sleep, tidying up toys and lately he can be seen pushing his aged body around a soccer field after an eight-year absence, as well as coaching the university soccer third team.

Mark Tallentire is a football journalist based in London and working on *The Guardian*. He is also the brother of the author and took her to her first Everton match in 1969 at Goodison Park against West Ham, a 2-0 win with goals from Alan Ball and Jimmy Husband.

David Tickner lives in Liverpool and has been watching Everton regularly since 1959 when Bobby Collins was signed. Needless to say he has seen far more lows than highs over the years, but the highs have been much higher than the lows were low.

Paul Tollet works for Microsoft and lives near Oxford. His finest moment as an Evertonian was the FA Cup Final 1995, just to see the United supporters' faces, and his worst was the 1989 semi-final against Norwich.

Matt Traynor was born at home, half a mile from Goodison. The first game he remembers was the 6-0 drubbing of Chelsea but his best match has to be the semi-final of 1995, and stuffing the dream final down the media's collective throat. Now living in London, he is an economist with London Transport.

John Walton is himself an Everton legend; he was the little skinhead ballboy in the opening titles of *Match of the Day* when Andy King scored against Liverpool at Goodison. Sadly, he never made the full team due to a cocktail of wine, women and song. John now looks after the engineering side of the J. W. Marriott Hotel in Dubai.

Nick Williams lives in Warrington and follows the Blues around the country because he can't think of anything better to do with his life. During the week, he is an e-commerce manager for a bank, but spends most of his day worrying whether Super Kev will be fit for the weekend.

Phil Williams lives in Chester and his all time hero is Mike Lyons. His first game was at home to Coventry City in the late 1970s when Coventry had that lovely chocolate away kit. His favourite moment was Graham Stuart's winner against Wimbledon in 1994.

Billy Williams is the finest German-English translator on the face of the planet, a chain-smoker and a heavy drinker (both of which sins he attributes to watching the utterly shite Everton teams of the 1970s week in, week out) he traded Wavertree for the cultural life of Cologne nigh on ten years ago.

Mark Wilson lives in Warrington, works in the Employment Service and is reputed to think of Everton more frequently than other notable subjects. He spends his life wandering up and down the country in search of the elusive 100 per cent 'away' record.

Neil Wolstenholme is a fourth generation blue, born on the Wirral, settled in North London, married to an Arsenal fan and struggling to bring up his young son in the true blue faith. He's set give up a lucra-tive finance career to experience poverty as a struggling writer.

Bradford Wood is American, based in Palo Alto, California, and has followed the Blues since Duncan scored in a derby game, then ran up the field with his jersey pulled over his head. His first live match was the 1999-2000 season, at home against Man United. This visit to Liverpool was augmented with a stop at world famous Netley on County Road.

Mike Wood was born in Liverpool but is now working in Zurich, looking after a bank's databases. His first game was against Spurs in 1964 – a 2-0 win with the memorable chant of "Don't say Brown say hopeless," aimed at Spurs goalkeeper Bill Brown (from the Hovis advert for the younger readers). Since leaving the UK in 1976, Mike has only managed about five games a season.

Si Wooldridge has tried to bring up his family of four kids in the Blue tradition but has recently lost the eldest daughter to the relentless MU bandwagon (the sooner Posh gets divorced the better...). His most prized possession is a signed photograph of Nev acquired by the missus while Si was serving Queen and Country in the Persian Gulf.

Liz Wyman was born in Southport and fell in love with Everton from the Top Balcony. Her first game was also Howard Kendall's first as manager. Living in Stoke-on-Trent, Liz works at Leek College, made an appearance on *Ready Steady Cook* and her favourite ever player is Adrian Heath.

and finally...

Goodison For Everton is a fan based group, which was formed due to the handling of a proposed ground move by former chairman Peter Johnson. The GFE has endeavoured to explore all avenues on the redevelopment front and have recently set up a dialogue with the new Goodison administration. Whatever the outcome, stay or move, the GFE assure us that the results will have been achieved in the correct manner, a manner befitting Everton Football Club.

Alan Ball

Born 12 May 1945
August 1966 to December 1971
£110,000

WE LOOK back on those good old days and we think the grass was greener, the shirts were bluer and the skies were brighter. And they were. It was August 1966 and, still flushed with victory from England's World Cup win, little Alan Ball was Goodison-bound. With a wave of his magic wand Harry Catterick had secured the mercurial talent from under the very nose of Don Revie for £110,000.

'I went back to Blackpool to start training for the new season and a phone call came. Before I knew what had happened I was at Everton and a whole new world opened up for me. It was really exciting for a young boy and an enormous challenge to be at a big club with such massive crowds. From my point of view, the World Cup was very quickly forgotten once I got to Goodison Park because we were too busy to think about anything other than Everton, and I can't express how much I loved every minute of it.'

The ginger genie had been let out of the bottle and nothing would ever be the same again.

And who couldn't love the tempestuous little redhead who burst into our lives, kicking and screaming? Feisty, hungry, fiercely competitive and only 5ft 6ins tall, the angelic upstart was to make his mark like no other.

Forever Everton, forever remembered and forever young – Alan Ball we prostrate ourselves at your little white-booted feet.

How much of his success as a player does he put down to his father pushing and encouraging him as a youngster? *Colin Jones, Mossley Hill, Liverpool*

My dad was the main reason I went on to become the player I did. He was always demanding and driving me on to get better and better. He knew that Everton was the place for me and I think playing on that stage on Merseyside improved my game more than anything.

Was 1966 the greatest day of your life? Were there any moments at Everton that

came close or even surpassed the feeling? *Frank Hargreaves, Anfield, Liverpool*
I think there are two different ways of looking at things. You play for your country and you're immensely proud, and 1966 was a fantastic time for England, but winning the championship with Everton and the Liverpool derby games, they were just something else and I remember them all very, very well. They were absolutely fantastic days and it's difficult to describe what it meant for me.

Was it over the line or wasn't it… and why didn't Roger Hunt make sure…? *San Presland, New Brighton, Merseyside*
It all happened so quickly that it would be difficult for me to say whether it had crossed the line or not. Roger is the one who said it was in and in his mind at that second it was and he turned away to claim it.

Did he ever regret not signing for Leeds and what did Don Revie say to him after he went to Goodison? *San Presland, New Brighton, Merseyside*
Once I'd made my mind up that I was going to Goodison the whole club just took over. You've got to understand that I'd had a very easy life at Blackpool. I'd been cosseted for four or five years and all of a sudden I was thrown into the deep end. It was really exciting and it happened so fast and I never had a chance to wonder what might have been.

What is his opinion of Tommy Smith? *Frank Hargreaves, Anfield, Liverpool*
I loved playing against him purely and simply because you knew what you were going to get, and I just used to think: "Come on then, Tommy, let's get it on." He was Red through and through and we were Blue to the bone and you couldn't have expected anything different. I've actually got quite a lot of respect for Tom; he was a good player and a great adversary.

In pre-Ball 1966 we played Liverpool in the Charity Shield at Goodison and lost 1-0. Just a few weeks later, with Bally, we played them off the park 3-1. What was his best derby memory? *San Presland, New Brighton, Merseyside*
I certainly remember that game. We already had a couple of balls in the net and it wasn't even quarter past three. I think that particular derby sticks in my mind the most because I'd probably only been there just over a week and the anticipation was enormous. I can remember going back to Blackpool that night and reliving it all. The hero-worship that I got around the ground was just awe-inspiring. After that, I used to think Liverpool were my lucky team. Anfield was a lucky ground for me and Liverpool where my lucky team.

Is it true that even when you were playing for Everton you would face the wrath of your dad after a bad game? *Frank Hargreaves, Anfield, Liverpool*
I could score a couple of goals and my dad wouldn't mention them, he would mention the ones that I missed or the passes I misplaced. He was seeking perfection from me right along the line. He was a hard mentor but, bless him, he was always doing it for the right reasons.

Who was the dirtiest player you competed against? *Ged Fox, Wickford, Essex*

Not so much dirty as tough and hard. Dave Mackay was particularly tough, but fair, and the really hard games we used to have were against Giles and Bremner and the other Leeds lads. There were a lot of tough players around in those days, but we had our own share as well and we were frightened of nobody.

Where did he get his incredible stamina? *Tony Field, Rotterdam, Holland*

That was down to my father, too. From day one he always said you've got to have certain attributes in football. Ability and technique are one thing, but you've got to have an engine and you've got to be able to sustain high-powered work and running. When I was a boy I ran a lot of cross-country, but I always loved my training. I loved the fitness side of it as much as anything else.

I have a photograph on my website, which I love, of him training with the Golden Vision. What was Alex Young like as a person and as a footballer? *George Lee Stuart, Lismore, Australia*

Alex and I were very good friends off the pitch. We used to go around a lot together and we shared the same love of racing. He was a magnificent footballer, a mild-mannered and lovely guy and terrific company. I feel privileged to say he was one of my friends.

Was Catterick a good tactical manager or just a good business manager? *Michael Dudley, Long Island, NY, USA*

He was a good manager. I think we sorted the tactics out, he just put good players on the pitch and we went and did the job.

It was 1968 and I was in the Paddock when I witnessed one of the most magical (if relatively meaningless) bits of football ever to grace Goodison Park. Alex Young was coming to the end of his time and Catterick had played him on the wing. Ball was alongside him at inside right. On a couple of occasions they took the ball from just in front of the Park End down to the Bullens Road-Gwladys Street corner-flag without it ever touching the ground, lobbing it from one to the other over defenders.

This hazy and golden memory prompts a question for Alan Ball: Does he remember the game in question and did he enjoy such a relaxed virtuoso demonstration as opposed to the usual combination of sheer graft and skill? *Paul Preston, Muswell Hill, North London*

I can remember lots of incidents with Alex, he was such a fantastic footballer. We tried to do everything correctly. If the game had to be fought and scrapped, then we could do that, but once we got on top we used to want to entertain the crowd. We felt we'd earned the right then to showboat a little bit, and there was none better at it than Alex and me – we loved it.

What did he think of Tony Kay and what kind of a partnership does he think they could have had? *San Presland, New Brighton, Merseyside*

I'd only played against him for Blackpool and he was a very good player, but he already had that problem when I went to Everton. I didn't know Tony at all but it would have been lovely to play with him. Sadly, because of the circumstances, that wasn't to be.

Best number-nine he played with? *Steve Kirkwood, Brentford, West London*
That's a hard one, there were an awful lot of good number-nines. I think Geoff Hurst was a fantastic player.

What went wrong in the 1968 Cup Final? *George Lee Stuart, Lismore, Australia*
A lot went wrong. It was one of those games where it wasn't to be our day. We created SO many chances. We were knocking it over the bar, from under the bar and I still say to this day that I've never been in a more one-sided game.
    If you remember, that year, we'd already beaten West Brom twice; we beat them 2-1 at Goodison and 6-2 at The Hawthorns and that just goes to show how bizarre football can be. Believe you me, we weren't overconfident, we went about the job properly, but it was just one of those crazy days when we couldn't finish off all our good work.

How much of a bribe did Don Revie offer him to sign for Leeds and why didn't he take it? *George Lee Stuart, Lismore, Australia*
He didn't offer a bribe or anything like that, but he pestered and pestered me. I wanted to stay in Lancashire and I wanted to be close to my family and I know I made the right decision. People say Ball, Bremner and Giles, what a three that would have been. It's hypothetical, but there's one thing I know for sure and that is it would have had to be pretty special to improve on what actually did happen between Howard, Colin and me.

How many more caps does he think he might have had if Don Revie hadn't got the England job? *George Lee Stuart, Lismore, Australia*
I think I'd have gone on and certainly got another ten or 15.

Why does he think Harvey-Kendall-Ball is still talked about in such revered terms, even after so many other great midfield players have been and gone? *Phil Bowker, Brussels, Belgium*
We were three young, hungry lads who worked well together and I think what the people loved was the fact that we played terrific football. We gelled and we used to say we could find each other in the dark.

If you saw Gordon West in a pub, would you buy him a drink? *Frank Hargreaves, Anfield, Liverpool*
I think I'd have to, the size of him.

How much did he get out of Hummell for wearing white boots? *Mark Tallentire, Battersea, South-West London*

I didn't get anything, to be honest. They had difficulties as a company and they went bust. I played for 18 months waiting for my cheque, but I never got a penny and that's the truth.

Did he paint his boots white? When I was young my great-uncle told me that Alan Ball used to wear ordinary boots and just painted them so that he would get the money from the boot company. *Ciaran McConville, Dublin, Republic of Ireland*

I did after a while because the boots weren't up to standard. I got away with it, too, until it rained, and then I was really caught out.

Who was the best Everton player you played with? *Ged Fox, Wickford, Essex*

We had a very good team, from Gordon West right through to Johnny Morrissey, but the two lads in midfield, Colin and Howard, were just an absolute dream to play with. The three of us knew each other's game inside-out from the minute we got on the training pitch together. We were so competitive to be better than each other, to be great for each other and to win, and it was a fabulous time in my life.

Why did everything go pear-shaped immediately after winning the title in 1970? *Ged Fox, Wickford, Essex*

My own thoughts on that are that Harry Catterick was a very, very good manager, but he was very strict and he ruled a little bit by fear. I think, as we got older, he thought he was losing his hold over the players and he broke the team up far too quickly.

Who in today's game would come closest to your style of play? *John Walton, Dubai, United Arab Emirates*

I think you would have to look at little Paul Scholes, and he's a redhead!

Which was his best performance in a Blue shirt? *Steve Kirkwood, Brentford, West London*

I think my finest hour was in the Charity Shield at Chelsea after we'd won the League, but there were so many. The fans always expected things from me and they got behind their team and they got behind me every time I pulled a Blue shirt on, but that day at Stamford Bridge we were brilliant.

When he gets the chance which team does he go and watch and does he visit Goodison much as a fan? *Colin Berry, Wavertree, Liverpool*

I just take in a cross-section of games, anything that interests me, really. I did have a spell of watching Everton quite a lot when I was doing some work with Radio City, and I watched them go through some bad times. I didn't enjoy that at all.

Ask Alan Ball if he enjoyed doing his column for *Shoot!* in the early 1970s when he addressed the Arsenal fans – who on one occasion memorably nicked his

hub caps outside Highbury? *Mark Tallentire, Battersea, South-West London*

I really enjoyed doing the *Shoot!* articles, it was nice to be able to get your point over in such a well-run magazine, and it was very popular at the time.

Do you remember Harry Bennett? *Frank Hargreaves, Anfield, Liverpool*

I think he was a big centre-half who came up through the ranks. I only played with him a couple of times; I think once was against Leicester away and possibly against Fulham at Goodison. He didn't seem to get many games if I remember rightly, but there was a lot of competition around in those days.

Does he realise how Everton fans feel about him and does he have fond memories of his days at the club? *Terry McWilliams, Ontario, Canada*

I am aware of what the Evertonians think about me because hardly a day goes by without somebody reminding me of my time at Goodison and what affect I had on people. I came as a young boy when Everton were looking for somebody to help overcome the dominance of Liverpool, and we had five fabulous years where we more than matched them.

How did he feel about the fact that although he had a sublime understanding with Alex Young, one of the greatest footballers of all time, the manager played them together relatively rarely? *Paul Preston, Muswell Hill, North London*

He didn't very often play us together, but that was for Harry Catterick to decide. I was in awe of Alex when I went to Everton as a 21-year-old and it was just great to be able to play with him. I thought Catterick should have played him a lot more, but, of course, he had a plenty of good players to choose from at that time. He had Alex Scott, who he could play wide, Johnny Morrissey, who could play wide left, and the three lads in midfield. I think with young Joe Royle coming through and Fred Pickering and Roy Vernon who played through the middle, it became increasingly difficult for Alex to get a game. Even when he did come in, he had to play wide on the right and Alex didn't really enjoy that very much.

Does he remember the goal he scored against Southampton in the 8-0 victory in November 1971? If my memory serves me correctly, there was heavy snow on the pitch and he ran from the halfway line to score in the Gwladys Street end to make it five. *Colin Jones, Mossley Hill, Liverpool*

We'd have beaten anybody that day. That was another weird game. I remember they played a very high line of offside, just inside their own half. I broke the offside with a late run and had a long time to think about how I was going to place it in the net. I think it was a really good goal for the fact that I had that time to think about things and I finished it off nicely.

Did he rate Alex Scott? *Kenny Fogarty, Amsterdam, Holland*

Yes, I did. He was a good man to play with. He was very quick, he would knock balls in behind full-backs and he used to chase things for you. He was a good player, Alex.

In the game that took place the Monday following the FA Cup loss to West Brom, Bally lost his rag and went to strangle somebody on the field. Who was it and what sparked it off? *Michael Dudley, Long Island, NY, USA*

I think that was Fulham. We won that one 5-1 and the fact that we'd lost at Wembley when we'd been by far the better side made it even more frustrating. That's the way I was – just so disappointed for everybody concerned, but I can't remember who it was I wanted to strangle.

How did it feel when you knew Everton no longer wanted you? Did you feel worse because it was purely motivated by money? *Frank Hargreaves, Anfield, Liverpool*

I was absolutely devastated. I couldn't believe that I was going to leave Everton. In fact, I said I didn't want to go, but Harry Catterick told me that at the end of the day he'd had some great years with me, we'd won silverware, we'd done fantastically, we'd been in Europe and he was getting double his money after five years' work from me. He said I had to understand that football is a business and I can honestly say that was the first time in my life I realised that.

When he was let go to Arsenal did he think it was a forward or backward move for him? *David Cairns, Co. Down, Republic of Ireland*

At that particular time there was only one thing I wanted to do and that was to stay at Everton, but it was taken out of my hands by Harry Catterick. He made me quite aware of the fact that it was time for me to go. My second daughter, Keeley, had only been born a couple of days earlier and the last thing in the world I wanted to do was uproot my family and move down south.

I took quite a while to decide about the Arsenal situation because Man United were reputed to be interested and they tried to waylay me so they could speak to me. I must admit, if they'd have got hold of me I would most probably have signed for them and I don't think that would have gone down very well.

So I went to Arsenal, and once again it was a new challenge in a big city and I quite enjoyed it. But once Everton has touched you, it never leaves you all your life.

Does he think nowadays, with players wearing blue, red and other coloured boots: "Hey, what a trend-setter I was," or does he just wish that he got the same sort of deal to wear the white boots that some of today's players get for their boot contracts? *Colin Jones, Mossley Hill, Liverpool*

Well, as things move on, the rewards for football are a lot higher. It would have been nice to get paid, but regardless of that I thought it was something I just needed to do at the time.

Was Johnny Morrissey really as hard a case as the legend says? What did

Morrissey do to Jack Charlton to earn the right to be jotted down in his infamous 'black book'? *Michael Dudley, Long Island, NY, USA*

He studded Jack Charlton before he got injured himself and Jack never forgave him for that.

Pound for pound, Johnny was a great footballer. He had a good brain and a fantastic turn of foot. He was a great one-two merchant, could cross the ball, and let's just say he was quite capable of looking after himself.

Looking at the old photographs, even of the 1969-70 Championship celebrations, in spite of the champagne flowing, Alan Ball is always holding a cup of tea. Is he an abstainer? *Liz Wyman, Stoke on Trent, England*

I certainly enjoy a drink, but I always had a cup of tea first of all, there's nothing quite like a cup of tea after a hard game. It just seems right somehow.

Who was the best manager he played under during his career and why does he think his own managerial career has never been particularly successful? *Neil McCann, Bangkok, Thailand*

All managers have their own qualities, but I think the best manager I ever worked under was Alf Ramsey.

I've enjoyed every minute of my own managerial situation and along the way I've brought some good players into the game. There are a lot playing in the Premier League now that I brought through as kids, so I like to look at the good side rather than the other side of it.

Could he have done the England job? Keegan, no trophies but he gets £1 million per year. *George Lee Stuart, Lismore, Australia*

Believe you me, the England manager's job is a very hard one. I spent a couple of days with Kevin and the squad before the Argentinian game, and with all the baggage that goes with it it's not the best job in the world, to be honest with you. I mean, everybody's looking to knock all the time, and it's just a shame we don't back our country as much as we ought to, especially the press.

Can you ask Alan if he had been offered the Everton job when Joe was sacked would he have taken it, or was it well known how bad things were behind the scenes at Goodison? *Eddie Pepper, Brighton, England*

I think if it had been offered there would have been no way in the world I would have refused it, even knowing that things weren't too good behind the scenes. But Walter's there now and he seems to be sorting it out, so hopefully they've got it right and Everton will go on and be great again.

Has he ever been approached by Everton to manage the club? *Lyndon Lloyd, California, USA*

No, never, never, never.

He's often said that he's happier on the pitch, coaching players. Would he ever

go after a job as a coach, especially a role similar to Colin Harvey where he's coaching the youth teams? *Kenny Fogarty, Amsterdam, Holland*

Colin's got a terrific job that he loves very much. It's very rewarding when you work with kids, to coach them and see them come through to the first team, and Colin's done that. To me, it's one of the most satisfying jobs in football, but it's going to be strictly golf for me from now on.

How hard is it to motivate players of today who are all multimillionaires and really don't give a toss about the club they're playing for? *Kenny Fogarty, Amsterdam, Holland*

It is difficult. Once you take away the hunger in any walk of life, people get a little bit blasé with what they're doing. I think the huge amounts of money that they're getting now allow them to become very comfortable very quickly, and if you take that hunger away then they're not quite the same people. That's when it's difficult being a manager.

Which of the clubs he has managed does he have the fondest regard for? *Colin Berry, Wavertree, Liverpool*

All of them, really. I'm very happy here on the South Coast. I've had good times wherever I've been, but down here I seem to have lasted the longest.

With your determined attitude, and some would say single-mindedness, there must have been many a good after-match 'chat'. Do you remember any in particular? *Frank Hargreaves, Anfield, Liverpool*

That was a big part of us. We were hungry, we didn't suffer fools and nobody could get away with anything – not even me. If I wasn't up to scratch, people were entitled to have a go at me. A major part of our success, and a big part of the dressing-room, was that we did sort each other out. But the important thing was that we all took criticism because we knew it was for the same ends. I used to blow my top when we were being inadequate, but I also had to take it. It was great for team spirit and that was why we were so good.

When you look back on those glorious old days what is your abiding memory of your time at Everton? *Adrian Evans, Eastcote, England*

I remember being completely overwhelmed with emotion on one particular Saturday when I got two goals against Liverpool. I was running back to the centre-circle after I scored the second one and pure elation welled up inside me. I remember thinking: "I just I love this place – I want this place forever." Once Everton has touched you, nothing will be the same.

A true Blue legend – Alan Ball, thanks for everything.

Paul Bracewell

Born 19 July 1962
May 1984 to August 1989
£250,000

HIS influence on the pitch was undeniable, his partnership forged along-side Peter Reid formidable, but the accuracy of his passing was nothing short of legendary. Paul Bracewell, the Wirral-born, 23-year-old traded Roker Park for Goodison Park in May 1984.

> **I knew Howard from my days at Stoke and I took him on his word that I was joining a good side. I met up with him again, just before the FA Cup Final, we agreed everything verbally and I signed a blank contract. I think quite a few people were surprised when I arrived because they hadn't really heard of me.**

A baptism-by-fire debut in the Charity Shield victory against Liverpool and Royal Blue glory ensued. With three England caps already to his name, Brace's future was so bright – he almost developed a squint. One crunching tackle later and the boyhood dreams, inspired by the fleet feet of Georgie Best, lay shattered somewhere near the halfway line at St James's Park.

> **Things were going great and I was very successful with Everton. The year before was included in the summer tour to Mexico and it was virtually the same squad that went out for the World Cup** apart from myself and Wrighty, who'd broken his leg at Southampton.
>
> I was enormously disappointed because I was out of action for two-and-a-half years, which is a big chunk out of anybody's career. No injury is good, but it did come at an especially bad time.
>
> If I hadn't been injured, who knows what might have happened, but you can't look back. After such a long spell out of the game, I was lucky enough to regain full fitness and play top-flight football again. I actually consider myself to be one of the lucky ones because I've played football since I was 17, which is 20 years now. And they were all very good years.

Philosophical, ambitious, and gracious, Fellow Bluenoses, meet the magnificent midfielder who took no prisoners and reinvented the mullet. Hold on to your hats, it's Paul Bracewell.

What were his feelings when he made his comeback from injury, coming on in the second half of a third round, third replay against Sheffield Wednesday at Hillsborough, with Everton 5-0 up by half-time? Did he ever think he or the team would get back to the top? *Matt Traynor, Finchley, North London*
You've always got to think that. I was out for a long time and it passes very slowly when you're on your own in the gym. I was just delighted to get back in. When we got to 5-0 I had my fingers crossed that I would get a chance to play. I remember I got a fantastic reception and we didn't concede any, which was brilliant or I'd have been remembered for that instead.

In this day of card-happy referees, how long does he reckon himself and Reidy would have lasted? *Pete Rowlands, Enfield, North London*
It was a hard game in those days. They've moved the goalposts a little bit with the interpretations of the rules and they've had to calm down a bit now. Football was always a man's game and I think sometimes that's been overlooked with players faking injuries or diving, but it's still tough. I'm not quite sure how long me and Pete would have lasted in today's game, I reckon it would probably be about ten minutes.

According to my records he was born on the Wirral, so ask him which team he supported as a lad – Tranmere, Everton or Liverpool. *Billy Williams, Cologne, Germany*
I was born in Heswall, but when I was younger it wasn't really a team I supported, I just liked George Best. He was the one I looked out for and watched all the time. It wasn't so much the club, just the player. Georgie Best was my hero

Was that haircut an accident with one of those Kirkby cleaner barber attachments and did he realise at the time that it was the death knell for perms, wedges and flicks? *Frank Hargreaves, Anfield, Liverpool*
I suppose I did become a bit of a trendsetter. My wife was a hairdresser and she decided to give me a new look. Nobody even recognised me when I went back and the commentators thought I was a new signing.

Does he realise that the ball he whacked on the volley over his left shoulder – about 40 yards across the pitch without even having to look up – right into the path of Trevor Steven, who went on to blast it into the top corner, was the best pass ever made? *Jason Palmer, Merthyr Tydfil, Wales*
It's always nice when people say that because I've often been asked whether it was just lucky. I did mean it, and I was delighted that Trevor picked it up, controlled it and stuck it in the back of the net, but it was most definitely intentional. Just lucky.

Does he feel a bit in the shadow when everyone goes on about Sheedy, Steven and Reid? *Clive Blackmore, Washington DC, USA*

No, I was part of a very successful side and I really enjoyed myself there. When I first went to Everton, people spoke about Harvey, Kendall and Ball, but people I talk to now mention Sheedy, Bracewell, Reid and Steven. There were a lot of good players and a lot of good lads at that time, but we were only successful because we made such a great team, one man on his own can't win things.

Does he ever wish that he had been selected for a shampoo commercial? *San Presland, New Brighton, Merseyside*

I'm not sure about that, because that would mean I'd been chosen for my hair and not my looks.

Did Brace and Reidy agree between themselves who would be Sheedy's and Steven's 'minders' and which of them would kick the shit out of the main midfield man of the opposing teams? *Osmo Tapio Räihälä, Helsinki, Finland*

Reidy and me used to complement each other. He would set them up and I would sort them out or the other way round, either way it got the same result. Kevin Sheedy was quality on the ball, so we used to do all the hard work and get him all the glory.

Given the fact that a midfield player who could not hold a candle to him in his Everton heyday, namely, Don Hutchison, is unsettled on eight grand a week, is he at liberty to say how much he was earning as a key member of the most successful Everton side ever to grace Goodison? *Billy Williams, Cologne, Germany*

I think it's always a bit prickly when players and supporters talk about money. To be honest, I can't remember, it was a few years ago now. Money's never really been the be all and end all with me. I've moved clubs and I've dropped down to come back up again. Football is a short career and players have to try and make as much as they can in a short space of time.

I saw him walk a goal in against Norwich rather than shoot past the 'keeper. He never seemed to take the chance to shoot when he should have. Why? *Steve Kirkwood, Brentford, West London*

If I'd have scored a few more goals my price tag might have increased. Being a goalscorer was never really my forte, so I was just making sure it found its way safely into the back of the net, with no mishaps.

Did he ever make a bad pass? (If he did, I expect he'd have caught the guy and tackled him within ten yards.) *Phil Bowker, Brussels, Belgium*

The training with Colin was first class, all pass and move, but we worked as a unit and that was one of our great strengths. We could play, and we would get it back quickly too.

How does he feel about being the classy catalyst we needed to tilt the balance and become the difference between also-rans and champions? *Kenny Fogarty, Amsterdam, Holland*

There are some very nice things being said about me, these people have obviously been doing their homework or they've got really good memories. There were also the lads who used to come in occasionally like Alan Harper and Kevin Richardson, they were part of it as well, and we mustn't forget about them.

Has he seen the picture of himself on the site *http:—www.mullets.co.uk*? **It's an Anglo-German mullet war.** *Jon Gard, Woolton, Liverpool*

I'm not really into the internet, but I'm sure somebody will fax or send it through to me, so I can have a look at it. In fact, I'm positive they will.

His goals were memorable, though infrequent. Does he have a favourite? *San Presland, New Brighton, Merseyside*

Well, there's that many that I can't remember. No, seriously, any goal that I score is very memorable indeed.

The first interview I remember by any football player was Brace's in a Finnish footy magazine, where he said: "We are the number one on Merseyside now." How did it feel? *Jonne Hellegren, Tornio, Finland*

Over the years, Liverpool had the more successful periods. When we won the Cup-winners' Cup it was the first time for ages that Evertonians had a chance in Europe. We'd won the League and we were the team to beat, it was a fantastic feeling and a great time to be playing for Everton.

How did he rate Ian Snodin, who was bought to boss the midfield in his absence? *Kenny Fogarty, Amsterdam, Holland*

Snods was another quality player that we picked up along the way. He was a good lad and came in for what was quite a bit of money in those days, about £840,000, if I remember rightly. He did his hamstring at a really bad time, because that weekend he had a chance to get called up for the England squad. He was out with his injury at the same time as me and it's really nice to see him doing so well at Doncaster now.

Who was his best mate during his Everton days, and does he still keep in touch with some of the 1980s team? *Matt Traynor, Finchley, North London*

I played alongside Reidy, we were good mates and I worked with him a couple of years as assistant manager at Sunderland, we still speak on the phone occasionally. I've still got my house up in the North-East and I keep in touch with Inchy who's working up there with him. Trevor Steven is a football agent and he used to be on the phone all the time trying to sell me players.

What is it about the Everton set-up that results in such a high number of career-threatening injuries? *Wayne Hughes, Paris, France*

I don't really know. All players get injured, and you've just got to get it sorted out as quickly as possible. Everton are a good club and you get the best possible treatment. You do need a little bit of luck in a football though.

Brace was a top player, but did he feel overshadowed by other less able players getting into the England side because they were London-based? *Steve Kirkwood, Brentford, West London*

At one stage we had myself, Peter, Trevor, Gary Stevens and Gary Lineker, so we had five players from the Everton set-up in there. This game is all about opinions; I managed to get into the squad to go to Mexico, but the following year I was struggling with my ankle and ended up needing an operation. It's just the way it's worked out. I was very disappointed.

You were Keegan's right-hand man. Having worked closely with him, were you surprised at the apparently naive tactics employed in the two Scotland games? *Wayne Hughes, Paris, France.*

I worked alongside Kevin at Fulham and I know that when you're the manager it's down to you to decide how your team play and who's in it.

You obviously need to surround yourself people who can offer help and advice, but when push comes to shove, you have to make those decisions. Kevin will get some good people around him. He's got a first-class coach in Derek Fazakerley, and there's Arthur Cox, who's working with Kevin in the England set-up and was director of football at Fulham.

In football, if you don't get the results people start looking for things to criticise but when things are going well, everything's hunky-dory. That's one thing I learned very, very quickly from the manager's side of things.

What was it that made Howard successful and Colin a failure as a manager? *Osmo Tapio Räihälä, Helsinki, Finland*

It's difficult for me to comment on that. I think probably the best person to answer that question would be Colin. From my experience of being a player-coach, you do make the step-over. I played with all the lads at Fulham from day one. You hope they give you respect, but it's all about results, and football will never change in that respect.

Who is the best player he has played or worked with? *Colin Berry, Wavertree, Liverpool*

There were a lot of great players. I believe that Neville Southall, at that time was the best goalkeeper in the world; he was dedicated and certainly one of the hardest workers in training, he was a total perfectionist. As a team, we were confident we could beat everybody because, even if they got past the lads at the back, they still had to beat Nev, and that was never easy.

Yes, it would have to be Neville Southall – he gets my vote.

Was Van den Hauwe hard or psycho, or both? *Colin Berry, Wavertree, Liverpool*

To be honest it was all bit of a front, but sometimes his reputation preceded him and that has disadvantages as well as its benefits. I think once he got amongst us and realised we worked hard and played hard and we weren't really all that interested in his image, he settled in well.

Has he ever lost a shoe in or near Goodison Park? *San Presland, New Brighton, Merseyside*
Not to my knowledge, but I'm sure somebody will come up with a story.

I recall being over for the Nottingham Forest game at the beginning of the 1986 season (2-0 if I remember correctly) and for the first time ever, I saw an Everton jersey with a player's name across the back. The name? Bracewell. *Colm Kavannagh, Co Wicklow, Republic of Ireland*
No, I didn't know that. That's great.

Has he always been philosophical about the injustice of Billy Whitehurst effectively ending the career of a truly talented footballer, one of the best ever to pull on a Blue shirt? *Phil Bowker, Brussels, Belgium*
It's all part and parcel of playing football, but I don't even think there was even a foul given on the day of the game. Having seen the challenge again on video, I'm very disappointed with it. I could never have known he would put me out for two-and-a-half years, but I wasn't surprised when I watched it again. Let's just say Billy Whitehurst is definitely not at the top of my Christmas card list.

Do you think that Everton need a bigger ground? Do you think we need to move away from Goodison Park? *Ari Sigurgeisson, Hafnarfjordur, Iceland*
I don't know. I always go back to my memories. I'll never forget the semi-final against Bayern Munich. Just getting down there and trying to get into the ground that night was ridiculous, it was a full house. The second half was unbelievable and that night will stay with me for the rest of my life. When you have nights like that to remember, you don't want to move to a new stadium. I've played in Cup Finals, but that for me was the most incredible night and most definitely my finest hour in a Blue shirt.

Does he think the current Manchester United team could have a chance against the 84-5 Everton side, or has the game changed too much? *Osmo Tapio Räihälä, Helsinki, Finland*
I think a lot of people talk about how it was different in the past, but I know for sure that our side of the 1980s would have given anybody in today's game a run for their money, without a doubt. I'd put money on it.

Martin Dobson

Born 12 May 1945
August 1974 to August 1979
£300,000

> I PLAY football with Daniel in the back garden – he's only seven, but he always beats me. Mind you, he cheats because he's the referee as well as the opposition. As soon as I put one in the back of the net he blows his whistle, insisting there's been some kind of infringement – I keep thinking he's Clive Thomas.
>
> Whenever I score and he hasn't disallowed it, I sing: "Everton, Everton, we're forever Everton." The other day, he looked at me and said: "What are you talking about, grandad?" I said to him: "Do you know they used to shout to grandad and sing his name? The boys in the Gwladys Street used to sing: "Martin Dobbo, Martin Dobbo, hello, hello."
>
> Oh yes, those were the days.

Martin Dobson glided into Goodison Park when skies were grey and socks were blue. It was August 1974. A natural-born worrier, the 26-year-old international soon realised that expectations were high.

> I came from Burnley, a small-town team, which was very friendly and a family club. Everton is a big-city club with 40,000-odd people watching every week, and I must admit that I found it tough at the start.

He needn't have lost a moment's sleep.

Our £300,000 record signing rose to the occasion with his unique blend of dignity, ability and commitment – oh, and a generous sprinkling of panache.

Martin Dobbo, Martin Dobbo, hello.

Martin, you were the most stylish midfielder in a decade at Everton. Did you know we loved you for that? *George Lee Stuart, Lismore, Australia*

I didn't know that. I knew in the beginning that some of the fans didn't rate me highly, and I must admit I found it very difficult even though everybody supported me at that time.

After the first season there were a couple of changes. The new manager came in and I realised I had to be more determined, a bit tougher and thicker-skinned. So I got stuck in and went about it the next season in a more aggressive manner and it worked for me. I started scoring more goals and we were quite successful.

Who else was in for him when he joined us? *Mark Tallentire, Battersea, South-West London*

At that time I'd just come back from the international scene. Tottenham came in and Leeds, I believe. Duncan McKenzie told me that Cloughie was asking about me – it must have been on one of the 44 days he was there. Now whether that would have come to fruition, who knows, but I was quite happy to sign for Everton. No regrets at all, I simply don't have them.

What was it like playing alongside Duncan McKenzie? *John Walton, Dubai, United Arab Emirates*

Frustrating sometimes, but he was a fabulous player and a crowd favourite. Duncan drove Gordon Lee mad, but the things he could do on the ball were just sensational. I think the game is there to be enjoyed, and he always had a smile on his face. He was terrific for the team spirit.

I was a big fan of Duncan and I was a good friend, too, but you could understand from a coaching or a managerial point of view that he wasn't going to be a regular player because he gave the ball away too much. But he was always going to do something that would make the hair on the back of your neck stand up, and that's what the fans wanted to see.

Did he really mean to score that cracking piledriver at Anfield in October 1976 or was it a complete fluke? And will he give me an apology on behalf of the entire Everton side that day for totally ruining me 100th consecutive Everton match celebrations by losing 3-1? *Billy Williams, Cologne, Germany*

I remember the game well. We were 3-0 down and we could have gone 4-0 down. I remember Dai Davis making a fantastic save and he got hold of the ball and he threw it to me just at the edge of our box on the left-hand side. I went to the halfway line and I was looking for somebody to pass the ball to, but everybody seemed to be away or marked, so I kept going. I remember coming on my right-hand side and opening up the goal and, again, I was looking for a player to pass to. I was knackered because I'd gone about 50 or 60 yards and it was unusual for me to run that far and I was never the quickest player. In the end I ran out of options and I thought: "Oh, well, I might as well just hit it," and it flew into the top corner. I got a bit of a bend on it as well, but it wasn't a fluke, I hit it well.

Latch cost £350,000 in a part-exchange deal, but I think Martin, at £300,000,

was the most expensive cash buy in the country at the time. Who broke that record and how long after? *Mark Tallentire, Battersea, South-West London*
I think it was Peter Shilton, who went to Stoke City from Leicester at 325,000 or 350,000 quite soon afterwards. It's a bit of a millstone, sometimes, when you've got a high price tag, and it affects some players, but after the first season I settled down quite well.

Blue or white socks and cuffs? *Mike Kidd, Pietermaritzburg, South Africa*
White cuffs, blue socks.

How do you think that the best Everton side you played in, which was swamped by formula, would cope in today's League with its mix of applied athleticism and flair? *George Lee Stuart, Lismore, Australia*
It always changes, nothing ever stays the same, and I'm not one of those players who look back on my career and thinks it was better then than it is now. I still get a lot of pleasure watching games, even though it's completely different. It's very quick, you've got to have good touch and you've got to be an athlete. In my day we had athletes, but we had flair players, too, so it was a more interesting blend.

Martin was one of my heroes while at school in the 1970s. Just tell him thanks for those occasional spells when we weren't in the shadow of them over the park. When he scored that hat-trick against Wimbledon was he a bit miffed that Bob Latchford got five, and thus the match ball? Did he score any other hat-tricks? *Andy Clarke, Billericay, England*
I didn't score any more hat-tricks, but I remember that game vividly. Latch, of course, stole the glory with five, and I remember the headline in the paper: 'Game, Set and Latch,' because were playing against Wimbledon.

I remember all of the goals I scored, but especially the one where I got it, flicked it over somebody's head, came inside and rifled it into the bottom corner. I was scoring goals in League games at that time, but to get a hat-trick was something special.

What did the team do the night of Bob's 30th goal? *George Lee Stuart, Lismore, Australia*
We all went out together. There was a celebration party at a hotel in Liverpool. I think the referee was fairly generous in that game. It sounds a bit crazy, because Bob was scoring all the goals right through the season; he just seemed to be on the end of everything. But that particular game against Chelsea was the last match of the season and he needed two more. We'd already notched up four, but Bob hadn't scored.

I got one and it just went over the line, but it was kicked out before it hit the back of the net. Luckily, the linesman had seen it and we were coasting. We got a dubious penalty and Bob took that one and got us to 5-0. Then, of course, he got on the end of another right at the end and that made the 30 goals.

It was great for him because there had been a lot of staid games, a lot of defensive matches and a lot of 0-0 draws, so for a guy to score 30 goals was a fantastic achievement. Bob was a great lad, as well; we were all very pleased for him.

My memory is bad, but I think that Martin Dobson was responsible for the first match which I had personally seen change from 1-0 down in about the 88th minute to win 2-1 at 90. Does he remember the match and whom it was against? *San Presland, New Brighton, Merseyside*

Was it Swindon Town in the Cup? I think we drew away from home, two-apiece, and then we came back to Goodison and I scored and Davey Jones got the winner. We went on to get to the semi-final that season under Gordon Lee, if I'm thinking of the right one.

What was Gordon Lee really like? I worked in Birmingham at the time and stuck the biggest team poster I've ever had on the wall behind my desk. All the Villa fans thought it highly amusing that Gordon Lee's head was cut out. *George Lee Stuart, Lismore, Australia*

Duncan probably cut it out. I liked Gordon. He'd had his success at Newcastle and Port Vale in management, and he was very honest and down-to-earth. He said it as he saw it and he wanted hard-working players with a good work ethic.

He encouraged players to go forward and score goals, that's why he brought wingers like Dave Thomas into the club, and it was never any surprise when we did score. Myself, Dave Thomas and Mickey Pejic on the left-hand side, and Trevor Ross and Andy King, were always looking to put one in. It was better to play in a team like that, particularly as a midfielder.

Where did he get those ridiculous boots with the orange livery? I think they were Gola, but they looked suspiciously like my Winfield (Woolworth's own brand) specials – at least that was what I told my schoolmates as I sought to justify my cheapo boots during games sessions on the Parish Field. *Mark Tallentire, Battersea, South-West London*

They were Gola and they were orange. If you look at the boots they wear now, though – bright green and gold and red – they were very tame.

I remember Bally used to wear white boots and I said there was no way I would ever do it, but then someone came along and said: "Look, Dobbo, there's 20 quid here for a season and one new pair of boots," so I took it. They were comfortable though, so I enjoyed playing in them and enjoyed a lot of success in them, too.

Was Martin Dobson pleased to discover that his namesake was playing in the Everton band over 20 years after his departure from Goodison? *Simon Burke, Toxteth, Liverpool.*

I appreciate that, that's very good banging the drum on behalf of my lad and me. I appreciate that, I'll have to come across and say hello to that gentleman.

In Martin's best year I felt that Gordon Lee put the mockers on our championship push by constantly criticising the snow-laden pitches. Did it blunt team moral when you all saw the snow on the pitch? *George Lee Stuart, Lismore, Australia*

I think that was one particular game when we went to Coventry and we'd gone about 18 or 19 without defeat and were into the top two or three. We went to Highfield Road and half the pitch was covered in snow and half had been swept away. Gordon quite rightly said: "Why hasn't all the pitch been cleared?" and he wasn't happy with the state of it.

I never saw him criticising any other conditions or teams, or anything, he was more or less focused on what we were trying to do. I think he was so honest that when he saw it he just asked: "What's happening?" perhaps without thinking of the psychological affect it might have on the players in the dressing-room.

Rollers? Perm? Or a real descendant of Caesar? *Frank Hargreaves, Anfield, Liverpool*

It was all natural, but I must admit to everybody out there that it's nearly all gone now – I'm a bit bald on top, but my wife cuts it short so it doesn't look too bad. But, yes, it was naturally curly with long sideburns and all that went with it in the 1970s. I remember Kevin Keegan got a perm and it was all the rage then. Perhaps I was one of the trendsetters, but I certainly didn't look at it that way.

That screamer you scored into the Kop, was that your best ever? *Steve Fairclough, Toronto, Canada*

I think it was, but I also remember one of the goals I scored against QPR at Goodison. That was another cracking game, it was 3-3 but we had been 3-1 up and we should have coasted the game. I just caught one, a half-volley on the edge of the box, and it flew past. I remember Phil Parkes was in goal then, and he was a magnificent goalkeeper and in the England squad, but it went past him before he moved. It was as sweet as a nut and I always recall that one with particular fondness.

What was the highest number of fags that Duncan McKenzie ever smoked in the half-time break? *George Lee Stuart, Lismore, Australia*

I think it was into double figures. Duncan used to smoke like a chimney and another old Evertonian, Keith Noon, did as well. When he came to Burnley he used to go in the little boys' room at half-time and have a fag, and Jimmy Adamson was quite happy with that because it settled him down. I think Duncan just relieved the tension a little bit. I remember one day him coming out in the second half and he'd forgotten to put his fag out. It was only when he got to the touchline that he realised and he had to stub it out straight away.

How did he feel scoring the best, most stylish goal in our 6-2 Boxing Day drubbing by Man Utd in 1977? *George Lee Stuart, Lismore, Australia*

I remember the lead-up to that game because we'd lost the first two games of the season and then we'd gone about 20 games without defeat. Man United were about half way in the division and we were maybe second or third and having a great run.

We thought we had a great chance of turning them over, but at Christmas you always get these funny results and we lost 6-2. I remember one of the goals from Lou Macari – it was absolutely brilliant. He came in from the right-hand side and he volleyed it from the edge of the box right into the top corner – it was one of those goals that you think: "Wow," and you have to stand back and admire it. I think it got to 5-1, or maybe 6-1, and I got on the end of a cross and I flicked it in with my head. You come in and have a bath after a 6-2 drubbing, but you think: "Well, at least I got on the end of something and I made some kind of contribution."

Why did Dave Thomas always wear short socks? Did he have 'kick here hard' tattooed on his shins? Or was he so good that nobody could ever kick him? *George Lee Stuart, Lismore, Australia*

Probably a bit of both. If the weather conditions were bad the pitches were awful in those days. Now, of course, they're magnificent and the same through the winter months as they are at the start of the season. But the thing about Dave was he always wore rubber-soled boots instead of studs, even when it was lashing down and the park was like a bog. I remember Dave when he went to Wolves. The manager, John Barnwell, said he had to get studs and he refused to play. So he went to Wolves for £200,000 and I think he only played about half a dozen games.

It didn't affect his play at all, he was just comfortable. He had great balance; he could go by defenders on both sides and was a fantastic crosser of the ball. They talk about Beckham and Giggs and how they cross the ball from wing positions, but Dave was fantastic. I was lucky to play with Leighton James, as well. They were both super wingers and that's where the goals came from.

Like Trevor Steven, he didn't run, he glided. Was it something in the water at Burnley? *Mike Owen, Childwall, Liverpool*

Sometimes you look stylish when you're coasting along because you've got a long stride. People used to say that I was running elegantly, but really I was running as fast as I could. Perhaps I looked as if I was keeping up with them, but I was really going hell for leather, all the time.

Was Martin still at Everton or was he replaced by Dave 'dwell on the ball' Clements when Jimmy Case ended Geoff Nulty's career? Did no one think to suggest suing Case or even charging him with GBH? *George Lee Stuart, Lismore, Australia*

I was back at Burnley then, but I think Geoff did take legal action and I think it was sorted out outside of court.

Geoff is a big friend of mine. We arrived at Burnley in 1967 – we were both free transfers, of course. He was from Stoke City and we became big mates and we're still in close contact even at this stage of our lives.

I remember seeing that game on *Match of the Day* and the challenge was tough and late. Players are very committed and there's so much adrenaline racing around there are always flashpoints. It's terribly sad when somebody's career is affected, though, and in this case it was.

I once saw him at Aigburth where Lancs were playing Hampshire and he was walking around the boundary with the most stunning-looking woman I had ever seen in my 14 years on this earth. She was wearing electric blue flares. Does he still enjoy the cricket and what became of la Dobson? *Mark Tallentire, Battersea, South-West London*

If I was at Everton, it was my wife. She's still my wife and she's still the most stunning-looking woman I've ever seen, and that's perfectly true.

I like cricket. I don't see too much of it these days, but I used to watch Lancashire quite a bit at Old Trafford because some of my mates, like David Lloyd and David Hughes, and, of course, Jack Simmons, used to support Burnley. They would come and watch Burnley play in the early 1970s, and in the summer I used to go and watch them. They had a great side at that time, too, with Clive Lloyd and Peter Lever. I don't get to see much cricket now, but I still follow it.

Where did Gordon Lee get his wonderfully stylish pacamacs? *George Lee Stuart, Lismore, Australia*

We weren't privy to that information, I'm afraid, but he did get a bit of stick for the clothes he wore. Big lapels and flared trousers were in, and Gordon would have the very tight gear and, of course, the other way round. He was slightly eccentric in that way, he used to wear what he wanted.

He had a car, I think it was a Rover, but he never used to put any oil or water in until it was due for a service, which was about every 25,000 miles. He was up and down the motorways all the time, and I think it blew up one day because he never looked under the bonnet. He didn't want to change his car because it was a good runner, and the chairman at the time was always on to him to get a new one, but he used to say: "No, we're winning and we shouldn't change anything." When it blew up we started losing games.

Given the fact that he was acknowledged as one of the most accomplished midfielders of his day, does he feel that he underachieved as a footballer in terms of honours and England recognition? *Billy Williams, Cologne, Germany*

Yes, we were almost, but not quite. After that period, of course, Everton went into the doldrums a bit, and it was only when Howard came back in the mid-1980s that they had great success, and I'd been gone about four or five years by then. But, yes, you go to a big club expecting to have a chance of winning all the top prizes. I felt it was a good platform to go on to bigger and better things, but there was a bit of a lull before they came good again.

My England chances are quite interesting. I've got five caps, but I played under three different managers and I don't know whether they got rid of me or I got rid of them.

I played under Alf Ramsey for my first cap, and it was his last game as England manager. We played Portugal and it was a 0-0 draw at the Stadium of Light and I thoroughly enjoyed it. Then the summer came along and Joe Mercer for the Eastern European tour. We played East Germany, Bulgaria and Czechoslovakia and we were very successful. Joe was a like an uncle, a friendly father figure. He didn't put any pressure on us, he just told us to go out and play and enjoy ourselves. The start of the next season, 74-75, Don Revie came over and I played in my first game at Wembley. We played Czechoslovakia and beat them 3-0, but I never had another game after that.

Again, there are no regrets because, on the other side of it, if I hadn't have had a free transfer from Bolton Wanderers to Birmingham when I was 19 I might have been out of the game at 19. So you look at it and think it's not so bad to have gone on and played for two superb clubs and in England internationals.

I know that I did my best and I know that I gave everything I had, and I was quite happy with my career.

Do you regret leaving Everton when you did, as you still had a lot to offer?
John Walton, Dubai, United Arab Emirates
Looking back on it, I think I would have liked to stay. I was 31 years of age then, and I was enjoying my game at Everton. I was settled there and had four or five years towards the end of my career, but I was looking for a three-year contract to see me through and I was offered a two-year one. I think that was the only thing that I was undecided about.

Leeds and my old club, Burnley, came in for me. You can look back and say that it didn't really work out for me at Burnley because they were relegated within 12 months. It would have been nice to finish playing at the top level.

Look at the players now, they're still at it at 38 and 39. Richard Gough is doing a terrific job there, and he's nearly 40. It would have been nice, but you can't have any regrets. I was very lucky in my career that I played for two terrific clubs in Burnley and Everton, and I appreciated everything that was done for me. You've got to work hard and there's always some criticism, but you have a go and see it through.

It would have been nice instead of being third in the division to be top place or to win the Cup. We were in the League Cup and we lost after a second replay, and we got to the semi-final of the FA Cup, but got knocked out by Liverpool in that shady one where Bryan Hamilton scored and the referee disallowed it for no reason at all. It was almost, but not quite, and I suppose these days it wouldn't be so bad to be second or third in the League, but it was a bit disappointing back then.

Many ex-Evertonians maintain high-profile contacts with the club and wear their blue hearts on their sleeves, but you aren't one of them. Who do you support

and how fondly do you remember your time at Everton? Your skill and elegance are fondly remembered by all of us. *Neil Wolstenholme, Chelsea, South-West London*

I do support the club, but the problem is that now I'm working elsewhere. I've worked abroad and in America, and I'm very lucky to still be involved with the game. I look for the Burnley result, I look for Everton and I like to watch the games at every opportunity. Of course, my son is a big Evertonian even though he lives in Leeds. He was born when we were over in that neck of the woods and he knows more about them than I do.

We talk about the team and we talk Everton all the time, but it's not quite the same when I get the black and white photos out and I say: "This is what I used to do in 1976, this is the goal I scored." Now, it's all on video, and it's fantastic for players to be able to build up their career on tape, match by match. But for us lot, it's the old photos and they're a bit crinkly at the edges now.

Andy Gray

Born 30 November 1955
November 1983 to July 1985
£250,000

' I WAS lying on my back with my head in my hands, shattered and absolutely distraught.

The Double was in our grasp and we never quite had the strength to make it through. Big Ron came up to me and said: "Never mind, Andy, we wanted it more than you." I managed to summon up my last ounce of strength to reply: "Fuck off, Ron, nobody wanted it more than me." '

Andy Gray arrived on Merseyside in November 1983 as his new club flirted shamelessly with the relegation zone. Even with his inherently 'dodgy knee' there was just something about Gray which captured Howard Kendall's imagination. "I knew he'd only managed around 20 games a season for the previous two years, yet I felt he was the kind of player who would make things happen. The club doctor passed him on the proviso he did extra training for his legs. If he could strengthen his quads it would help support his bad knee."

The bet had been placed and the deck duly shuffled.

Straight flush.

Fellow Bluenoses, it's my pleasure to introduce you to Andy Gray, passionate, dedicated, fast-talking, much funnier than Freddie Starr and the man who still believes that only the best is good enough

Listen closely, Andy, and you can still hear that Goodison roar.

When he joined Howard's band of misfits in the early 1980s, did he really think that he could be the last piece in the jigsaw that would turn them into Euro-beaters? *Lol Scragg, Arbroath, Scotland*

I always remember being interviewed on the day I arrived at Goodison. A journalist asked me why I'd signed. I told him I'd come here to win things and he actually, genuinely looked surprised at my answer. He said he'd heard it before and the only thing I could think of to say was: "Yes, but you haven't heard it from me. I like winning and I want to win things and I think we can win things," and I really believed that. I'll tell you what though: I never thought we could have achieved the things that we did in the two years. To sweep the whole of Europe with the football we played was beyond all of our wildest dreams.

When he arrived at Goodison did he have any inkling of the potential that was there? When did he realise that they were on the brink of something special? *Richard Marland, Waterloo, Liverpool*

I knew there were some very good players there, but I didn't know how good, and the first time I thought we were on the brink of something special was in the build up to the 1984 Cup Final. We turned the season in January 1984 and we started on that run. The closer we got to the Cup Final I began to think that this was a team which had the potential to go on and sweep the board.

You were credited with lifting the morale of the club both on the field and off. How bad was the atmosphere in the dressing-room when you first arrived with the team struggling in the bottom five? *Rob Bland, Morecambe, England*

The atmosphere in the dressing-room was actually better than anyone could have imagined, but I think that's true for every club that struggles. It's not the atmosphere in the dressing-room you have to look at; it's the confidence and the atmosphere on the pitch. What I think I did, along with Peter Reid I have to say, was encourage people to want the ball in training and in games and remind them that they were good players. I decided that if the gifted players could see somebody like me wanting the ball all the time when I didn't have half their talent, then it would help, and I remember they started gaining confidence pretty quickly. That was the major turn in the team. The morale was always good, but the confidence was pretty low when I arrived. As soon as it picked up at the turn of the year there was an incredible transformation.

What kind of lunatic scores a half-volley with his HEAD? *Phil Pellow, Waterloo, Liverpool*

A lunatic that was useless with his right foot. I'll never forget that game against Notts County, because as Kevin flipped it in, Graeme Sharp went to the near post and just got slightly underneath it. I actually thought he was getting it, so when it dropped over his head I was half back on my heels and the only thing I could think of was throwing myself at it – it was purely instinctive, there was nothing premeditated about it. I just thought if I could throw myself towards it and get a bit of my head on it, it could go in. Luckily enough, I managed to get a good bit of my head on it and direct it wide of the goalkeeper. It was an extraordinary goal and everyone always talks about it.

Why did he look like shit the morning before the 1984 Cup Final when the BBC cameras were roaming around the team hotel? *Lol Scragg, Arbroath, Scotland*

I not only looked like shit, I felt like shit, too, and I'll tell you why it happened.

Freddie Starr had appeared at our hotel on the morning of the match to do his bit of comedy and we were all awakened early by this noise out on the lawn. I swear I'd only just fallen asleep because I'd been sharing with John Bailey and anyone who's ever shared with John Bailey will tell you he never shuts up – he even talks in his sleep and he's a nightmare to sleep alongside. That's why I looked like shit and that's why I never shared with him after that again.

Did you know who Hafnia were? *Clive Blackmore, Washington DC, USA*
A Scandinavian food firm, I think.

When he leapt like a salmon and the ball bounced off his golden locks to beat the Watford 'keeper, had he any idea where it was going? *Tony Field, Rotterdam, Holland*
I had, actually, because the only one who didn't fall or lose his balance in the challenge between Sherwood, Terry and myself, was me. So as soon as it hit my head I knew it was there and all I could think was: "Please God, let it have enough strength in it to get over the line." I've scored two Wembley Cup Final goals, the League Cup and the FA Cup, and I don't think either actually hit the back of the net.

Ask him how amazed he was that his goal against Watford in the Cup Final was allowed? *Ste Daley, Speke, Liverpool*
I wasn't amazed, I was surprised, because often when you go up for a ball the likes of which Trevor Steven delivered into the area that day and the goalkeeper goes down under pressure, then nine times out of ten you do expect the whistle to blow.

I have to say, and I've said this from day one, that I didn't touch the goalkeeper, and I defy anyone to look at the video of the match and actually say where they saw any contact because there wasn't any. I just got lucky and I stuck my head in there. I hit it with my head rather than headed it and it dropped over the line, but the goalkeeper actually clashed with Terry, who was the centre-back that day at Watford, and both of them went over and I was the only one who didn't make contact with anybody. So the referee actually made a great decision. I have to say the majority of the time it would probably have been disallowed, but as far as I'm concerned, if you look back in the history books, all it says is Sharp and Gray, and that's good enough for me.

On the coach back from 'The Oxford Match', a few of the lads (one I remember was Tommy Wright's brother, Roy) said Andy Gray and John Bailey had won all their money from them in the afternoon at either snooker or pool. Did he ever think of taking up any other sport as a pro? *San Presland, New Brighton, Merseyside*
Absolutely not. Football was my life and there was nothing else that came even remotely close to threatening it.

Was his goal in the European Cup-winners' Cup Final his most important ever? If not, which was his personal favourite? *Vince Balfe, Wicklow, Republic of Ireland*
Goals in Cup Finals are always important, but I think the goal that was probably

most crucial that year might well have been the first one against Bayern Munich at Goodison in the semi-final.

We were sitting at 1-1 and that meant that the Germans would have gone through if it had finished there. I think the goal that put us 2-1 up was the one that killed the Germans off. We went on and got a third, but I think the second goal was probably the most important with regard to going on and winning a European trophy.

I only pick out the European trophy because we were the first Everton team to get to the Final and to win. I always like going down in the history books, and so does every other player. No one can ever take that away from the team who won in Rotterdam. We've gone down in Everton's history as the first team not only to qualify for a European Final, but to win it, too.

As a player, what was your first ever pay packet (sorry to be so personal)? *Phil Williams, Chester, North Wales*
I don't remember my first, but I remember my first as a pro with Dundee United, it was £16 a week. Six quid of it had to go on 'digs' money and I was left with a tenner to do me the rest of the week. That was in 1973, so it was quite a while ago, but it's quite extraordinary when you see players of 17 and 18 now and they're getting £10,000 and £15,000 a week – I don't think inflation's gone up that much.

What was Jim McClean like? Did he try to sign him up on a 25-year contract? *Mark Kenyon, Minnesota, USA*
Funnily enough, no. Because freedom of contract wasn't in when I was there. Thankfully, it came in just after I left Dundee United and that was when Jim started signing up the players on long contracts.

Jim McClean couldn't have been better for me if he'd have tried. He coached me on his own in the afternoons and he used to take me out on the pitch and hit cross after cross after cross and pass the ball up to me to control and lay off. He worked selflessly and tried to build my ability. After two years he said he couldn't do any more for me and that he was going to have to sell me to an English club. He said he would only hold me back if he kept me there and, bless him, he did sell me. I went to Villa and history tells you the rest. I wouldn't say one bad word about Jim McClean. Many will, I know, but I won't be one of them.

Looking back with hindsight, does he believe that the celebrations after the tremendous Cup-winners' Cup Final victory against Rapid Vienna had an effect on the FA Cup Final performance and cost us an historic treble? *Colin Jones, Mossley Hill, Liverpool*
I don't know what you mean by celebrations because we certainly didn't celebrate. Our schedule for that time was ridiculous. The only thing that stopped us from getting the Treble was time.

We were better than Manchester United that year. I know that because we'd already beaten them 5-0 at home and drawn at Old Trafford, so we were certainly better than them. The thing that beat us was the ridiculous task of having to play two Cup Finals in two different countries in different parts of Europe within three days of each other at the end of a very long season. But, unlike today, you didn't hear us complaining about it, we got on with it.

We had to fly from Rotterdam straight after the game and we got into Speke Airport at about two o'clock in the morning on the Thursday. Howard gave us the Thursday off to sleep, which we did. We woke up on Friday morning, went into training, got on the coach and drove to London, went to bed that night and got up to play in the FA Cup Final – we just never had enough time to recover. I can assure you there were no celebrations after the Cup-winners' Cup Final except the one glass of champagne, which Howard allowed us on the plane, and that was it.

Did Terry Darracott really write the hotel's name on his head in Glasgow? *Clive Blackmore, Washington DC, USA*

He did actually, yes, it's a great story. When we went out we would get rather worse for wear. Terry got a felt-tip pen out and wrote the hotel and the room number on his head he said that if he was drunk and we all left him, at least he would get home.

If Moran hadn't been sent-off in the Final, would we have won? *George Lee Stuart, Lismore, Australia*

It's a tough question to answer. I don't know, but I do know that the sending-off certainly lifted them. If we had gotten another game, another 90 minutes after seven days of rest, then we'd have beaten them in the replay.

I didn't think we were ever going to score in the game, to be honest. We played with a tiredness and a lethargy that was unusual for that season, but I do think if we'd managed to scrape a 0-0, we would have gone on and beaten Manchester United in the replay. I really do believe that, because we were better than them.

Was the EFC team of 1985 the best team he's played in? *Vince Balfe, Wicklow, Republic of Ireland*

I think it would have to be. It had everything, brilliant defenders, a great goalkeeper an exciting midfield and two Scots up front. It really did have it all, it was entertaining, it could score goals, it could defend, it could play every type of football – and it could raise it's game depending who it played against. You look at the records, I think it shows we scored more goals than anybody else that season and conceded fewer than anybody else – it was just an incredibly talented side.

How does he feel about his Scotland career, and about that of Graeme Sharp? Surely they both deserved a lot more caps than they got? *Martin Smith, New Jersey, USA*

That's probably the one disappointment I have, having been capped first of all at 19 and lastly at 29 and in the ten years in-between I only amassed 20 caps. Sometimes you're dependent on the manager. Each manager has different opinions of different players, and I got a bit unlucky at times. I missed out a bit, too, because of injury, and that didn't help me. I think I was good enough to have gotten maybe 50 or 60 caps, and certainly Graeme was. Alan Hansen's another who's a 20-cap man and should have had nearer 100, but that's what happens when you play for Scotland. I missed out on important internationals and competitions, and it is a big disappointment to me that I've only played just over 20 times for my country.

It's Leicester City away, 1984-85 season. Andy Gray scores to put us in front and promptly head-butts the post and falls over. He subsequently has a storming black eye. Later on, Steve Lynex equalizes controversially, but we go up the other end and Gray scores a belter to win the game for us. As the players go back to the halfway line, Gray points at the bench aggressively mouthing obscenities. Add this to the image of him with a black eye and it was one of the most frightening things I've ever seen on *Match of the Day*. I want to know what he was saying, and to whom, please. *Stuart Roberts, Guildford, England*

I can always remember Jimmy Hill on *Match of the Day* showing that shot of me strutting over, snarling and pointing. He said: "Look, there's Andy telling his bench that he can still do it."

I wasn't pointing to the bench at all. It was a controversial goal by Lynex, we all thought it was offside and I was walking over and pointing at the linesman, who'd kept his flag down. I actually shouted: "Stuff you, you bastard," or something like that.

What does he think of claims that Newcastle, Man United, etc. have the best, most passionate fans? How do we compare to other supporters he played for? *Martin Smith, New Jersey, USA*

I always say Everton supporters are certainly the best with regard to loyalty to their team and standing by them. I don't know any other side that I've played for that would get 35–40,000 every game when they were struggling in the League, as Everton have done at times over the last four or five years, but their crowds continue to be absolutely incredible. An old club of mine, Aston Villa, has trouble getting 30,000 into their ground at the moment, and they're in the top six of the League. Imagine if Everton were up there, you couldn't get a seat in Goodison. I think Everton supporters have always been fantastic. I always thought they had a great knowledge of the game and their loyalty was unquestioned.

Does Andy remember the lads hanging from the trees in Stanley Park when we beat QPR 2-0 to take the title, and does he ever wonder what happened to the one I saw fall out when Mountfield scored? *Neil Wolstenholme, Chelsea, South-West London*

I can just remember everyone from every vantage point available that day. That they could see anything at all is astonishing. That was a fantastic day and I remember I got incredibly drunk afterwards.

We went back to Southport, me, Graeme Sharp and a few of the lads, and all we went into this Italian restaurant, a big bunch of us, and we kept singing: "Hand it over, hand it over, hand it over Liverpool…" There was about eight of us and how we never got duffed up by a load of lads I don't know. It was a great day all round.

Did he think, as ITV, among others on Cup Final day in 1984, that he and Peter Reid looked like Freddie Starr? Does he think that Suker looks like Peter Mandelson? *Jon Berman, West Derby, Liverpool*

We used to be called Freddie One and Freddie Two at Goodison. Peter always maintains that I'm more like Freddie Starr and I'm convinced that he's more like him. When I arrived at Goodison in 1983 they said: "Oh, my God. We've got a problem now, Freddie One and Freddie Two."

We do both concede that we have a slight resemblance to Freddie. We both think we're funnier than him, of course, and you can't argue with that. As for Suker looking like Mandelson: yes, I would go along with that, that's not a bad shout.

Was he 'Fred One' or 'Fred Two'? *San Presland, New Brighton, Merseyside*

Fred Two. Reidy was there before me, he was Freddie One.

Who was he most respectful of as an opposing centre-half? *Steve Kirkwood, Brentford, W. London*

I gave everyone respect, but I never went into a game thinking I was frightened of anybody. I always thought I could handle most of them and sort them out if need be. There were some great centre-halves around, like Hansen and Lawrenson, but I always felt I could physically intimidate those two. Kenny Burns was tough, Larry Lloyd when he was at Forest, Dave Watson at Manchester City. I always found Dave a tough opponent, but I never, ever worried unduly about facing centre-backs, I always thought I could look after myself.

Does he have a sly chuckle now when he sees how overprotected goalkeepers are these days? *Ste Daley, Speke, Liverpool*

They were always protected. I always thought they were overprotected then, and they're a lot bigger now than they were in my day. Neville, who we always thought was a big goalkeeper, is a lot shorter than the Schmeichels and the Schwartzers of today. They're 6ft 3ins, 6ft 4ins, they're giants now, and yet they still come out like big nancies and want for all the protection that they can from referees. I suppose, in the modern game, you're not allowed to just give them a whack, you're not even allowed to challenge them now. It's been a gripe of mine for a number of years and will continue to be.

I remember seeing a picture of Andy Gray in a Wolves shirt made out of the same material that they make vests out of – you know with holes in it. Ask him if that shirt was worse than the Everton shirt with the white V-neck insert and if he liked the tight shorts that went with it? *Mike Kidd, Pietermaritzburg, South Africa*

I never liked those tight shorts that went with our kit. I was always a baggier shorts man when I first came to England at 19. Somehow, the style changed to tight shorts, but now it's baggy again, which I'm sure the players of today are very happy about. Everything was geared for tight then, it was almost like a second skin. Those shirts we wore in the Everton days – those so-called Aertex ones – were supposed to let you breathe, but you actually sweated more because of them. Companies fiddle about with kits all the time, but we were unfortunate to be in the era of the tight-fitting shirts and shorts and they were very bad.

Am I correct in thinking that in the interview after the 1984 Milk Cup Final you were drinking Heineken? *George Lee Stuart, Lismore, Australia*
Probably.

How did he feel when Howie told him he was being sold? Had he any prior warning or was he as shocked as me? *Neil Wolstenholme, Chelsea, South-West London*
I was disappointed. Howard didn't want to sell me, he wanted to keep me with Gary Lineker, but he said he was going to start the season with Gary and Graeme and I thought that was unacceptable after all I'd achieved and contributed to our success.

Howard came round to my house. I'd only just moved about two weeks before and half my stuff was still in packing cases, and I turned to my girlfriend at the time and said: "Don't unpack any more of those, I've got a funny feeling we won't be here." I just knew Howard had come to tell me something. Managers don't come to you in pre-season unless they've got some bad news. We sat and we talked and had a glass of wine and he offered me a new contract and I said no. He said: "I'm going to get slaughtered for this," and I said: "I hope so".

He said he'd had a bid from Villa and did I want to go? I said: "No. Why would I want to leave this club, I love it here, we've won everything, we've got great players and I get on brilliantly with the supporters, why would I want to leave Howard? You must be mad." He told me he was buying Gary Lineker, so I said I'd think about it. I phoned him the next day and told him I'd go and make it easy for him, but I was really disappointed and choked.

What would he have given to stay on at Everton after that glorious season? *Darryl Ng, Southampton, England*
Pretty much everything, I think. People who remember that glorious season of 1985 will be aware that I broke a bone in my foot up at Newcastle when we beat

them 3-2. I was out for five or six weeks and in that time Adrian and Sharpie had forged a quite incredible and successful partnership. In turn, it meant that when I was fit, I spent 12 games sitting on the bench. Then Adrian suffered that horrific injury against Sheffield Wednesday when he shattered his knee. I teamed up with Graeme and history will tell you what we went on to achieve.

I just felt that if Howard was bringing in Gary Lineker I wasn't prepared to sit on the subs' bench again. I thought I'd served my apprenticeship. Sharpie and I had showed for two seasons that we were good enough to cope with anything, but Howard obviously wanted something different. I didn't fancy playing in the Reserves so that was the basis of my decision to move on.

Was he pissed off Barcelona didn't make a bid for him after his great season at EFC à la Lineker? *Mark Kenyon, Minnesota, USA*

No, I wouldn't have gone abroad then. Absolutely no chance. When Howard decided to bring in Gary Lineker at the end of that brilliant season I had the chance to go and join PSV where Marco van Basten, Ruud Gullit and Frank Rijkard were all playing but at 29 I felt I was too old, so I decided to go back to Villa. It wasn't a great move. Let's put it this way, I'd have loved to stay on at Everton I still think I had a lot to give, I certainly had another couple of seasons left in me.

Can you please tell Andy that I have met him in Birkenhead back in 1984-85 and would like to echo the sentiments of one Pedro Bishop (see *Shades of Gray*). He should know what you are talking about. *Steve Jensen, Wamberal, Australia*

Bishop sent me a letter when I left. There was a poem which I can't remember now, but it was along the lines of: "We love Andy Gray so much that if I found him in bed with my wife I'd tuck him in and make sure he didn't catch cold."

What did he think when he heard about another player named Andy Gray and what happened to him? He played for Aston Villa, too. *Ari Sigurgeisson, Hafnarfjordur, Iceland*

I think the other Andy Gray is now a footballing agent. He played at Aston Villa and Crystal Palace, but I don't know where he went after that.

Does he think the producers of *Sporting Triangles* saw how he inspired the Everton revival from under the shadow of Liverpool and hoped he could do the same thing to arch-rivals *Question of Sport*, and does he consider it one of the big failures of his career that *Sporting Triangles* flopped abysmally? *Ray McNamara, Co Clare, Republic of Ireland*

Sporting Triangles did NOT flop abysmally; I'll have you know. It used to get great ratings, there were millions watching it every week. Unfortunately, it only flopped because they didn't want to fund it. I enjoyed it, I recorded three series of that and I thought it was fantastic. The thing is, you're up against an institution called *Question of Sport* and every sporting quiz show is going to be judged against it. I really enjoyed it and it's as simple as that, and I don't regard it as a failure – far from it.

How gutted was he when he got booed during the first live Sky game at Goodison after the manager fiasco in 1997? *Lol Scragg, Arbroath, Scotland*

I was a touch disappointed, but I happened to think that the reception I got was mixed rather than total condemnation. I think the people who knew me as a player there knew that what had been put in the press was a fabrication of what actually took place. Peter Johnson had manipulated the press to mislead people. He told the supporters that I had a contract that was done and dusted and it was only a matter of just coming up and I would be the manager, but that wasn't the case.

I think a lot of the fans who knew me and knew what I was like didn't believe the stories that they'd heard, but the younger brigade, who'd never seen me or met me, did. They didn't give me a rough time at all, and I didn't feel that bad about it. I don't think anything that happened then, has tarnished the image the supporters have of me, though. At least I hope not.

Whilst working in the studio for Sky how does he manage to avoid cracking up at the mere sight of Richard Keys' bodily hair? *Colin Berry, Wavertree, Liverpool*

Just because I'm used to it, really. He's the only man I know who has a 'body hair-dresser' – he is indeed the hairiest man in the world.

We've got a great working relationship and Keys is a football fanatic, although that sounds strange when you consider he supports Coventry. But he does love his football and he's got a strong connection with Merseyside, of course, because he worked up there as a young 'cub' reporter on one of the local stations. He's got a great affinity with Merseyside, but, sadly, he's a bit of a Red – although he wouldn't want that publicly known – so we do have our odd battles. He's a good lad and a great pro and we've had nine years of working together, but he is hairy, I'll give you that.

What was his opinion of Peter Johnson during the talks they had re the manager's job and what is his opinion of him now? *Kevin Hazard, Sumbawa, Indonesia*

I was never sure of Peter Johnson.

I did have an interview with him, well more of a chat, really, and I was never quite sure of his intention and I never quite believed what he was saying. Subsequently, I have to say that the man did put an awful lot of money into Everton – he did get an awful lot back out, but I never believed he was a true Evertonian in the sense that somebody like Bill Kenwright or Philip Carter are, for instance. I don't think the Everton supporters ever believed he had the best interests of the club at heart, either. I only met him once, I never really saw enough or talked enough to form a complete picture of him, but, certainly, I didn't always believe what he was telling me.

Was he really serious about managing Everton or was he simply using it to screw a better deal out of Sky? *Stuart Ainsworth, Basingstoke, England*

When I got a call from Peter Johnson to ask if I was interested in the manager's job I turned to my girlfriend at the time and said: "I'm going, I cannot allow this chance to pass me by," and that was on day one.

On the Monday afternoon I went to meet Peter Johnson and three of his directors and we sat and chatted for over two hours. Everton had been without a manager for about two months, I think, and they were three weeks away from pre-season. We sat and we talked and he asked me what my philosophy was about the game and how I believed it should be run, and all that kind of stuff. I told him that if I had a chance to run a club the size of Everton, I'd do it this way and I'd bring in this and I'd do the other and I'd need this amount of money to spend. At that particular moment if Peter Johnson had said to me: "There's the contract, sign it," I would have done so, there's not a doubt in my mind about that, but he didn't.

I was going to La Manga the following day for five days and I found it quite extraordinary that Everton, who hadn't had a manager for so long, were going to allow me to go to Spain for five days without me making a decision. I thought they would make a decision there and then and say: "Let's talk about this," but they didn't.

All the time I was in La Manga I had chance to think about everything and take the whole picture into consideration. I have a daughter who was five at the time, who I spend every other weekend with, and because my job at Sky is a Sunday it means I can have Friday, Saturday and Sunday morning with her. I suddenly realised I wouldn't be able to do that and everything else came into focus. I'd heard one or two stories about Peter Johnson from pals of mine who were in Liverpool and phoning me up, and I was told to be wary.

When I came back, because I was contracted to Sky I had to meet with the bosses and they made it quite clear that they weren't going to allow me to go. They made me a new offer and I accepted it.

So I was never offered the job at Everton, I never agreed a contract with Everton and I never, never turned down an offer of a job at Everton.

All these stories came out that I had let the Everton fans down. All Peter Johnson was doing was covering his own backside, but I knew the truth and he knew the truth. The thing that disappointed me the most during the five days I was away in Spain was this: We had left that room on Monday and Peter said to me: "I hope this conversation remains within these four walls." I told him I was going to Spain and so I wasn't going to tell anybody, and all I had for the next five days was people phoning me from England and relating the tales about players I was going to sign. Those stories could only have come from one person, and that was Peter Johnson, so he had been leaking stories in the press, building up the supporters' hopes in the belief that I had already agreed to take the job when nothing could have been further from the truth.

I actually don't think Everton could have afforded me because the difference between the salary of a manager and the salary of a self-employed person would have been huge and there would have been a problem in agreeing a price, but it never got to that stage. I think I made the right decision. Everton is very much the right club, but very much at the wrong time, and you never say never, but whether I get the opportunity in the future, who knows?

Was he surprised Howard took the poisoned chalice? *Mark Kenyon, Minnesota, USA*
No, Howard is an Evertonian. They say you should never go back, but he not only went back a second time, he went back a third time as well, but Everton were struggling to find someone. There had been total mismanagement from the day that Joe left. Everton had gone three months with Dave Watson in charge, then they'd gone two months of the close season with no manager, which is probably the most important part of a team's preparation when the manager gets his players in, buys his players and tries to organise a pre-season tour, so at all these important times of the year Peter Johnson had no manager.

At the end of the day, they went to somebody who they knew would come back and who would give them an answer quickly. I think he was Bill Kenwright's choice anyway – over and above me. I think Bill always wanted Howard back at the club, I think he was the one dissenting voice with regard to me coming back to Goodison, and because we were the only two names in the frame, once I was out then Howard got the job.

How did he really get on with Howard Kendall? *Keith Giles, Perth, Australia*
Very well. I fell out with Howard twice in two years. Once when he became the first man to drop me just before we played Gillingham in the first replay down there in the FA Cup. He came to me during the pre-match dinner and said: "I'm not playing you tonight." I was absolutely staggered and flabbergasted and disappointed. We were hopeless, too, and almost went out. He picked me for the second replay and we won 3-0, and I think I created all three goals.

The only other time I fell out with him was when he decided to sell me, so I got on great with him in general. I thought he was a wonderful man-manager and I thought the blend of him and Colin was ideal. Colin was certainly quieter and more studious and very much a coach. Howard was very much a manager and I had the utmost respect, and still do, for Howard Kendall.

On the Mark and Lard show on Radio 1 the other day you were a question in a quiz. The question?
Which cartoon character does Andy Gray sound like when he sings.
a) Betty Boop b) Hong Kong Phooey c) Marge Simpson
The answer was Marge Simpson. Have you any comment to make on that? *Jon Gard, Woolton, Liverpool*
Marge Simpson? Well I thought I sounded more like Ronan Keating, to be honest.

Big Nev or Schmeichel? *Phil Williams, Chester, North Wales*
I've always said that Neville Southall was the best goalkeeper I ever played with by a distance. In the mid-1980s, he was just sensational; he was the best in the world.

Peter Schmeichel was the same, but ten years on. I think he's the modern equivalent of Neville, but he's about 6ft 4ins and that's what a modern-day goalkeeper needs to be. I think they're both on a par with each other and both the best in their time, and I can pay no greater compliment than to say I couldn't choose between them.

Did he really ask for appearance money when he was invited to the Hall of Fame Dinner? If not, why did he not turn up? *John Quinn, Tewkesbury, England*
Did I ask for a fee? No. I didn't turn up because I wasn't available – it's as simple as that. I was either working or away. There's absolutely no way if you get into a hall of fame like Everton's you don't turn up. The person who asked the question is obviously someone who doesn't know me at all, because that would never enter my head. I have work commitments and family commitments, and assuming that none of them cross over then I'd love to go up to the next one – there's no doubt about that.

Can you put in a good word for me with Kirsty Gallagher? *Rob Bland, Morecambe, England*
Tell him he'll have to get in the queue. And there's an awful long line in front of him, too.

The media is bringing a huge amount of money into football. In Andy's opinion, has this changed the game as we know it, making it less personable/intimate, and more of a product and commodity? *Bradford Wood, California, USA*
Yes, it has, at least I believe so. I think that the top players' rapport with the fans has gone and the gap is getting wider and wider. Footballers have become like pop stars now, almost untouchable. We only ever see them on stage, which is the football pitch, and not really anywhere else. I think that's sad. I believe football is all about the relationship between players and supporters. Throughout my career I always had a great laugh with the supporters. I gave them time and space to talk and sign autographs and take photographs, and I do think that it's become more of a product and less of what it was. It's not necessarily a bad thing, but it means that football has changed dramatically over the last six or seven years, there's no doubt about that.

Would he be offended by the fact that my wife described him as "a big soft kid on the loose in the sweet shop" when she first saw him playing with his video thingy? *Neil Wolstenholme, Chelsea, South-West London*
No. Since I was able to walk all I've ever thought about being involved in or wanted to be involved in was football, and when you stop playing you have to find something to give you that kick of adrenaline. Television has given me that, certainly Sky with all the stuff that we've brought into the coverage of football and the groundbreaking stuff we've introduced, and it's been great for me because I go on there to express myself. I am like a kid in a candy store at times, but I think it's been good for football in many ways and good for the armchair

fan. We've always said that what we want to see is bums on seats and once we've filled the ground then we'll happily show the game.

Please could you ask him whether he thinks things like Sky's Monday Night Football and other bizarre kick-off days and times are fair on those supporters who actually go the match, especially away fans? (And please don't let him cop out by claiming it is the clubs who agree to this.) *Nick Williams, Warrington, England*

I actually think that people like Monday night football. It was always a night when people had nothing to do. People have come to terms with it and it's all part and parcel of modern football these days. They go to the pub and enjoy the fact they can watch the match. But we don't have total power at all, otherwise we would schedule matches for whenever we liked – we would not show Liverpool v Man United or Man United-Arsenal on a Saturday morning at 11.30, but because the authorities want it shown there, we show it. It helps teams like Manchester United to play slightly earlier because it gives them more time to rest before European games. If we can play a game on a Sunday and a Monday, then it helps the team to rest if they played in Europe on a Thursday.

There are lots of other factors involved, too, but Sky do not dominate football. The Premier League dictate what happens and the clubs are happy to go along with it, and I think most of the public is.

Are Evertonians merely paranoid or does the media slight Everton by not giving us the same type of coverage that other teams enjoy? Bang to the point, Andy, is there a media conspiracy against EFC? *Ken Myers, California, USA*

Well, I can't answer for the written press because I'm not party to what they write or what their feelings are. I live in the Midlands now so I don't get to see or hear the regional coverage. From a television point of view, from where I stand, obviously, there's not a negative slant, I could never be negative about Everton when we cover them.

Certainly, as far as Sky are concerned, the amount of games you're on depends on how you're playing at the time and which games are most important. If everyone is to be honest, over the past four or five years Everton have been fighting more at the bottom end of the table than the top. If Everton were playing like Arsenal and Chelsea they would be on television far more than they are now, possibly even double the amount they are at the moment.

I don't think there's an anti-Everton conspiracy amongst us at Sky, and when Everton's fortunes change, as they seem to be doing now, they'll get far more favourable press than they have been doing. I don't think it helps that Peter Johnson managed to alienate a lot of people in his tenure there as chairman.

Did he feel the slightest bit of sympathy for Bolton after he had used his magic technology to prove that they had scored against us before they got relegated? *Si Wooldridge, Chippenham, England*

No, because the game took place halfway through the season, it wasn't the last game of the season. People look back at that and say Bolton went down by one point, but had this goal been allowed in November, or whenever it was, they would have stayed up. I don't go along with that school of thought because you play 38 or 40 games and that determines whether or not you're good enough to stay up. So, one decision that goes against them, you can't look at that over the course of a whole season and say that cost them relegation. A team that gets relegated gets relegated for one reason, and that is because they're not good enough to stay up, and that season Bolton weren't good enough. Happily, Everton were ...just about.

How much did he enjoy Nathan Blake's goal at Anfield earlier this year? *Phil Bowker, Brussels, Belgium*
That's a terrible question. How can you ask somebody who works in the media how they enjoyed a goal at Anfield?
    It was actually very good.

For all the extra cash and raised profile that Sky has given football, how does he justify the complete power it has over the Premiership re the rescheduling of matches at short notice, regular Sunday football, etc., giving the impression that Sky couldn't give a toss about the people who go to games, they only care about the ones who watch footy on telly. *Phil Bowker, Brussels, Belgium*
That's utter toss for a start. We don't reschedule games at a moment's notice. We can't reschedule a game at a moment's notice, it's not allowed.
    Premiership games are agreed something like eight or ten weeks in advance of when they're showing – that's Sunday and Monday, only the ones late on in the season get moved when you get to the beginning or end of May, because, obviously, we don't know who's going to be challenging for the title and who's going to be struggling against relegation. Those are rescheduled slightly then.
    We used to have Sunday football, when ITV were showing games live they were on a Sunday, so this is nothing new. We don't reschedule games at a moment's notice, we would never be allowed to and we will never be allowed to.

Does the white marker pen actually detach? *Clive Blackmore, Washington DC, USA*
Yeah, it does, but it doesn't work when you detach it, it needs to be linked up to the screen.

Tricky one here: Who was your best ever partner? Pre-Everton is OK. *George Lee Stuart, Lismore, Australia*
That's a difficult one because when I first came down from Scotland Brian Little, at Aston Villa, made me, there's no doubt about that. We were different – he was small and had incredible ability in movement with the ball and he could conjure up so many scoring chances. I was just very straightforward and relied

on people providing crosses and passes for me. I wouldn't have achieved half of what I have if I'd have been with another partner as my first one, but after Brian, Sharpie would have to be the one.

Everyone thought we were too similar to play together and we'd get in each other's way, so it gave us both a great deal of satisfaction that we were able, not only to not get in each other's way, but that we could get so on so well that we almost completed the treble.

How does he contrast the (allegedly) more drink-o-centric-Chinese meal team spirit approach to management of Kendall-Reid-Bryan Robson to the Evian-Caesar salad-my-body-is-the-tool-of-my-trade approach of Wenger-Vialli-Johnny Foreigner? *Phil Bowker, Brussels, Belgium*

It was obviously different in our day, and I think because of the fitness levels they have to look after their body more now. Ask me if I played now would I drink, I would have to say no, but I do enjoy a glass of wine and going out and enjoying myself, so it would be hard.

People have to have their beliefs in the game, in what they should do and how they should treat their body, and it is different – I accept that diet is an important part of being a footballer now, but I still like the old ways of Peter Reid. He has adjusted his way of thinking to complement the modern game.

How does he feel about Duncan Ferguson choosing not to play for Scotland? *Martin Smith, New Jersey, USA*

Surprised and disappointed. I understand Duncan's reasons, but he doesn't seem to understand that it's not the SFA he's letting down, it's the whole country and the whole footballing nation of Scotland. I've tried to talk to him about it, I said: "Listen, son, you're going to regret this when you've retired and your kids ask you why you only played half a dozen times for Scotland." It's going to be hard for Duncan to justify why he chose to turn his back on his country, and I just think he's missed out. He made his point, he made his protest. I know he felt let down by the SFA, and I understand that totally, but it's not the SFA who are hurting, it's every Scotland football supporter, and I include myself in that band at the moment. How I wish over the last two or three years he had picked himself or made himself available, because I do think he would have made a huge difference to us.

I would like to ask his opinion of the coaching staff at Everton. Does he rate Archie Knox? Walter puts great store on his ability, but some of the play maybe indicates a problem? *Mike Coville, New York, USA*

I've got a great deal of respect for them. Funnily enough, I played with both of them at Dundee United when I went as a 17-year-old. They were in the twilight of their playing days, and because I was young and fresh, I added another couple of years on to both of their careers – they would have retired long before they did. I've known them for years and I was with Walter at Rangers when he was with Graeme Souness, and Archie and him took over there.

You work as a team and you put trust in people you know, and Walter feels comfortable with Archie as his number two and his ability to put across what he wants to do. They're both great lads and I shouldn't imagine there would be a problem about the coaching. Walter knows a great deal about football, he's fully qualified and he's an excellent coach, and I don't think there will be a problem if he gets the right type of support financially. I think they could do a really good job at Everton.

Graeme Sharp or Duncan Ferguson. Who's the better player? *Darryl Ng, Southampton, England*

Graeme was top scorer in the top division and Duncan hasn't achieved that yet. Graeme won championships, and I know Duncan won the FA Cup in 1995, but he hasn't quite gone on to scale the heights that Sharpie did. His record is still there to be shot at. There is no doubt that Duncan at his best is a threat, but Sharpie was a fantastic centre-forward, absolutely fantastic.

Which is the team he looks out for first on Saturdays, Everton, Villa, Rangers, Wolves or Dundee United? *Jon Berman, West Derby, Liverpool*

I was born, bred and grew up in Glasgow as a Rangers supporter, so that's the first result I look for and no one would be surprised at me saying that. Rangers is my team and it's as simple as that. I think Villa and Everton are very close, but for different reasons, and I remember Howard came up with a great analogy, which I think applies to me: I would say that Villa was like a wife to me, but Everton was like a mistress, and that probably sums up the relationships I had with both clubs. I couldn't really split my affinity between one and the other.

Would he realistically take the Everton job if offered it at some point in the future? *Keith Giles, Perth, Australia*

I know Walter well and I'd like to think he'll continue to turn the club around. He just needs to get some money to spend and then that question will never come up. I've got a lot of time for him and it would be great to see him restore Everton Football Club to its former glory.

I know two things in life, I know about football and I know about television. If television doesn't want me, or if I don't want it, then maybe, before I hang up my football boots forever, I might try management.

I don't regret the decision I took three years ago, but you sometimes only get one chance and that might have been my opportunity. If it turns out that way, then so be it, but I can't help thinking that things that special only ever happen once in a lifetime.

And we're so glad that you happened in ours. Thanks for the memories.

Adrian Heath

Born 11 November 1961
January 1982 to November 1988
£700,000

'IF I close my eyes, I can still picture it now – playing in little triangles, Trevor Steven, myself, Sharpie and Peter down the right-hand side and Pat Van den Hauwe and Sheedy on the left. Andy Gray and Reidy warned me that when I hung my boots up it would never be the same again, but I didn't really believe them and just kept on taking it for granted. Of course, they were right and sometimes I feel envious to the point of jealousy when I see players running out on a Saturday now, because no matter what you achieve in management, it's always second best.'

Dinky Adrian Heath arrived at Goodison just days before his 21st birthday. Only 5ft 6ins, ten stone and with the face of an angel, he may have had trouble getting served in the pub, but on the park he was as brave as a lion.

An almost extra sensory understanding and striking partnership with Graeme Sharp was soon developed, and the goals just kept on rattling in. Nothing on earth could curb the diminutive dynamo and everything in Inchy's garden had a delicate rosy hue.

It was three days before he should have made England debut, when a wrenching tackle by Sheffield Wednesday's Brian Marwood smashed his knee and his international dream. He never did get his England cap.

Fellow Bluenoses, it's my great pleasure to introduce you to the man whose astonishing contribution plotted the history of our great football club. Congenial, articulate, gracious and still no bigger than a tuppenny rabbit: Adrian Heath, you have our undivided attention.

Was he surprised that Everton came in for him when he was at Stoke and was he shocked at the price they paid for him? £700k was a lot back then. *John Staines, Adelaide, Australia*

I wasn't surprised, because Howard Kendall was the manager and he played with me at Stoke City. He went to Blackburn, but we kept in touch and he told me if he got a big job he would come and get me. I didn't know where that would be, but when he went to Everton I kept my fingers crossed that he would come back for me, which he did.

With regard to the fee, I think it was the second highest in the country at the time. It was an awful lot of money in those days, but considering I was there for six-and-a half years and they got nearly all their money back when they sold me, I'd like to think that I represented good value.

How did he feel about getting displaced, first of all by Andy Gray and then by Gary Lineker? *Richard Marland, Waterloo, Liverpool*

It was strange really with the Andy Gray situation. Originally, when he was bought, Sharpie was left out. Howard played Andy and me for a few games, and then he played Sharpie and Andy together with me wide right if we had a few injuries. I suppose, me playing out of position so much is what split Andy and I up.

I thoroughly appreciate what Andy Gray did for us though. The big fella along with Peter Reid was the catalyst to everything we did. We were certainly a good set of young players, but I think the introduction of Peter and Andy Gray made us a proper team. They taught us what playing football was all about, in terms of winning.

Gary was a little bit different because he scored the goals, but I don't think that we ever reproduced the football the supporters at Everton liked to watch. Shall we say I was more than a little bit satisfied when I got back up front with Sharpie and we won the title again by playing some great football.

That goal at Highbury in the semi-final, does it stand out as one of his finest, not in quality, but because of the reaction? *Pete Rowlands, Enfield, North London*

When I get asked which is my favourite goal, I mention that one and people say it wasn't particularly great, but the importance of it and the reaction of our supporters make it so special to me. Add to that the fact that we were going back to the final in the FA Cup; it signalled the beginning of what was a very successful period for us. I was delighted that we'd got to Wembley – I knew our fans, who'd been so special to the players, had got a great day out to look forward to. Prior to that, we'd just been watching Liverpool go to Wembley every other year and winning something and it was our turn at last.

Is it fair to say that Peter Reid used to look after him like a big brother on the pitch? The Sheffield Wednesday game springs to mind. Reidy went in and battered Marwood shortly after Inchy was taken off. *Martin Smith, New Jersey, USA*

Well, he says he's still looking after me now by giving me another job.

I'd been told by Bobby Robson the week before that I was in the next England squad, so I think at the time he felt guilty because he'd played me the ball, which was a little bit short and it got me in trouble. Every time I see him, I remind him that he cost me my England cap and my career, and he's still paying for it to this day.

No, he used to look after us all, Reidy. Him and Andy Gray made us grow up very quickly. We were afraid of nobody and people forget we were so young. Trevor, Gary Stevens, Sheeds, he'd hardly played any football. I was only 21, Sharpie was, too, and Derek Mountfield. It was young side, but those two made us grow up into men.

An Evertonian mate of mine – reliable source since he is from Derry, the first real Christian city west of Rome – contends that Adrian Heath was never the same player after the dreadful injury which resulted from Brian Marwood's reckless (to say the bleedin' least) tackle which put Inchy out for a long while. Said mate reckoned the bad tackle was deliberate on Marwood's part. Any comment? *Charlie Deeney, Ottawa, Canada*

I don't think it was deliberate, I think it was just a mistimed tackle. One or two people said the same thing about my comeback, but all I could do was play on to the best of my ability at that time. I was playing the best football of my career when I got injured, so coming back and being a bit rusty after being out for so long, people obviously made that comparison.

Did he see Marwood face to face after that 'tackle' and if so, what did they say? *Osmo Tapio Räihälä, Helsinki, Finland*

I have seen him, yes, he works for Nike, and Sunderland have done a deal with them for next year and so I'll be seeing a lot more of him in the future.

The first time we met it was a bit embarrassing, but Reidy had already made him pay for that tackle and in a few games after that some other players did too.

I've never put anybody out for that length of time, but I've also made tackles that I've not been particularly proud of.

Has Peter Reid got a dictionary? *Phil Pellow, Waterloo, Liverpool*
Yes, he has, but it's an abridged version.

Is he bitter on missing out on the European Cup-winners' Cup Final and the run into the championship season? *Pete Rowlands, Enfield, North London*

The League was different because I played a significant part, I'd scored quite a lot of goals and I knew that injury was part and parcel of the game, but I have to say that I was very upset and emotional in Rotterdam.

I'd played in the first two ties, but I had to sit in the stands with Mark Higgins for the Final and I felt as if I was a million miles away. I was made up for all the players and the supporters, but for my own personal and selfish reasons I was gutted.

We finished so high in the League, we should have played in the European Cup ties, the UEFA Cup and Cup-winners' Cup, and we had that cruelly taken away from us with the disaster at Heysel. I didn't know then that it was to have been my only opportunity, so I feel cheated to have been robbed of what should have been a very special night for me as it was for the rest of the players.

What did you think of Lukic, the Arsenal goalkeeper, when he lifted the ball just to show everyone your height? P.S. you were big to me. *Ari Sigurgeisson, Hafnarfjordur, Iceland*

Ha! We used to beat Arsenal for fun in those days, I remember beating them five at Goodison and three away, so it was probably the only way they could get anything back on us. They never liked coming to Goodison, that's for sure.

How did he feel in May 1987? He had won the League on his own in the end. *Osmo Tapio Räihälä, Helsinki, Finland*

I think Gary Lineker had come and scored all those goals and it made it seem impossible for me to get back in the team. As it happens, I played an awful lot that year in different roles, but for me to go back up front with Sharpie and win the League gave me a lot of self-satisfaction.

Nobody can disregard Gary's qualities and his contribution to the club the previous year, but I think we did lose a bit as a team. Trevor Steven didn't weigh in with the same amount of goals; neither did Kevin Sheedy or Derek Mountfield. As a whole, we were a better team when Sharpie and I played up front than when he was there with Gary Lineker, and as a collective group we were a bit more pleasing on the eye. It was not only great to be starting up front, but to win the League again was very pleasing indeed.

Sharpie and I were close on and off the field, but to play alongside him was tremendous. He was a dream of a target man and he was always prepared to share the burden.

One of my best mates is a Portsmouth fan and he wants me to say thank you for scoring the goal that beat Southampton in the 1984 FA Cup semi-final – a sentiment I definitely wish to echo. *Neil Wolstenholme, Chelsea, South-West London*

It will always be special because of the timing. To score a goal in any FA Cup semi-final is very emotional and you know the importance of it, but to do it two seconds before the end of the game is tremendous. It's something that I'll never forget, and I'm sure it's something that the Portsmouth supporters won't forget either.

Did that nickname ever get on your nerves? *Ste Daley, Speke, Liverpool*

I've had it from the age of about six. I was always the smallest in the class. I went on holiday one year with a group of friends and my friend's father said I looked like an Inchy, little Inchy and it stuck, I've been Inchy ever since. Everybody knows it, so it's nothing I've ever been embarrassed about or too bothered about really.

Was the cracker from 35 yards against Liverpool in the 3-3 draw in 1982 the best goal he ever scored? *Osmo Tapio Räihälä, Helsinki, Finland*

No. I think I would have to say for an actual goal, beating Norwich at Goodison when Neville Southall half-volleyed the ball down to me on the halfway line. I ran it in-field and played it to Kevin Sheedy, who stood on it for what seemed an eternity before scooping it over all the defence. I raced round and volleyed it in from about 17 or 18 yards, it was a terrific goal and something that I can still re-run in my mind in minute detail. It was my best goal, not in terms of importance but certainly in terms of it being a classic goal.

Does he feel that he never got the credit he deserved for Everton's success in the 1980's? *Martin Smith, New Jersey, USA*
We had a terrific set of players then. I think people forget that we were very young when we got there and most of them went on to play full international football. There was an awful lot of competition, to say the least.

Whether or not I had enough plaudits isn't important, it's the fact that my team-mates and the supporters appreciated what I did.

I still get a lot of mail from Evertonians and I'm delighted with that. In fact, I was in Spain recently and an Evertonian came up to me in the street and said: "Thanks for scoring all those goals for us," and we're talking 12 years on now, so the fact that they all still remember it will be good enough for me

When he left us to join Español did he feel sad, or simply relieved that he would get first team football again? *David Chow, Manchester, England*
First-team football was the main reason for leaving. Colin had turned the team round a little bit and he brought Tony Cottee in to replace me, and Stu McCall to replace Peter. Having had the injury, I couldn't afford to be sitting around and not playing. I'd got myself going again, and we'd won the League the year after. I knew Colin wanted to change the team a bit, but I wasn't prepared to sit there week after week watching other people play because I had a lot to offer. The thought of playing abroad always appealed to me, so I thought it was a good opportunity to leave.

Did he learn any Spanish or Catalan while at Español? *Osmo Tapio Räihälä, Helsinki, Finland*
I learned Spanish and it's still quite good because I regularly go to Spain. Catalan was a bit more difficult, but I could say the usual stuff – good morning, hello and where are you from? But there the majority of the people spoke Spanish.

I thought it would be easy for me to learn Catalan, being in a working environment, but they all wanted me to speak in English with them so they could practise on me.

Having now spent several years in management and coaching, what do you think is the essential ingredient in making a star player out of a young hopeful? *Phil Pellow, Waterloo, Liverpool*
In the modern game every player needs to have a major strength. Whether it be dribbling, tackling, heading, pace, or exceptional touch and vision like Zola, but

I think if you're going to make it to the top now and be a top Premier League or international player you certainly need one major asset in your armoury.

The game is getting quicker now. I'm not saying it's getting better as a spectacle, but it's certainly getting quicker, and power and size are becoming more important. Players are finding it more difficult to make a real impression in the game now, but you do need an outstanding talent of some description and a little bit of luck.

How would he compare Nick Barmby of today with himself in, say, 1984? *Osmo Tapio Räihälä, Helsinki, Finland*

We're similar in terms of the way we play, although I think I played a little bit further forward than him. Nick is an intelligent footballer, and I know that because I've worked with him, so they think he can cope with anything. He plays wide left, he plays wide right, and he plays behind the front two in the middle. I think he gets shifted about a little bit too much for his own good at times

Nick is a good pro, he works hard at his game and I feel there are a lot of similarities between us. I think it would be better for him if he settles down in one position and then he might realise more of his potential.

Just why did Gary Speed go? HK and Speed seem to have sworn Trappist vows, but the little man may be willing to at least provide a few hints. *Neil Wolstenholme, Chelsea, South-West London*

I think it got to the stage where Gary thought he needed a move. We were disappointed at the time because he was an integral part of what we were trying to build there. It's been well documented since that we didn't have any money and it was very difficult, and the last thing we wanted to do was sell what was one of our best players. The fact that he's still playing so well for Newcastle proves that.

Certainly, from a personal point of view, I enjoyed working with Speedo. I was really disappointed that he left, but if anything was said it was between the manager and the player. I'm not really sure there was anything else other than Newcastle coming to him with their interest and he got on with it – he felt a move was the right thing at the time, but I was certainly sorry to see him go.

Was it a hard decision leaving his managerial job at Burnley for a lesser job at Everton? *Chris Lord, Morecambe, England*

I had a terrific job in Burnley. I'd started well there, my first year we got down to the play-offs, I was in the process of building a team to get them out of that division and it was a good club. I gave that up to go back to Everton with the promise of £20-odd million to spend, then got there and found that there was actually no money at all. I do feel a little bit cheated.

Did it give him great satisfaction to see Waddle balls it up the season after he left? *Chris Lord, Morecambe, England*

To be honest, I was a little bit disappointed when I saw what money was available to him the following year, but I always wanted the club to go on and be successful.

At Christmas that year we'd got ourselves up to third in the division, and if we'd have had a little bit more money to put into the team I'm sure that we then could have gone on and maybe finished in the play-offs. No, it didn't give me any satisfaction, other people thought that considering he'd spent all that money he didn't do a particularly good job, but I was pleased that they stayed up because I had three or four really good years there.

Was he like me? A few days after the Coventry game did he feel just a little bit embarrassed at actually CELEBRATING the lap-of-the-gods escape? *Frank Hargreaves, Anfield, Liverpool*

From my point of view, celebration isn't really the word, relief was.

I remember being very emotional after the game with Big Duncan, because in the week prior to that I've never been as nervous in all my life. Everything I'd ever done for Everton, and I'm sure Howard Kendall felt the same, would have paled into insignificance if we had been in charge of the club when it went down. Certainly, Everton should never have been down there, but to be in charge and responsible would have been an absolute disaster for me, and I just couldn't have coped with that. So my feeling was relief more than anything else.

I can't express what it was like on the day in the dressing-room before and after. I just hope that no Evertonian, in any capacity has to go through it again because it was horrible.

We stayed over the night before on the Wirral and I remember the supporters lining the streets all the way from the tunnel. I looked at some of the players, and to be honest with you I felt a bit frightened for the likes of Gareth Farrelly and John Oster because it was the first time the enormity of the game and the size of the club had really dawned on any of them. I just hoped they could cope with it, and they did.

It was a terrible day, especially with the news of what was going on else-where. You get people telling you things, which aren't true, like Bolton were winning. I remember getting home and I was drained but I couldn't sleep, my mind was just racing and reliving it all. It was certainly the most emotional and traumatic day I've ever had in football and I wouldn't wish it on anybody.

I ask this as a fellow dwarf: Did Inchy ever get pissed off with always being 'little Adrian Heath'? *Charlie Brewer, Seoul, South Korea*

If I'd been called 'that fat bastard' or something like that it might have been a problem for me, but 'little' was a word that described a characteristic so it didn't bother me at all – much.

In January 1991 he played for Manchester City at Goodison alongside Peter Reid. During the first half, Sheedy banged in an absolutely classical half-volley. Everton still had Nev, Sharpie, Ratters and Watson in the side. What was the

feeling, playing against all these people and at Goodison? *Osmo Tapio Räihälä, Helsinki, Finland*

I'll say this now – I still think that Goodison Park is the greatest ground for atmosphere in the country and you always get a good reception from the fans. I think they appreciate the effort you put in while you were there and it was nice to go back and see old friends, but I did wonder if I was playing for the wrong team.

When I look at what players did after they moved on from there, Trevor Steven and Gary Stevens had eight or nine good years up at Rangers, I still had another four or five years left in me, and Sharpie left a little bit after that, and I still think, with hindsight, that the team broke up earlier than it should have done.

Now that Nev is back in the Premier League and the Blues have signed Richard Gough and Mark Hughes, are you getting the boots Dubbined up again? *Phil Pellow, Waterloo, Liverpool*

I said that the other day. I went to watch a First Division game in Scotland and I turned to Alex Rae, who's one of our Scottish boys, and I told him I'd decided to get my registration back out because I think I've got another five years left in me.

But all joking apart, I think it's a great testament to the players. Obviously, Neville's was an emergency. Had he been playing regularly he would have been in better physical shape. But, certainly, looking at Richard Gough, and even Waggy to an extent, I think it's a testament to their professionalism.

I played myself until I was 36, so I can't complain, especially being my size and at the sharp end where it is a little bit more physical, but I've had my day now and, hopefully, I can help get some of these younger players to have theirs.

Was he secretly happy to see Sunderland tonked by Everton on Boxing Day 1999 until he had to face Reidy, or was Reid also thinking: "Well, fortunately it was Everton." *Osmo Tapio Räihälä, Helsinki, Finland*

I think Peter made that comment. He would have rather it be Everton than anybody else.

Before the game I said to the players that I used to love playing at Goodison on Boxing Day – I don't know what it is, but Everton always seem to play well on Boxing Day, there's always a bit of magic in the air and we had some terrific results there if you look back over the years.

I told the players that Everton would be fired up and it would be a full house and to make sure we started brightly. Unfortunately, we didn't. Everton got an early goal and in the end we were fortunate to get away with five.

Obviously, these people pay my wages now, so my allegiance has changed. We want to win games, but if we were going to lose a game I'd rather it was Everton.

Nothing ever gave me greater pleasure than running out at Goodison Park. I used to especially love playing mid-week games under the lights. Howard

Kendall told me that no matter where I go, it would always remain under my skin, and it does, it's a special place and I loved my time there. I feel very humble when I go back, and no matter where I am or what I do, I always look for their result first. Walter Smith seems to be doing a fantastic job over there. I wish him the very best of luck and I can't help thinking that for Everton Football Club, the only way is up.

Inchy, we'll wait here for you to come home again.

Howard Kendall

Born 22 May 1946
March 1967 to June 1998
£80,000

 WHEN they knocked on the door of my house, my father immediately asked: "Is it Liverpool?" They told him it was across the park.

And that, my friends, is quite literally how close it came.

It was one day before the 1967 transfer deadline when Howard Kendall signed for Everton, leaving Bill Shankly wringing his hands in despair. That weekend, Everton beat Liverpool at Goodison Park in the fifth round of the FA Cup – a screamer, courtesy of Alan Ball. Cup-tied, Howie watched from the stands. The die had been cast.

That day was to herald the dawn of one of the greatest love affairs in football, which would span the next 31 years. And who could ever have dreamt that the 20-year-old Tynesider with a heart full of ambition, a headful of hair, with 60 quid a week in his pocket, would go on to navigate the uncharted waters of unprecedented glory.

Fellow Bluenoses, the stage is set for the most revealing interview of his distinguished career and it gives me the utmost pleasure to introduce you to the captivating, charming and charismatic man who led Everton Football Club in its finest hour.

Howard Kendall, the floor is yours.

People go on about naming stands, gates and statues in honour of football heroes, how would Howard like to be remembered? *Frank Hargreaves, Anfield, Liverpool*

I would like something at Goodison Park, or the new stadium if they move, that would be a tremendous honour. Alex Young was at Goodison a few weeks ago for a presentation and I thought then how proud he must have felt.

I've been in Dixie Dean lounges and Joe Mercer suites and would be deeply honoured to have something named after me. I don't want it after I've gone though, I want to see it or walk into it myself before I depart this world.

Ask him how surprised was he was to end up on the blue half of Merseyside given that the press already had him down as having committed the heinous crime of signing for Liverpool. *Les Anderson, Keighley, England*

It was well known that after playing in an FA Cup Final for Preston when I was 17 a lot of the top clubs were coming for me. I was continually linked with Liverpool, but I got the impression that so many players had left Preston for Liverpool, such as Gordon Milne, Davey Wilson and Peter Thompson, that they didn't want to be classed as a nursery team. Jimmy Milne, the Preston manager, approached me and he said: "I've got a club for you." I was totally surprised that it was Everton.

I've never regretted it for a moment, although at that particular time I would have signed for Liverpool because all I wanted to do was play in the top flight and play top-class football. Everton gave me that chance.

Ask him about his early months at Goodison when he replaced folk hero Jimmy Gabriel and was constantly jeered for the impudence of stepping into the boots of a legend. Did he really think he had a future with us then? *John Quinn, Tewkesbury, England*

When you go to a famous club it's always dangerous when you're replacing somebody the fans love, and Jimmy Gabriel was a great player when Harry Catterick sold him to Southampton.

I was cup-tied when I arrived at Everton and I didn't make my debut for a little while. When I arrived at Goodison Park for my first game, there was a telegram waiting for me from Jimmy Gabriel. I thought that was a lovely gesture from him, and he remains a tremendous friend to this day.

But time goes on, and Harry Catterick was wanting to rebuild, he'd already won the Championship, which was an absolutely unbelievable feat as a manager, and he felt maybe he had to bring some younger ones in. He brought Alan Ball in the early part of the season, Colin Harvey was emerging as one of the best midfield players in the country and he felt that maybe I made up the balance. It all turned out to be very successful.

Can you ask Howie if he remembers a game in 1972 against Derby when he tried a one-two at the Street End, he didn't quite catch the return and smiled after having come so close. Does he remember some little bastard in the first couple of rows shouting: "It's nothing to laugh at Kendall."? If he does, does he forgive me? If he doesn't forgive me, tell him my dad battered me in the ground and it might make him feel better. *Brian Parkinson, Doncaster, England*

It's lovely that, I've never had a question like that asked before. Sometimes, when you used to play at Goodison Park, there could be 13 or 14,000 people in a 40,000 stadium, you can not only hear the abuse, you can pick him out, but on that particular day, Derby County, I can't think of the person you're talking about.

I had a bad injury at Derby County, I clashed with Roger Davies and I was out for a long time after that, then when I came back I actually scored in that particular game, maybe that's the game he's talking about. I put one in from about

25 yards, and although I think we lost the game, maybe the little lad in short pants giving me the abuse inspired me and I gave him what he deserved in return. And of course I forgive him.

How did he feel, never getting the England recognition he deserved? *Jim Lynch, Southport, Merseyside*

That was always a disappointment because I had a lot of media push in terms of being selected. In 1970, I was selected for the England squad against Yugoslavia at Wembley. I thought that was going to be my big one.

We trained in the morning at Roehampton and when we came out to the coach afterwards, Alf Ramsey said: "I'm going to name my 12 players," and I was about the fifth name mentioned. I always remember looking across at Bobby Moore and he gave me the thumbs up. Then Alf sat down. I thought: "Yes. I'm in, fantastic, I'm playing tomorrow." Then he stood up again and said: "Rodney Marsh, have I named you?" He said: "No, Alf." "Oh, sorry," he said, "you're my twelfth man," so I thought: "Brilliant. Rodney Marsh is substitute."

I telephoned my father and family and everyone came down to London. The next morning Alf said: "If Colin Bell fails his fitness test, Howard Kendall will be playing." Now, I knew Colin Bell was playing and I couldn't believe that he'd done it in that way, and I was sub. He promised me that if he made a substitution in the 90 minutes, I would go on. And he didn't make one, and that's the nearest I think anybody can get.

It is a regret and something which is disappointing, but I wouldn't have liked to have gone on for a few seconds or a few minutes, I'm a person who would like to have earned it by being selected from the start, but it was 'that' close. Admittedly, Alf Ramsey did stick with his tried and trusted, he was a very loyal manager, and there were a lot of top-class midfielders at that particular time. He used to talk about caps being given away in cornflake packets and that became the case. I wouldn't have liked mine to be dragged out of a cornflake packet; I wanted to be selected and to deserve it.

Ask him if he remembers being Everton's number-three batsman and number-three bowler in the Peter Lever benefit cricket match against Man United at the other Old Trafford on 16 July 1972. He does? Right, Mr Kendall, your starter for ten: How many runs did you score and how many wickets did you take? And your 'Billy bonus' question is: who won – Everton or Manchester United? *Billy Williams, Cologne, Germany*

I do, indeed. I don't think I took any wickets and I might have scored 60 or 70 runs. Actually it might not have been as many as that, but I'm sure it was over 50. And we won, of course.

Did he feel that the midfield of him, Bally and big John Hurst was the best there has ever been at Goodison? I have fond memories of John Hurst going off for stitches to a head wound and then returning wearing a scrumcap. *Tony Field, Rotterdam, Holland*

I don't think John Hurst would regard himself as a midfield player, I think he must mean Colin Harvey, but I do remember John in one particular game going off for stitches, but that was the professionalism, that was the way they were in those days, nobody wanted to miss a game or even a minute of a game, we wanted to be put back on the field as soon as possible because we wanted to play. John Hurst was a central defender, not a midfield player.

Ask him does he remember missing an absolute sitter on his debut against Southampton, when he spooned the ball over the bar from about four yards out? *Tom Davis, Texas, USA*

I most certainly do. I'd waited so long for that debut, and when I played in that game I don't think Everton had been beaten at home all season. I went out there and I had leaden legs, and I mean leaden legs – it was awful.

I remember missing the opportunity and I remember us losing the game. My late father was at the game, we were going back to Preston and we called into the garage for petrol. It was pouring down with rain and I just wanted to sneak away and forget about the day. All right, I'd made my debut and it was out of the way and I just wanted to go home.

I looked over and there were some Everton fans, they saw me and just bowed down in these puddles of water on the forecourt of the petrol station and paid homage to me. I said: "I had a nightmare, we lost because I missed that opportunity," and they said: "No, it's OK, thank you for coming here," and I thought: "That's me now, that'll do me."

Was Alex Dawson really as good as Pele? *Charlie Deeney, Ottawa, Canada*

Quick answer? No! But I'll tell you something now, Alex could have sprung as high as Pele when he nodded that one in, oh dear me! Alex was superb in the air. He was only about five feet nine or ten, but he was the best in the air I've ever seen. I was a kid when I joined Preston and just to look at him play was amazing. He used to practise it every day, crosses came in and up he went, neck back and wallop. He was fantastic. Alex and Pele were different players, though, and I don't think Pele would have signed for Preston, would he?

Who did he most fear as a player? I can't believe he feared anyone, but ask him anyway. *Iain Cooke, Basel, Switzerland*

It wasn't so much fear; it was the element of expectancy really when you played against Leeds United, because they were renowned as people who didn't take any prisoners. I've been on the end of quite a number of challenges from the likes of Norman Hunter and Johnny Giles. They were so apologetic afterwards and you tended to forgive them, but on that field they were ruthless. Apart from being top-class players, Don Revie's Leeds was the crudest team you've ever seen. I'll tell you what, you wouldn't get many of them playing for 90 minutes today.

I rate you as the Evertonian of the century – you're the greatest. Who was the most talented player you played with? *Ari Sigurgeisson, Hafnarfjordur, Iceland*

When I played in the 1970s with Everton, I felt Alan Ball was one of the most influential players that Everton really have ever had, he was so consistent, he was a great motivator and a great pleasure to play alongside.

The best I've played against was George Best. Dear me, when you played against someone like that, you'd walk off the pitch at the end of the game and tend to be a few inches smaller, you'd know you'd been up against the best. My claim to fame is that we share the same birthday.

Given his obvious talent as a footballer, how much does he regret the fact that most Evertonians regard him as a manager first and foremost, eclipsing his feats as a footballer? *Les Anderson, Keighley, England*

When Merseyside started to do the 'Sports Personality of the Year' with the *Liverpool Echo*, I was the first one to win that award, and that meant so much to me because it was something from the fans.

We move on, the kids now won't have seen me play, but their fathers will tell them how good we were and compare us with certain players of today, that's normal. All I can ask is that I was appreciated when I was playing there.

Who was his best signing, would it have been Nev? *Osmo Tapio Räihälä, Helsinki, Finland*

I think so, yeah. When you look at signings, you could name so many players because a lot of them did absolutely brilliantly. Neville Southall, I honestly believe was the best in the world at one stage, so if you look at the price you paid, the years' service he gave, and the Footballer of the Year award, he's got to be rated as the best signing I made, yes.

Do you think it's necessary or desirable for Everton to leave Goodison Park in order to succeed commercially in the modern game? *Phil Bowker, Brussels, Belgium*

When we talk about the successful times and what Goodison Park means to a lot of people, it would be a very sad day if suddenly that was taken away from them. I think that a lot depends on where the new stadium's going to be, but if you asked the likes of Bolton Wanderers supporters or Derby County or Sunderland, they'll tell you that once the dust has settled, it's not so bad after all.

I've been up to the Stadium of Light, it's absolutely fantastic and I'm certain the facilities would be as good. You ask a Sunderland supporter, they've forgotten all about Roker Park now, and that's a compliment to the way the people have built the place, they've built a stadium which is brilliant and they've got a successful team at the minute now, too, that's also important.

Was he aware at the time that the Birmingham City footy kit of the mid-1970s was an abhorrence, or did he think it looked kinda cool? *Les Anderson, Keighley, England*

I remember going down to Birmingham City, I'd gone there from Everton and was a big money signing in a deal including Bob Latchford and Archie Styles.

We got to this air-raid shelter, which was supposedly a training ground; it was at Elmdon Airport or nearby. The players immediately came to me and asked me to have a word with the boss about the kit and I thought: "What's wrong with it?" I had a new fresh kit on and they had on something like you wouldn't believe, they were caked in dirt and so filthy. I couldn't believe they were going out there wearing all this dirty gear, especially as I'd been used to special treatment at Everton. I said: "No, I won't have a word, but if it's like this tomorrow, I will."

It was a horrible kit, though, now as I think about it, blue and white and shite.

What was his greatest moment for Everton Football Club as a player? *Iain Cooke, Basel, Switzerland*

There have been so many. I think the best moment as a player was to win the Championship in 1970. I remember talking to Bally about five minutes before the end of the game when he came running past me. I asked him how it felt to be Champions, and he just clenched his fist and said: "YES. We're the best now." The game hadn't finished, but we knew we'd won it.

His finest moment as an Everton manager, was it winning a particular trophy or something like the Bayern game? *Antony Richman, Johannesburg, South Africa*

As a manager, I think you always remember the first trophy you win at a particular club. You have the excitement of winning a semi-final and you know you're at Wembley. That 1984 Cup Final, we had to win that because it meant Europe and it meant the first trophy for me as a manager, nobody then, in the future, could ever take that away from me, I'd won a trophy with Everton Football Club and I would be written in their history. It's gone on from there, but I think the first one is very special.

Did the mistreatment of you and your family by some so-called supporters in the early days have any influence on your decision to leave for Bilbao? *Mark Kenyon, Minnesota, USA*

None whatsoever. I understood the fans' frustration in terms of not being successful.

I kept the Everton Board of Directors in contact with any move I was making, I didn't do anything out the back door. The year before, I signed a provisional contract to go to Barcelona, and they understood that. It was nothing to do with a Lineker link or whatever, I signed a provisional contract when Terry Venables was the manager at Barcelona. He was about to leave and they wanted me to take over and I told Everton Football Club.

The European ban was in place and I just wanted more of Europe, I wanted to further my education or whatever you want to call it and Barcelona were the biggest club in Europe. Then that broke down when Venables elected to stay, so I stayed, too, and we won the Championship in 87 again.

Then Athletic Bilbao came in and sold me the idea of me going there. I thought: "Well, we're Champions again," and I missed Europe. I believe that the team I had after winning the European Cup-winners' Cup would have gone on to better things – I really and truly believe that. They themselves going out on that pitch never believed they would be beaten, and as the manager I put them on the pitch with that belief, it was fabulous.

I don't regret going to Spain, I've never been a person who regrets what I've done. I came back from Spain and went to Manchester City and things were going all right – they were struggling at the bottom, but they stayed up, and the next season they were up there and I got the call to come back to Everton again, and I thought: "Yes, I'll do that." Now, maybe I should have stayed there, but I've never been one to turn round and say: "I shouldn't have done that." I've got on with it, and a large percent of the time it's been successful.

Thank him for all the good times, and very happy memories, and ask him would he ever come back in some capacity? *Iain Cooke, Basel, Switzerland*

I'm not sure about 'any capacity'. but I don't think you can about spend so many years of your life, successful times and difficult times, without it becoming a part of you. I certainly wouldn't want a job in the hot seat again.

I'm hopeful that the club has sorted itself out at the top level, because if it's stable up there, it works its way through, it helps the manager, helps the players, helps everyone and, well, who knows....If there's a part to play, yes, absolutely, I would love to be connected, but for the good of the club and nothing more. I would hate to be an interference, and I think that that's a danger if people thought that maybe I was nosing in or waiting in the wings, but I would come back to help in some capacity.

Did he watch the 1986 World Cup and see the basis of his team playing for England and think: "I want the England job"? *Dominic McGough, Rickmansworth, North London*

When I came back from Spain, and it was before Graham Taylor took over, Peter Swales was on the management committee and I was at Man City. I'd missed club management in England and I was enjoying Manchester at that particular time. There was a short list of three people, and I was one of them, and I said to them: "I don't want it, I want club management." I think the England manager's job is a very lonely one and I was very, very happy in Manchester.

There was another time when I was doing particularly well at Sheffield United. I had a call from someone who was elected to appoint the next England manager before Glenn Hoddle took over and I said no. He said he thought the other person wanted it more than me, and so I told him to let him have it, but it was nice to be considered again.

It should be the best job, it should be the job that everybody wants, but it's a totally different job to being a club manager and it takes a special person who'd want to do it.

Bearing in mind that he was considered for it in the 1980s (according to his book), how does he rate Keegan as England manager? *San Presland, New Brighton, Merseyside*

I don't think Kevin likes the day-to-day hassle of a club, so that's a lovely job for him, when you get to play every two or three months. I think he does love his job, because you don't have to win Saturday, Monday, Wednesday and Sunday, you've got a delay and you've got separation.

Does he take it as a compliment that so many of the players who played under him have gone into management at other clubs? I mean, Reid plays an identical pattern, shape, style and formation at Sunderland as we did in the mid-80s heyday. *Nick Williams, Warrington, England*

I think that's very nice, yes, it was a lovely compliment.

I was invited up a few months ago. We were in the boardroom and the chairman of Sunderland said: "The master and the pupil," and I thought that was nice, but I don't think Reidy would have read it like that because he's a master of his trade now. It's taken a little while, but he's done a hell of a job up there and I'm delighted to have helped him in terms of recommending Gavin McCann. I told him not to hesitate, to just go and get him and he did. I wasn't taking him away from Everton Football Club because they should never have sold that player in the first place.

Sheeds at Tranmere, Kevin Ratcliffe at Shrewsbury, Dave Watson, and Peter Reid, they're all doing really well for themselves. I think what I did was I gave them an insight in terms of not only playing and enjoying it, but it was the way that I felt professional footballers should be treated and I think that gave them a guideline for when they went into management.

How would he compare the Everton Championship sides of 62-63 and 69-70 with the great teams of the mid-80s? *Nick Williams, Warrington, England*

I joined Everton in 67, so it was the tail end of a very successful period in the club's history, really. In terms of the adulation of playing with the likes of Alex Young, Jimmy Gabriel, Brian Labone, and people like that, they were idolised by everyone and it was a great honour to actually play with them towards the end of their careers. To go on to the late 60s, I thought we played probably the best football that I've ever played in my life, and I'm talking about teamwise. We lost the Cup Final in 68, but 69, that was absolutely unbelievable, it was superb and it was a great pleasure to be part of such a tremendous team. Our Championship win in 1970 was fully deserved because we were the best. It all broke up too quickly and it was a very sad day when it happened.

They talked about Everton being the team of the 1970s, and in 71 we were nobodies, we'd lost out on the European Cup in the quarter-final and we lost out to Liverpool in the FA Cup semi-final at Old Trafford, so there was nothing then, and it broke up, similar to Crystal Palace – they were the team of the 1980s and they went down in 1981, relegated. A bit like the Manager of the Month or when you win a trophy and you parade round before the game – it's a jinx. Mind you, I'd settle for a trophy nowadays, I don't mind where I parade it.

Why didn't he rate Paddy Nevin? *Osmo Tapio Räihälä, Helsinki, Finland*

That's totally wrong, that. All players, if they play at that level and they've represented their country, have got particular skills, and to say I don't rate him is totally not right.

It depends on the club's particular position at the time and if he's got a place. What is he? A wide right-sided player, a floater behind the front two, is he a striker?

Sometimes, you have to make these decisions and you think maybe you'd be better off without. But Paddy had some great skills and he's a smashing lad, as well. Sometimes, you just have to make very difficult decisions.

What was the best overall team performance any team of his was responsible for – Bayern, 5-0 against Man Utd or the Sunderland game? *Osmo Tapio Räihälä, Helsinki, Finland*

You've mentioned a few crackers there, by the way. Sometimes you're sitting there, whether it be in the stand or the dugout, and you're marvelling at what you're actually seeing on the pitch. I think if you ask most Evertonians, even the players, they'd talk about Bayern, they would talk about the night that we beat Bayern and everything that went with it.

It was a packed-out stadium and everybody was on a high, the players were all Evertonians at the time, too. Nobody remembers this you know, but the draw in Bayern, 0-0 in Bayern, was an absolutely unbelievable result because we did our homework and we did it right. Of course, we wanted an away goal, which would have been even better, but 0-0 in Bayern, the Olympic Stadium in Munich, was a great result because they were the best team we could face in that competition.

To go 1-0 down was a nightmare because we knew then we had to get two. We were going towards the Gwladys Street in the second half, and at half-time I told the lads the crowd were going to suck the ball in and to keep their confidence. We hadn't done anything wrong, we did everything according to plan, apart from putting the ball in the back of the net.

There are certain qualities that players have that can cause an opposition some grief, and Gary Stevens had a long throw and he used it a couple of times at the start of the second half and it caused them mayhem. We got down to a really dangerous position, he tossed it in and we got a couple of goals and they were rocking. Andy Gray was on a high, their centre-back came up and there was contact made, he certainly had to have attention to his nose a few times. When Trevor Steven came through on that third goal, the whole place erupted.

I knew we'd win the Final because I'd seen Rapid Vienna and I knew we were better than them, we'd already beaten the best team in that competition, so the Final was Bayern. That night, if you ask the players, and I think supporters as well, they would turn round and say that was one of the best nights they ever had at Goodison Park.

Many thanks for managing the best Everton side I have ever seen, Were you surprised at Dalglish's departure after the 4-4 draw? *Phil Bowker, Brussels, Belgium*

He knew we were going to win 1-0 in the second replay, so no wonder he left.

No, I was very surprised; in fact I think everybody was stunned. We were behind four times and we clawed it back. It must have been a nightmare for Kenny. If you reverse the roles and put me in his place, I'd have been livid, because they scored great goals and we scored scramblies. I don't think it was just that result that made him resign, it was probably the build-up, in terms of what he felt and the pressure of the job. It's not an easy job, by the way.

The daft thing that happened at that time was this: we were drawn against West Ham away in the next round and everybody thought: "Ah, yes, Wembley now we've beaten Liverpool." We thought we were there, and then we went to West Ham and lost. You can't take away the 4-4, but it's not one of those that lasts in the memory because we were chasing the game all the time.

Who was the biggest nutter in the dressing-room in the 1980s, the real narky, angry fella no one messed with? *Colin Berry, Wavertree, Liverpool*
Kevin Ratcliffe was more than a captain. I always remember one player I disciplined (Pat Van den Hauwe) and dropped for the game coming into the dressing-room about 20 minutes before kick-off. He went up to Kevin for his complimentary tickets and Kevin just said: "Piss off, you know what time I give tickets out, now piss off," because I'd explained how much he'd let me down and the reason I was leaving him out. My captain was doing my job for me and that was the way it was. My ethos was that if you're not a good pro, not prepared to pull with the lads, not prepared to weigh in all you've got, there's no room for you in my team.

Did EFC make any attempts to overturn the Heysel-inflicted European ban in view of our exemplary behaviour in Rotterdam? *Paul Christopherson, Nottingham, England*
I'll tell you the thing that bitterly disappointed me: everyone was aware there was a disaster, everyone was aware there was a tragedy, but when that five-year ban was lifted, Everton Football Club, regardless of who was the manager or the owner, should have been the first team back in Europe whatever their League position.

They should have gone into the UEFA Cup, or something like that. Everton Football Club, footballwise, were the ones to suffer professionally more than any other club in the League. They should have been allowed entry into some competition, but when the ban was lifted, who was the first team in? Liverpool. Now, I'm not having a go at Liverpool, but what I am saying is that they were involved in the tragedy and they were the first ones back in Europe. I wasn't involved with Everton Football Club at that time, but I thought that was terrible.

Did he think that the adaptation of our style to accommodate Gary Lineker harmed us as a footballing side? *Richard Marland, Waterloo, Liverpool*
It didn't harm us, but it changed us. We had five players the season before who'd scored in double figures. We had Trevor Steven, Kevin Sheedy, Adrian

Heath, Andy Gray, Graeme Sharp and Derek Mountfield. Derek's were from set pieces mostly, but we had five players who'd scored tremendous goals.

Gary Lineker, I won't take away from what he did, but nobody else could join in with them. We changed our style because of his pace, and when Sheedy picked him out over the top, nobody else could catch up and he'd go on and score. But although Lineker went out and got the goals, nobody else could get any. I felt that it wasn't a case of losing out in the Final to Liverpool or finishing second in the League either, we'd changed and it wasn't a coaching change, the players changed and I felt we suffered as a team.

Lineker was absolutely superb, but when the offer came in I felt we'd go back to what we were doing for the benefit of everybody. We weren't the team I wanted to be. I've taken a lot of criticism on that one, but then my answer is that we won the Championship the year after, playing the way I wanted to play and with a lot more players, too. We really scrambled that one, but we deserved it because we had something going within the club.

After you'd completed the Joe Royle-inspired signing of Bilic, how long did it take to see you'd be done over? *Phil Williams, Chester, North Wales*

I can't answer that, the people who have to answer that are the chairman and the Board of Directors. I did a monthly report, and not just about Slaven Bilic, about every player I inherited or signed, and I have a monthly report which is minuted at Everton Football Club, so I'll leave it at that.

If we'd lost the Oxford League Cup game, in 84, would you have resigned? *Stuart Roberts, Guildford, England*

I'd have been sacked, or at least that's what people tell me. I knew we had a good nucleus of players, but any manager will tell you, you just need a little bit of luck to get the odd result at the right time. But I knew what I was seeing at the training ground, and that wasn't bad, and I thought: "Just give me a little bit of time."

If we'd lost at Oxford, maybe someone else would have come in and reaped the benefits. That would have been sad for me as I would have missed out on all that glory. Someone else would have taken over and enjoyed it all instead of me.

What did he consider the key ingredients that turned the corner for us back in 84? I reckoned it was a mixture of Peter Reid establishing himself, the promotion of Colin Harvey and the signing of Andy Gray. What did Howard think they were? *Richard Marland, Waterloo, Liverpool*

I think you've hit the nail on the head there. If you're talking about taking chances and going for little ingredients in terms of: "I know what I've got and they need a little bit of a boost," I got two players who, at that particular time, were renowned for not being 100 per cent fit. They both had injury problems, Peter with his knee and Andy with his knee. I took a chance on both of them, and in the early stages it looked like the gamble had failed, then all of a sudden they got stronger and made so much of a difference that it was unbelievable.

People don't think about this either, but what happens in the dressing-room matters, too, and that dressing-room was alive with those two. They really helped promote the younger players, who were lacking confidence at that time. They then went on to play for England, Gary Stevens and people like that, they just needed some help, some guidance. The manager can give it on a day-to-day basis, but on the field Peter Reid and Andy Gray took over.

Without a doubt, that was the turning point and whoever asked that question is spot on with his theory.

Can he elaborate on his abrupt dismissal from the Notts County hot seat? *Paul Christopherson, Nottingham, England*

Can I elaborate? I'd rather not. I wish him all the best. If he supports Notts County, then he knows Mr Pavis and I don't need to answer the question.

Is it true that Terry Darracott once wrote his hotel room number on the top of his head before a night out in Glasgow so he could get back if he forgot where he was staying? *Mark Kenyon, Minnesota, USA*

I'm just so pleased he didn't write my number on his head. The gentleman must have been in Glasgow at the time, that's all I'm saying.

I only really have one question for Howard and that is: Will we ever get to know what happened behind the scenes during his reigns, or did he have to sign a confidentiality clause? If not, there must be a good book in there some-where – perhaps something Becky could do? *Andy Richardson, Hackney, North-East London*

My answer to that is that I'm sure Becky will do a great job.

No, I didn't sign any confidentiality clause; I've never been a person to write an article for sensationalism just for the sake of a few bob at the time. Maybe, in the future, there will be some opportune time to tell you how it actually happened.

Is it possible to describe what it was like sitting on the bench at Wembley in the FA Cup Final watching Liverpool rob us of the Double? Did the fact that it was the Red Shite make it any harder for you to take? *Phil Bowker, Brussels, Belgium*

Yes, it did. I don't appreciate the words, though, because you have to respect the opposition and they're not shite, they're a very professional football team who on the day beat us.

What was more difficult was that it was all organised before the game that, whatever happened, it was a parade around the city, and that was very, very difficult for our lads to take. We'd just lost out on the League and to lose the Cup Final as well and to be on the same bus as Liverpool, it was very difficult for a lot of people.

Peter Reid disappeared because he couldn't cope with it. In all fairness, I respect how he felt, but at the same time I don't respect him for doing that because I had to do it and so did the rest of them. We could have all disappeared and not want to be seen round Liverpool, but we didn't.

Did he leave the first time in charge because he could see the cracks forming in the team he put together? *John Staines, Adelaide, Australia*

No, it was the European stuff. There's not many times when a manager takes over a team who are the Champions, you get appointed by a club because they're struggling. Man City, Sheffield United, and so on, and they give you 18 months or two years for you to sort them out. I don't have any regrets about leaving in 1987 because Colin took over the Champions and there are not many managers who can say that.

Who, if any, is the one player you wished you hadn't sold in any of your terms at Everton? I just hope he doesn't say Mike Newell." *Phil Williams, Chester North Wales*

Martin Keown, I think.

Would he like to expand on his mysterious comments on TV after he left the first time to the effect that his reasons would become apparent in time? *Tony Field, Rotterdam, Holland*

If I did say that, then it would be to get a taste of Europe, and nothing more. I just felt I wanted to sample something and get it out of my system, I suppose.

What was the score with the racing trip before the Coventry game? A lot of snidey tales surround this trip. The beans on this little episode, would he care to spill 'em? *Les Anderson, Keighley, England*

Yes, I will do. One 2 One, who were our sponsors, arranged this day because they wanted to have some publicity. It was organised before we lost at home to Sheffield Wednesday, it was on the Monday at Pontefract, and it was part and parcel of the sponsorship of the football club.

It was nothing to do with having a great day out or a reward for losing, or anything like that, it wasn't a time to celebrate because we knew we were down there and in trouble, but it was just a time to honour our sponsorship deal for Everton Football Club. I'm delighted with your question, but sometimes when you reply to them people don't believe what you say.

Which player was the biggest challenge to manage? *Richard Marland, Waterloo, Liverpool*

I've not had real problems with anybody because I've tended to try and treat them as I would like to be treated myself. There have been awkward sods and you've got to fine them, but as I tended to try and treat them as human beings, they've been fine. We all have to discipline players when they're out of order on the pitch, but off the pitch I've not had any great problems.

Why did the board renege on buying Dion Dublin? Did they not believe he was

as good as Howard's assessment (thus drawing Howard's judgment into doubt), or was it really, as some have hinted, a racist thing? *Roy King Miaa, Kristiansand, Norway*

No, it was never a racist thing. The club was financially not too brilliant at that point, at the same time, because I was involved in all Board meetings and financial situations I knew how much money was available for me to spend.

Alex Ferguson did not want to sell Dion Dublin because at that particular time they were in Europe and the English players were invaluable to him, though the rule's been relaxed since then. Dion was longer term and, OK, you agree a fee, and maybe you pay a little bit over the odds, but I spoke to my Chairman, I spoke to my Secretary, and we agreed the deal with Manchester United and agreed the method of payment as well.

Dion Dublin wanted to come to Everton, in fact he was desperate to come. This was the second time I'd tried to sign him, so when you talk about the racist thing, forget all about that because I tried to sign him from Cambridge.

The next morning, I went into the training ground and the chairman, David Marsh, telephoned me and said: "I've been round with the Board of Directors and we don't like the Dublin deal – it's off, you can't go through with it".

So then I had to go through telephoning Alex Ferguson and telephoning the player to say sorry and that the Board had blocked the deal. I had a couple of days to think about it and I felt so strongly about it – maybe they had financial difficulties at the club, or whatever, but no one came and talked to me about that. In effect, they had told me I was no longer the manager of the football club because they'd blocked something I wanted to do.

I knew that we were capable of financing that deal or I wouldn't have entered into it in the first place. I just thought, watching Dion Dublin was similar to an Andy Gray situation, we weren't bad up to the penalty area, then we just needed something to happen. A big lad would have made it happen, I'm certain of that; it would have improved us, just like Andy did. We were putting quality in there, but who was on the end of it? Nobody, and I felt Dion Dublin would have taken care of that.

I'm so delighted, not for me for a pat on the back or anything, but that the lad has gone on and had a tremendous career.

When you accepted the job third time around you must have been aware you weren't Peter Johnson's first choice. You must also have known Andy Gray had walked away, suggesting there was something rotten at the club. Are there any circumstances when you would turn down Everton if they approached you to get involved again – say as director of football or some such? *Neil Wolstenholme, Chelsea, South-West London*

No, I wouldn't turn them down, I'd listen to what they'd say. Look at the situation at Sheffield United, for example, the club I came away from to join Everton. At that particular time we got in the play-off final and lost out in the last minute. We could have been a Premier League club, now look at it and the change that has happened there.

If you're a football person, a fan, all you want to talk about is your football, go to your game, discuss the game, have a go about the players and then go home. There are so many factors that are involved with football now, it's not nice any more.

Westlife, Cliff or the Cuban Boys? *Les Anderson, Keighley, England*

Hhhhmm… I know Westlife. I don't like the Cuban Boys. I am 'with it'. I can't say Cliff, though, can I? But poor Cliff has been knocked like you wouldn't believe, why knock the man? You've got to respect what he's done over the years, not knock him. I'm not having that, actually, I'm sticking with Cliff.

Can you ask Howard what his views are on the Bill Kenwright takeover? Good thing? Bad thing? *Frank Hargreaves, Anfield, Liverpool*

Bill's a fan and Everton Football Club deserves someone who's got a passion for the club to take over, yes, I think it's about time someone took over who feels for the club, the club's interests and the fans' interests.

You have dealt with a variety of chairmen at Everton, including Sir Philip Carter, Dr David Marsh and Peter Johnson. Do you have a good word to say about any of them? *Neil Wolstenholme, Chelsea, South-West London*

Of course I have. Sir Philip was superb. He wasn't a football man, but he was a fabulous person. Normally, with Everton Football Club, the Littlewoods Organization was behind the appointments of the Goodison Chairman, the MD of Littlewoods would normally be the chairman of the football club. We went through a bit of a difficult time early on, but he backed me up and I think I repaid that. David Marsh, I don't think he had any responsibility whatsoever, I think he led the line for others. We're working our way down the list now, aren't we? I think I'll stop there.

About modern professionals, are they artisans who deserve every penny they can get, or overpaid wankers who wouldn't have lasted five minutes in his day? *Les Anderson, Keighley, England.*

Overpaid wankers? Nah, that's not right. I don't begrudge anybody who's really top-class earning what they are in the modern day. What I don't agree with is agents pushing ordinary players, and consequently they're earning too much – because they don't deserve it. Top players should earn it, but I think that average players are earning too much.

Did he really not rate Hinchcliffe at all as a player, or was it an attitude thing? *Col Berry, Wavertree, Liverpool*

I sold him from Man City to Everton, I didn't have money at Man City when I was there. Colin Harvey loved Hinchcliffe and I needed a goalkeeper badly, so the deal was I took Neil Pointon from Everton, I rated him; I thought he was a superb player. Hinchcliffe went to Everton and that gave me enough money to buy Tony Coton from Watford, so I got two for one and I thought that was great business.

Now, whether I like Andy Hinchcliffe or not doesn't matter, but when I came back to Everton the media feeling was: "He'll be the first to move, he doesn't like him." That wasn't the case, the lad has great qualities, I'm not saying he was my ideal defender, but he's got a sweet left foot and he's played for his country. It was circumstances, that's all. I had Michael Ball coming through and we needed the money, and all of a sudden it was a case of: "Who's available? Andy Hinchcliffe? Somebody wants him, how much?," and then it's a deal, because I've got a ready-made replacement and I could go and spend the money somewhere else.

In the present day, as a manager when you've not got money to spend, you move out certain players and bring in others. Selling players to strengthen your squad is all part of being a manager, there's a lot of wheeling and dealing going on.

How good could Billy Kenny Jr. have been? *Richard Marland, Waterloo, Liverpool*

Who knows, all you could say was that he was on his way through the youth team and forced his way into the first team. He naturally had talent or he never would have had that opportunity. It's sad that he's not still there, doing what he was good at, and that's playing football.

In retrospect, does Howard think that playing in so many different positions so early on damaged John Ebbrell's career? *San Presland, New Brighton, England*

John Ebbrell's career wasn't damaged at all. I signed him for Sheffield United Football Club, I got the steal of the century and he only played half a game. I'll tell you something now about John Ebbrell, he's one of those players that players appreciate, managers and coaches appreciate, but sometimes not the fans, but there are players who are so important to your team and I couldn't believe I signed him for £900,000. Unfortunately, the lad's career has been cut short by injury, but he was a great asset.

Would Andy Gray have made a good Everton manager with you as general manager? *Mark Kenyon, Minnesota, USA*

Andy's his own man. I think if he'd taken over Everton he'd have wanted to do it his own way. He would have wanted to be the one who was responsible for the success and not have me in the background. I don't think there was any possibility of myself working with Andy.

Who was the player who he really wished he'd signed, the one he had the chance to, and didn't, or the best one who turned him down? *Col Berry, Wavertree, Liverpool*

My disappointment was that when I first went to Everton I didn't sign Bryan Robson because that was my real target, I wanted to sign him from West Bromwich Albion, he was the real one that got away. Nobody left me, though, unless I wanted him to go.

What is the dark secret surrounding him and Gary Speed, you know, the one that made Speed leave? *Ste Daley, Speke, Liverpool*

All I can say is that Gary Speed wanted to go to Newcastle. Kenny Dalglish chatted him up and when I spoke to the agent to see what was going on he told me that Speed wanted to move on. I told him that I wanted Speed to stay, I'd made him captain the first day of the season and I definitely wanted him to stay. I spoke to Kenny and he said: "It's nothing to do with me, but he was on our list last year." Speed had been got at, without a shadow of a doubt, and it came as no surprise to me.

What did surprise me was when he refused to go to West Ham. You know something, there was a lad called Griffin from Stoke City, he was told not to play in a game and he ended up at Newcastle, too. You look at the record books, it's a fact. That was an awful way of pushing through a transfer, to say you don't feel mentally well enough to play, and where did they both end up? Newcastle. Gary Speed? I'll leave it to you.

Who was the young player he was convinced would make it and didn't? *San Presland, New Brighton, Merseyside*

That's a good question. To be honest, it's a very difficult question. It's not the perfect answer, but there was a player at Everton once called Jimmy Paige and everyone was chasing him because his ball skills were incredible, he could juggle the ball like you wouldn't believe. Everton pushed the boat out, gave him a contract and signed him.

He never grew, he didn't get any strength, and in the end all he was doing was juggling the ball about. To be a judge of people or players at that age is crazy because you just don't know, you could have the best skill in the world but you may not become a player.

In your opinion, who is the better centre-forward, Sharpie or Dunc? *Phil Williams, Chester, North Wales*

I definitely couldn't compare people like that. When you're talking about strikers, it depends on the service they get, too, don't forget. Sharpie, I always felt, could do more. I didn't feel he scored as many in the six-yard box as he could have, the little tap-ins.

Now Dunc didn't score enough goals. He never got into goal-scoring positions as often as you'd have liked him to, although he had a presence.

With no hesitation, I'd say Sharpie right now, but I'll say this, now, too, without a problem: I've got so much time for the Big Man, and I'm talking about Dunc, when he gets over his injury he'll be a sensation, he's absolutely unstoppable at times, but over a longer period of time, Sharpie would come out on top.

Why did you bring Cleland in when O'Kane seemed to be doing so well? *Phil Williams, Chester, North Wales*

It was the end of Cleland's contract, anyhow, so he wasn't going to cost a fee.

We felt we needed more experience, and although Cleland had played for Rangers for a good many years, he was still a young lad so there would be a sell-on effect on that. He could play right or left side, so I felt he'd be a nice addition with no attachments involved and without any disrespect to John O'Kane.

Does he ever reminisce and think of what might have been if he'd have signed for Liverpool? All those trophies as a player, must have had him thinking 'if only' now and then? *Les Anderson, Keighley, England*

No, I'm not a person who looks back, to be honest with you. I've worked hard, had a very lucky career and when you talk about success, I can hold my head up high.

When I signed in 1967 as a player I never thought for one minute what would have happened and that I would have spent 17 years, once as a player and three times as a manager, and enjoyed so many successful times.

I have the honour of being the most successful manager in the history of Everton Football Club, one of the greatest and the biggest clubs in the world. It's a tremendous honour and I don't regret for one minute anything or any decision that I've made.

And that, my friends, was the enchanting and honourable Mr Howard Kendall. The man, the myth and the legend.

Brian Labone

Born 23 January 1940
July 1957 to September 1977
Straight from School

IN the splendid days of yore when football was still a gentleman's game, the fulcrum of our defence was an articulate and noble man named Brian Labone. A local lad made good, an Evertonian who'd spent his formative years in the Gwladys Street boys' pen watching Dave Hickson score his magnificent diving headers with astonishing regularity.

Labby went on to captain his team for six years and leading by example picked up only two yellow cards in his esteemed 14-year career. The 'one club' man was to represent England 26 times, including the 1970 World Cup Finals. It was the kind of stuff that fairy tales are made of.

> **I joined Everton straight from school, so I didn't cost them a penny. I was given 20 quid as a signing on fee, which was immediately confiscated by my dad because he didn't want it to 'go to my head'. After that I was on seven quid a week, but don't forget, you could have a great night out for ten bob in those days.**

Ladies and Gentlemen, here is the man once billed by the legendary Harry Catterick as 'The Last of the Great Corinthians', Public Relations maestro, joker and raconteur, take it from me, you would buy your insurance from this man.

Brian Labone, step into the limelight.

I believe he was booked twice during his career, which was remarkable for a defender. Can he remember the two incidents? *Phil Pellow, Waterloo, Liverpool*

I thought it was only once actually and that was against Newcastle United. Their centre-forward was Wynne Davies, I'd been heading his shoulder blades all night and the referee penalised me for the umpteenth time, I suppose I would have been sent off these days – but I disagreed with the decision, as you always do, and threw the ball down in disgust, it bounced about 30 feet in to the air and I was promptly booked.

I believe the second one was against Arsenal at Highbury but I don't really recall that, I just remember the one at Goodison.

Brian Labone

My dad always compared him to Tommy G. Jones, was he influenced by him at all? *Mike Wood, Zurich, Switzerland*

Funnily enough, there was a dinner at the Adelphi the other week and I met the great man for the first time. He's 85 now and he looks fantastic.

His great friend was Gordon Watson, he was a trainer at Everton for years and he used to always say to me: "Brian, you're not bad but you'll never be as good as T. G." My entire career at Everton, I had to accept that I was never going to be as good as T. G. Jones. I never saw him play but I believe he was brilliant, so it's not too bad an insult to be rated in the same breath as T. G. Jones.

Which was the better side the 1969-70 one or the 62-63? *Richard Marland, Waterloo, Liverpool*

It's easy to say 1969-70 and don't forget we had the holy trinity then; Harvey, Kendall and Ball – we were the only team who ever won anything with only three players.

But the 62-63 was a fine side, it certainly had the best goalkeeper in Gordon West and the best centre-half in Brian Labone. I believe we were the only two who played in both teams too.

I think the current Everton side might just about beat our side from the 60s but only because we're all in our 60s now.

Is it true that Gordon West could be the dressing-room joker? *David Tickner, Bowring Park, Liverpool*

He was a joker, but on the day of a match he certainly wasn't. Gordon did get worked up and quite often he would make himself physically sick before a game.

We used to have funny meals in those days before a game to help us perform, like steak. It's since been proven that steak is the hardest thing in the world to digest. I remember when we went over to Italy we were given spaghetti and we though they were trying to fatten us up and put is off.

When Everton bought Tony Kay, I was disgusted that the fast improving Brian Harris was to make way for him, and during his brief career at Goodison, I always felt Kay was a bit nasty for the royal blue shirt. How did Brian rate these two players? *Phil Pellow, Waterloo, Liverpool*

I didn't think we needed a replacement for him and it's a pity we couldn't have played Brian somewhere else in that team because he was a marvellous asset. He was very versatile and could play anywhere.

Catterick used to keep his cards very close to his chest, he told us it was only a rumour about Kay coming.

Brian's a very good friend of mine, and on a Friday, we used to do what every intelligent footballer did in those days, which was to go to the Tattler to watch cartoons. I was with Brian this particular day and he'd been assured by the immortal Harry Catterick that there was no truth in the rumour we were going to sign Kay and when we came out of the news theatre we bought the *Liverpool Echo* and there it was – 'Everton Sign Tony Kay'.

Now Tony was a great player, you've got to give him that, he was an arrogant player a hard man and I suppose nasty, a bit like Roy Keane. But that type of player is only nasty when they're in opposition, they're hard players when they're on your side.

It was sad for Brian, but he got over it and Tony Kay unfortunately only played about 60 games until his misdemeanours at Sheffield caught up with him. Harry had been Tony's manager at Sheffield so he knew what a good player he was. In fact I think Tony could have gone on to play many times in the England team, but unfortunately that was not to be. Now, they would have slapped his hands, fined him and suspended him for a couple of games but it was a lot different those days.

You scored two goals in your time at Everton; do you remember them? *Liz Wyman, Stoke on Trent, England*

I only ever scored two but I saved thousands!

I remember them with great clarity; they were both against Lancashire clubs and both headers.

One was at Burnley – I had to score that because I gave a penalty away. I equalised with a header from a Jimmy Gabriel free-kick. The other one was against Blackburn Rovers from a Derek Temple corner at Goodison in the Stanley Park end. It was a rule that centre-backs would only go up at the last minute if the team were struggling, because we had centre-forwards who could score goals in those days. We would always stay back except in dire emergencies.

I remember one game against Wolves at Molineux, Bally hadn't been with us very long and Peter Knowles gave him a bit of a jostle. The next thing I saw was you and Jimmy Gabriel kick the soon-to-be-a-Jehovah's Witness up in the air. Do you remember it and do you think you influenced him into turning to God? *Tony Field, Rotterdam, Holland*

I don't remember that incident at all. I tried to play the game fairly if I could but you can't play centre-back without fouling or inadvertently kicking a few people. I think that particular incident, I'd probably passed Knowles on to Jimmy Gabriel who kicked him because he was the hard man in the half-back line and I was a gentle giant. I would always pass them to the side so Jimmy would do all the dirty work and get sent off.

Now, if Jimmy Gabriel had kicked him, it could certainly have hastened his entrance into the church.

Labby played with some of the greatest players ever to wear the royal blue: West, Wilson, Young, Ball, Kendall and Harvey to name a few. Who was the best 'unsung hero' of the Everton teams he played for? *Roy King Miaa, Kristiansand, Norway*

I suppose you could put Johnny Morrissey and Brian Harris in that category, they were very good players who were never really rated with star quality but turned in a consistent performance every week.

He always seemed such a gentleman on the pitch, very much in the 1960s as Waggy became in the 1990s. Was he really such a clean player or was there a dark side we never saw? *Mike Wood, Zurich, Switzerland*

I was always accused of being too soft. As a centre-back you always came across these bruising centre-forwards and had take them on with a bit of skill. You always got a chance to whack the opposition if you bided your time though. If the centre-halves wanted to mix it, we always got a chance to slide tackle the centre-forward and clatter him into the half-time results at Goodison Park – which was usually rusty and could inflict terrible wounds. That was in the days when you could tackle, but now you're not allowed to any more.

Perhaps you can clear this up for us, once and for all. You were probably the closest player to Harry Catterick when he was 'assaulted' at Blackpool. Some say he slipped on ice and fell, but H.C. swears hooligans attacked him. Come on Labby; spill the beans. *Adrian Evans, Eastcote, England*

I don't think it was ice because it was in the summer time.

Harry had dropped Alex Young to make way for a young Joe Royle and Alex was a very popular player with the fans. Harry definitely stumbled – he wasn't kicked, it may have been a jostle, but that's all.

More has been made of it than actually was, because I was right behind him. I think the only person who would have kicked him that day would have been Alex Young!

Could you have made it in the modern game – did you have the necessary pace for this day and age? *Richard Marland, Waterloo, Liverpool*

I think so. I think there are still slower players out there now – I know that's true because I watch them every Saturday.

I was never the quickest thing on two legs but I had a good eye for reading situations, or at least I like to think I did. That was a big part of the game as a centre-back – looking at situations and reading the play, I had to anticipate what was going to happen.

When I look at old games now, they look so pedestrian and slow but if we had the same training as they do now it would have been different. The training in our day was lapping and heavy endurance work, we had heavy pitches to play on so we had to have tons of stamina, we didn't have the pitches like they do now, which look the same at the end of the season as they did at the beginning. And while the game is quick now, I'm sure if we had trained, we would have adapted to the conditions.

They always say a good player would last in any era and I like to think I was good. You don't play for 15 years in the top division without being consistent and a reasonably good player. In those days the First Division wasn't dominated by three or four teams, if you look back at the records, any team could win the League and the Cup in those days. It was only in the 70s that Liverpool started dominating and that began in the late 60s when all the big money clubs were getting the best players and the cream was going to the top.

Does he remember, going to Evered High School and presenting medals in the 1960s? *Tommy Davis, Texas, USA*

When I was at the Collegiate, it was with a great friend of mine, Ken Robson. He played in the same old boys team as I did in the late 50s and went on to became the sports master at Evered. He coerced me into doing a presentation there during the 60s, so I do indeed remember it.

I remember your quote in the Golden Vision about a win at home and a draw away was championship form, do you think that with a little luck either way on the away games that that statement could still hold true? *Tony Field, Rotterdam, Holland*

Don't forget in those days it was only two points for a win, so I think now you've got to do more than draw to win the Championship. You've certainly got to win all your home games but now you would need to mix a few wins in with draws in your away games. Having said that, you still probably wouldn't win the League, because the three-point situation has changed everything. If you win three games now, you'd be miles up the table, if you lose three you'd be down in the relegation zone. If a team could win all it's home games it should be fine, but the way Man United play these days it wouldn't be a guarantee at all.

In retrospect, does he consider ruling himself out of selection for the 1966 England World Cup squad by refusing to change his wedding plans was an error of judgement? *Billy Williams, Cologne, Germany*

It was probably the first in a long line of bum decisions that I made in my life. Well, there was no way we were ever going to win the World Cup in 1966 was there?

To be perfectly honest with you, I may have played the odd game there, but Jack Charlton was in at the time and when I wasn't in the original 28, I was a bit disappointed and that was why I went on to make marriage plans. I probably would have been in the squad, and it's only when I see the likes of Ian Callaghan getting invited to these 'old boys' dinners that I feel a few pangs of jealousy.

Now and again I do wonder if I made a stupid decision, but let's be honest, at the time Everton had just won the Cup and England weren't going to win the World Cup so it was a calculated risk – that' s why I don't back any winners when I go to the races – I always make the wrong decision.

Having said all that; I have a beautiful daughter as a result of that marriage so who can say if I made the right decision or not.

How did it feel to have to wait for a place in the England team when Jack Charlton was in his place? *Mike Wood, Zurich, Switzerland*

Well it was funny because the centre-half slot was up for grabs really but Jack got in at the right time and did very well.

It was unfortunate timing for me because Alf Ramsey's first game was 1963 in Paris, just after the English ice age. The League programme was cancelled for months because of the frozen grounds and I didn't have a particularly good game, in fact we got beat 5-2.

So that was Alf's debut and I didn't see another England shirt for about three years after that, by which time Jack had gone into poll position. Jack was a very good centre-back but we did things a different way.

What on earth motivated him to announce in the autumn of 1967 that he would soon be retiring from the game when he was at the peak of his ability? *Billy Williams, Cologne, Germany*

I wasn't playing particularly well at that time and my father had a successful central heating business. Believe it or not, being a local boy and playing for your local team, there's a lot of pressure on you and I was always a bit of a worrier. I thought it was only fair to tell Everton that I was going to retire and give them a chance to replace me. I wasn't on ten grand a week and it's easy to make decisions when you're on £70 a week.

We had Roger Kenyon who was 'up and coming' and I didn't want to just spring it on them. After that, all the worries seemed to leave me, my form improved and I got back in the England squad so I changed my mind. But that was the reason, I had somewhere to go, I was getting on for 30, which in those days was quite old and I'd done everything really, we'd won the Cup, the League, and I'd won England caps.

Football is a glamorous life but when you're doing it every week it does become rather arduous and boring at times, but I'm quite a bouncy person and I changed my mind and that was it.

Does he think Gordon Banks was nobbled in the 1970 World Cup? *San Presland, New Brighton, Merseyside*

I've often been asked that question. I don't know. Gordon used to like having a bit of a sun tan and I'm not too sure whether one day he didn't sneak away and lay himself out for a couple of hours. We all know what happens when we go to Spain for a few weeks, you get a bit of sunburn and you drink cold water, you end up with an upset stomach. We did stay in top-class facilities but nonetheless, Alf Ramsey took all our food and drink over to preclude us from eating any chillies and whatever else they eat over there and from drinking their water.

You could put it down to those Mexican people trying to nobble him but it seems strange that he was the only one it to go down with Montezuma's Revenge.

Personally, I put it down to his sun-worshiping. When we were in Brazil years ago to play Mexico, Gordon would disappear, get the lift up the top floor, strip off and top up his tan in the roof garden and that's all I'm saying.

Does he recall Germany's third goal in Mexico in the 1970 World Cup? The one where he stood and watched the German number 10 nod it to Muller who volleyed past Bonetti? *Paul Tollet, Oxford, England*

I try never to recall it. I've never watched the recording of that, I've seen bits of it but I've never watched the whole game. I had a pretty good game, if I remember rightly, and that was Muller's only kick – but it was a great finish, as you know. The ball was crossed from Grabowski to the far post; Keith Newton always reckons he flicked it against the fella's head and it came back across, but anyway, Muller wasn't going to miss it in the six-yard box. I'm not criticising Peter Bonetti but any ball in the six-yard box should really be the goalkeeper's – but I should have been marking Muller, so there you go.

I'm really too young to remember seeing you play (though I must have done a few times) but my dad tells me that pairing you at your peak with Kevin Ratcliffe at his peak would have been the perfect combination – do you agree? *Neil Wolstenholme, Chelsea, South-West London*

I wouldn't disagree because he only scored two goals too. His speed would have been a great asset, he was much quicker than me, in fact he was probably one of the fastest defenders ever. I was born about 20 years ahead of him but that wouldn't have been a bad combination because I think I could head the ball better than Kev, but he was certainly the quickest back four player I've ever seen.

How is the plumbing business these days? *Paul Tollet, Oxford, England*

That was my father's business and it was bought out just before he died. My father died very young, he was only 50, so when I came to finish football, I would have gone into the business.

I went to see them when I retired through injury and even though the company carried the name J & B Labone and I was the B, they couldn't fit me in – even as an office boy – so I told then to go and stuff themselves, well not exactly those words but...

Did you find most of your work was for Evertonians, and on the off chance that you accepted work from RS households, did you deliberately bugger it up? *Paul Tollet, Oxford, England*

Oh no no no, money is money and business is business. In fact a lot of my friends are Liverpudlians and Ian Callaghan is one of my best friends. I work in insurance now and a lot of my clients are Reds so I'm afraid I'm strictly neutral when it comes to that side of things.

Does Labby still panic when he flies on an aeroplane? He and most of the other passengers went very quiet, when the plane took off for Rotterdam, the night EFC played Rapid Wien. *Tommy Davis, Texas, USA*

I don't think anybody's particularly enamoured with flying – I'm all right at 35,000 feet but it's the getting up and coming down that bothers me.

On the way back after that magnificent victory I could say none of us would have particularly cared if we'd have crashed and we certainly wouldn't have felt it, we were all nicely sluiced and I think it was a very lively flight home.

I'd like to apologise for being one of the many delirious blues who swamped you as you left Elland Road after the 1995 Cup semi-final victory. Do you realise your grin was so wide it looked like you were swallowing the stadium? *Neil Wolstenholme, Chelsea, South-West London*

I remember that day very well, it's the best I've ever seen an Everton side play away from home and that probably includes when I played as well. And to think that we were supposed to just be there to make up the numbers against Tottenham. I seem to recall that they were going to do all sorts to us and we turned them over 4-1 – we took them on and murdered them. It was a brilliant day. We had to face United in the final and as you know we beat them too, but Elland Road was a fine performance.

If he was playing now how does he feel that his game would have differed if at all? *San Presland, New Brighton, Merseyside*

I think you have to be much more athletic. The defences tend to play very square these days so you have to be more athletic and you would need to speed up a bit, but fundamentally the game's the same.

They call it different things now; 4-4-2 and 4-3-3, but a team might play all those formations as the game runs its course. I think if you play in defence, you play as a unit. Look at Arsenal with Adams and Dixon and Winterburn, they're falling apart a bit now but all in their 30s and they're all pretty formidable. It's a matter of reading the game and having good communication with your fellow defenders but I don't think you would need to change your game at all.

Since the early 1960s, I reckon that we've only had three goalies worthy of the title, Gordon West, George Wood and Big Nev. How does Labby rate Paul Gerrard and Tommy Myrhe against them? *David Tickner, Bowring Park, Liverpool*

It must be very difficult for a goalkeeper now, I've never seen the penalty area so full of players crowding in on the near post for these flicks on – it must be like a market place.

Keepers can't get much of a run at the ball these days, I don't think centre-backs can either but I've never seen so much pushing and pulling of shirts. It can't be much fun for them.

I admire Paul Gerrard for having stayed in the background for so long and going out on loan all over the place, he obviously never doubted his own ability and it looks like Paul's going to get the place now with Thomas out, and I do rate him highly.

Does he have any good stories to tell about Westy? *San Presland, New Brighton, Merseyside*

The first time Gordon was in the England squad was for the England v Scotland game at Hampden Park which used to average around 120,000 spectators.

We'd been training at Lilleshall but Gordon had travelled up independently and we met him at Glasgow airport. He was always my roommate at Everton and we were staying at the Marine Hotel in Troon.

Anyway, we get up on the day of the game and we've got our suitcases and just before we embark on Hampden, Gordon and I go to the gents. So I'm on the coach and Harold Shepardson, who was Alf's number two for a long time, decides to do a head count – and of course there's no Gordon. We were only about a mile down the road so we turned back and there's Gordon West, literally running down the road with his two suitcases.

Knowing Westy like I do, he was such a panicker; he'd have definitely run all the way to Hampden Park.

So Gordon gets on the bus and we all take the mickey and eventually we arrive at Hampden and make our way to the dressing-room, and we're all getting our shirts out and ready. Banks was in goal, so Gordon didn't think he was going to be a substitute. In those days the rules were different, there weren't substitutes as such, but these were the European nations game so they decided that they would be able to substitute the goalkeeper at any time. Westy gets a shirt thrown to him. Now I won't say he dropped it but I will say he held on to with great difficulty and it was only then that he realised he had to tell Alf Ramsey that he'd left his boots on the bus.

We had to tannoy for our driver who'd probably just said to his mate: "Right, I've got rid of those English bastards, let's go and have a pint." And this poor fella had to go all the way across the compound and find our bus. Now bear in mind there's a 135 000 gate there so you can imagine how many charabancs there are. This poor guy had to go and rummage around and get Gordon's boots and bring them to him.

And all that was before he'd even made his debut.

What is the Corinthians outfield playing record that Waggy is approaching?
George Lee Stuart, Lismore, Australia

I played about 450 League games and I think Waggy is approaching that now, but he's getting near to retirement so I think I might be able to hang on to that record a bit longer.

Do you remember the very first Friday lunch that the players had with the supporters in January 1995? There were about half a dozen fans and the entire Everton team, plus Royle, his staff and you. What puzzles me is, that when I asked to take your photograph, you introduced me to your son-in-law, and I have since wondered whether he was someone I should know? *Marko Poutiainen, Oulu, Finland*

Did you say son-in-law? I haven't got a son-in-law or a son.

I do remember that Friday lunch thing though and I think they've carried that on. I didn't think Friday was a particularly good day to do it, myself. The day before a match, I used to try and concentrate and psyche myself up.

It was a good lesson in PR though because I do feel the players have drifted away from the fans a bit – they're film stars now. In the old days a fan could meet a player walking down the street, but now they get into their big limousines and go home to their haciendas.

I don't know when, but he was dropped for the first time since becoming a trophy-winning captain and his career was virtually finished. The *Echo* devoted half of the back page to a very cruel picture of Labby standing alone in his half of the pitch defending a totally empty Goodison Park... it was the saddest thing I have ever seen – a fallen giant. Does he remember the picture and did he retire too late? *John Quinn, Tewkesbury, England*

I think that particular picture, if that's the same one is of me leaning against the goalpost was after I'd retired, well I didn't retire as such, I snapped an achilles tendon when I was 31, so I suppose I may have been coming to an end then but I was basically retired through injury.

Harry Catterick is supposed to have called me the 'Last of the Corinthians' but to me he used to say: "Brian look on the bright side, if you'd have been a race horse, they would have shot you."

If it's the picture I'm thinking of I'm wearing a sports jacket and I had long brown hair in that style of the early 70s – the flower power look. It was taken in a poignantly 'empty' Goodison if I remember correctly, but I was still in the first team until I snapped my Achilles and I didn't really come back from that.

My records tell me that Labby wore the royal blue shirt on 520 occasions, is there a particular game that sticks in his memory? *Rob Rimmer, Aintree, Liverpool*

Definitely winning the Cup against Sheffield Wednesday in 1966. It's great to win the League and a lot of people say you've got to be a better team to win the League and maybe it's true because you have to perform well over a longer period. But some of the greatest players in the history of English football never got a Cup winners' medal. To win the Cup you have to win five or six consecutive games and once you're out, you have to wait another year to do it. I don't know if it was one of my better games but getting there and getting a medal was the main thing.

If I had my time over again, what would I change? I'd like to have been born 20 years later and earn a few bob more per week. Other than that, I don't think I'd change very much at all, in my personal life I'd probably try and make a few correct decisions but I've got no complaints really.

Brian Labone, as ever, it was a delight to be in your charming company.

Duncan McKenzie

Born 10 June 1950
December 1976 to September 1978
£200,000

SOME suggested he may have been more at home in the circus ring than on the football pitch with his breathtaking ball trickery, but Billy Bingham wasn't one of them. In a frenzied retail therapy session, he recruited the nimble-footed Duncan McKenzie from Anderlecht for £200,000 on the same day he signed Bruce Rioch from Derby. It transpired that this was one of his last acts in his capacity as manager – he was gone within the month.

The replacement ringmaster was Gordon Lee, and his no-nonsense, hard-working team plan had no vacancy for a jester – lets just say, they didn't really see eye to eye on certain issues.

' There was always someone in Gordon Lee's life he had to bemoan. He didn't want them to be the star because he wanted to be it. I think we just got rid of him in time or he would have taken us off the coupon, never mind out of the First Division. A lot of the fans were on my wavelength about how we thought football should be played, though, and to hear them cheering me on, well, there was nothing quite like it. '

Arriving through the door marked 'Entertainment', Little Dunc was a crowd-pleaser of the highest order. His chicanery enhanced his impact and the fans never roared louder than when Jumpin' Duncan was on the ball.

Raconteur, radio and TV pundit and after-dinner speaker:
Duncan McKenzie, let the show commence.

Did he practise a lot as a kid, or did those sublime skills just come naturally?
Mark Kenyon, Minnesota, USA
When I was a kid I used to live with a football; I used to sleep with it, too. I don't

think I learned anything after about eight years of age; by then there was no trick I couldn't do with a ball; I could catch it on my head, juggle it on my shoulder throw it in the air, catch it on my thigh and let it balance there, and I could trap a ball between my heel and my bum when somebody threw it to me. I used to love playing and I suppose I did nothing but train by just messing around with a football all the time.

When I became a professional, I didn't really like training. I liked the crack of it, but I always used to go in goal for a laugh, I love playing in goal. I can't understand how anybody can complain about playing too many games, I would rather have played every day and never train.

Where did the idea to jump over cars come from, and since the Mini is no longer in production does he think he would have been up to jumping over today's Super Minis? *Rob Bland, Morecambe, England*

Well, the truth is that I could actually jump over the big Mk 10 Jags too – I was a regular jack-in-the-box. John Barnwell, the Leeds secretary, called me a physical freak.

I used to jump over this five-bar gate and the reserve team goalkeeper at Leeds was a fella called Brian Williamson, he said that the coach had a Mini and it wasn't as big as the gate. He told me if I jumped over it, he'd give me a fiver. So one day, I turned up for training and the Mini was in the middle of the car park with a yellow bow on the top and all the lads had cleared the decks. I went and put a tracksuit on and hopped over it and they were satisfied, but they didn't pay me my fiver, which is not unlike professional footballers.

I ended up doing it at Paul Reaney's testimonial in front of 13,000 people who'd paid a pound each to see it.

Ask him why Gordon Lee ruined the best years of my life by selling him to Chelsea. *Sid Martin, Sandwich, England*

Gordon Lee caused his problems at Newcastle as well. I think the biggest problem with Gordon Lee was that he wanted to be a star and I think he was a little bit upset when one or two of his players gained more headlines than he did. The amazing thing was that after he got rid of me, he turned on his favourite, Bob Latchford.

It's difficult to be playing in a team and knowing that the manager doesn't want you. Every time journalists ever asked him about Duncan McKenzie, he would turn round and say: "There are ten other players, ask about them," because he didn't want to speak about me. He had no reason to have a go at me because I never caused him a bob's worth of trouble in all the time that I was there, but I used to love winding him up when I was on the pitch.

Does it surprise him that Gordon Lee would not sign my programme after the first replay against Aston Villa, in the 1977 League Cup Final because it had a photograph of Duncan McKenzie on the page? I quote the Screaming Skull: "I'm not signing that piece of shit," after I pursued him with my programme waving in the air. I had the foresight to look down at it and there was a picture of little

Jumpin' Duncan. We all knew then that his tenure at Goodison was to be very short-lived. *Charlie Brewer, Seoul, South Korea*

No it doesn't surprise me at all. I remember scoring the winning goal in the FA Cup against Cardiff, where I'd pinched it off their centre-half. I ran into their penalty area and I took the goalkeeper on about eight times before he eventually fell over. I couldn't stop laughing because five defenders ran past me and didn't even try to get the ball off me, they just went and stood on the goal line. When I got through, I miskicked it and it went through somebody's legs and in the back of the net and we won the game 2-1. That was the winning goal and afterwards Gordon Lee told the press that he was going to ring the FA and ask them to take that goal off me. Gordon Lee? The hamster died years ago but the wheel's still going round.

How much did he enjoy teasing Denis Smith when we played Stoke in the Cup just after he joined? I remember him playing 'keep ball' for about 40 seconds before Smith put him over the wall and into the Enclosure. Smith didn't look at the ref, he just walked off. *Paul Tollet, Oxford, England*

I'm not sure it happened exactly like that, but somebody said to me that I had the ball longer in one go than most players get it in an entire match. That was just me, I loved it and I used to love upsetting Gordon Lee.

One of my other favourite moments was when we played Newcastle, the last match of the season, and we beat them 2-0 and Gordon Lee had spent 45 minutes in the team-talk raving on about Geoff Nulty and Alan Gowling to our team. Bruce Rioch threw his boots at Gordon and shouted that he'd never heard so much crap in his life. He pointed to me and said: "He will murder Geoff Nulty," and pointed to Mick Lyons and said: "Gowling won't get a kick against Mick Lyons," and that turned out to be the truth.

Hugh McIlvenny wrote a piece in *The Observer* saying that his abiding memory of the 77-8 season would be Duncan McKenzie dancing away and entertaining the fans on the far side of the ground and Gordon Lee clutching his head in his hands in the dugout.

On his Everton debut away to Coventry in December 1976 did it come to his attention that the Everton Blue Streak (football special) crew had invaded the Coventry City end of the ground en masse? *Billy Williams, Cologne, Germany*

I don't remember any of that at all, but I remember we lost 4-2. Bruce Rioch and I debuted on the same day, I scored a goal but it was disallowed for offside. It probably was offside, because the refs were quite decent in those days. Andy King scored one, it was a belter – the Everton fans must have thought it was worth the entrance fee just for that. Although we had a few problems at the back at that time I knew then that we had the makings of a half-decent side.

Which Everton centre-forward that he has seen or played with does he think he would have linked best with? *San Presland, New Brighton, Merseyside*

Bob Latchford. Joe Royle is a good pal of mine now, but he was an opponent for me in the old days. I didn't play with Joe, but I played with Bob Latchford and I'd put him right up there with any centre-forward I've ever played with. I played with Alan Clarke at Leeds, who was a great finisher, but Bob was immensely strong. I'm probably one of the only Evertonians who still keeps in touch with Bob, he's a very dear friend.

Who were the players he admired when he was younger? *Rob Bland, Morecambe, England*

Denis Law was my hero, and that was almost tongue-in-cheek to begin with because everybody supported Spurs. They were the great 'double-winning' team of 1961 to an impressionable school kid, and they all supported Tottenham. So I went the other way and supported Man Utd. I can almost hear the boos and hisses now. But it's true I was a Man United fan, Denis Law was my hero, and after that it was Alan Ball because of the World Cup in 1966.

Would he agree that the overall standard of today's Premiership is way behind the quality of the top division in the 1970s and 80s? *Mark Wilson, Warrington, England*

I think it is in terms of skill, it's got so quick now that I think it's got too fast for it's own good. I'm not saying it should ever have been as slow as my style of playing, but it's so athletic now that it's difficult to be as classy when you play at that pace.

Could you ask him, in his opinion, why don't players nowadays seem to get as much fun out of the game as he obviously did? *Rob Sharratt, Narara, Australia*

This is the great shame. I do commiserate with the fact that they live in a goldfish bowl these days and everything that they do is monitored and watched, and they finish training and go running off to their ivory towers with electric gates and electric fences. The human side of it is down to them, though. The public haven't changed, but the players have. I think if the players went out to their public the way that we did, with a good heart and a smile on their faces, it would be a good start.

I can remember making an award in one of the pubs at the bottom of Everton Valley and it was so packed they picked me up and passed me over the top of the crowd to the front. The fans love it when they get a chance to meet with the players. One of the saddest things I saw was quite recently when I arrived at the same time as the visiting team and they put out two runners to the bus so that the fans couldn't even see the players get off and go into the ground. I think it's crazy, it's like they're saying they don't want anything to do with the public. You only need one superstar to go out there and meet the fans once a week or something, sign a few autographs and chat with them, and I'll tell you what, so much faith will be restored, and what's more amazing is that the players might even find that they enjoy it. I know I did.

Did we lose 6-2 to Man Utd on Boxing Day 1977 because our players had such bad hangovers? *Osmo Tapio Räihälä, Helsinki, Finland*

I don't think so, I thought we played very well on the day. Gordon Hill scored two volleys from the left wing, that Subbuteo player, Lou Macari, scored a hat-trick, one was a header and a couple of volleys, and the quality of their goals was stunning. We murdered them and lost 6-2. It doesn't happen too often but it did that day.

If he hadn't smoked 60 a day "to give the rest a chance," he would have been able to convince even Gordon Lee that he was the best thing since powdered milk. *Sid Martin, Sandwich, England*
Do you like powdered milk? The worst thing I ever did in my life was smoke that many fags, it's as bad a drug as you can get. I used to smoke at half-time, immediately before the game kicked off, I was even smoking in the tunnel, it was dreadful – the best thing I ever did is pack it in ten years ago. But would he have liked me more? I doubt it, I think he was very set in his ways, and if you weren't very workmanlike then you weren't going to be one of his players.

How did he feel watching Everton beat Chelsea 6-0 without him playing? *Osmo Tapio Räihälä, Helsinki, Finland*
It was great, actually. I was biting my nails for Latch to make sure he got the hat-trick because prior to that we were dribbling round goalkeepers and waiting for him to come lumbering up to tap it over the line, so we considered it to be a team effort throughout the season, and, of course, we were delighted for him. That was an awesome feat in those days, you know.

Would 'Fat Latch' have become a success on the continent? *Osmo Tapio Räihälä, Helsinki, Finland*
Oh, he would have been. I was awesome in the air when I went over to Belgium – they weren't very good at heading in the mid-1970s, it came later on. They didn't like it at all. Latch would have been a sensation; he'd have scored even more goals over there than he did here.

Well, I guess I'm in a minority on here as I think that the Gordon Lee team would have been better without this clown arsing about. I'd like to know whether he has always wanted to hog the limelight and why he always played for himself, not for the team? *Neil Wolstenholme, Chelsea, South-West London*
Well, that's your opinion, and it's not really something I can turn round and defend. If somebody's decided that's what you are, then that's it. But you have to speak to people that you played with as well for their opinions, and I always got on very well with my team mates, who seemed to appreciate what I had to offer.

Has he met Clive Thomas anywhere else and found out the real reason why he disallowed Hamilton's goal in the FA Cup semi-final? *Clive Blackmore, Washington DC, USA*
I never spoke to Clive Thomas, but there's a story there. I went to speak at a

sportsmen's dinner at the Park Hotel in Cardiff and after I'd finished this little guy came up to me and said: "I'm ever so pleased to meet you, I worked for Clive Thomas and if it's any consolation, he's as big a bastard as a boss as he is as a referee." And I thought that just about summed it up.

Does he think that referees who own sports shops and have lots of horrid red jerseys that they need to shift should be allowed to referee FA Cup semi-finals? *San Presland, New Brighton, Merseyside*

Well, this is it, isn't it? And you can bring the story right up to date now, because what is really upsetting when you're a Bluenose is when you've got a referee in the guise of Mike Reid who's doing a lap of honour when Liverpool score a goal, and I think it's getting a bit above and beyond. Referees do worry me; look at the Paul Alcock instance with Di Canio. If David Ginola had taken a dive like that he'd have been packed off back to France. The problem is that the referees think they're stars these days.

Does he feel that the balance of power on Merseyside would have shifted sooner if Hamilton's goal had stood? *Clive Blackmore, Washington DC, USA*

We'll never know. We all knew it was a goal because Liverpool didn't complain and they were very good at that in those days. People often ask me who was the best referee in Europe, and I think Tommy Smith would have been up there with the best of them. He used to sway their opinions and make decisions for himself. I don't know, I felt that one retrograde move was when Gordon Lee had the chance to enhance that team by buying Peter Shilton. He was at Stoke and a pal of Mick Pejic and he wanted to come to Everton, but Gordon Lee wouldn't pay £200,000 for a goalkeeper.

Does he remember having his picture taken with an Evertonian clad in a horrible bright yellow leather jacket and scruffy Everton scarf after the pre-season friendly at Nuremberg in August 1977? And if so, would he like said picture complete with my autograph? *Billy Williams, Cologne, Germany*

Tell him no! No on every count. I remember Nuremberg, though, because Gordon Lee drove us round the bend. We stayed at a training camp called Mettmann, near Dusseldorf, and the lads were topping themselves playing Scrabble – I think they'd been to the Don Revie School of Boredom. Eventually, we got a day off and were told we could go out shopping. So we shopped at every bar in Dusseldorf.

Is his wife still in the fruit and veg game? I was one of those urchins who used to hang around the shop in Jason Walk waiting for a glimpse of our hero. How good did he feel wearing his tweed jacket, Harold Ian printed shirt and big flared jeans (26 inches if ever I saw it)? He looked cool to us, anyway. *Frank Hargreaves, Anfield, Liverpool*

Oh, when you look back it's criminal, isn't it? That hair. And those sideys, which made it look like you were on the phone in both ears. Fashion is so ridiculous when you think about it, but it will probably come round again. No, my wife's not in the fruit and veg game anymore. That was Dot's mum's shop in Jason Walk. I used to go there when we were courting 30 odd years ago. I don't have a business now; I just sell myself.

Steve Claridge is in trouble for allegedly having a bet that his team would win a match.

Knowing how many players like a flutter, do many wives bet on matches? *San Presland, New Brighton, Merseyside*

I don't think the wives do have a bet on the games; they're all on that much money they don't need to go out gambling anymore. When I played, we used to bet on ourselves to win, we never bet on ourselves in a negative way. I can't see a problem in betting on yourself. In fact, I always thought that the best wager you could ever have would be on your own ability.

If you like a flutter, I always think that the safest bet is on someone like Dave Unsworth. Put your money on the penalty-taker. Even though he's got nine goals, he's still about 12 to one for every home game with Ladbrokes to score the first goal.

Who was the manager he played under who encouraged him to go out there and show people what he could do? *Rob Bland, Morecambe, England*

Dave Mackay was the one, really, when I was at Nottingham Forest. He was the first one that actually said: "Go out there and use your skill." Later on, Brian Clough said exactly the same. He'd taken me to Leeds and he got the sack, and when he was leaving, he turned round and said: "You, you little bugger, with all your fancy flicks and your back heels and your nutmegs. Never change." I thought that was wonderful.

What is Duncan's opinion of Gordon Lee, and did he take any satisfaction out of the decline in his career after being sacked by Everton? *Colin Jones, Wavertree, Liverpool*

There are people who you might think you absolutely loathe, and at the time you can bear a bit of malice towards them. But further down the line you don't want to see them struggling or out of work. The bottom line with Gordon Lee was that he was a very good manager at a certain level, which was around the Second or Third Division. He was terrific, he could work on a shoestring budget and get the maximum out of players with limited ability, but when you're at the highest level you need players who've got a little bit more than just hard work in them, and Gordon Lee couldn't see that.

It appears that he still has Everton very close to his heart, apart from living locally what other factors does he put this down to when he had so many other clubs? *Colin Jones, Mossley Hill, Liverpool*

All you bloody lot out there who listen and write in and make Everton the most talked about club on the Internet. I've never heard a better expression than Joe Royle's and that was: "Once an Evertonian, always an Evertonian," and I think that's true. I love going to the match, I love the crack, I think the people behind the scenes are fantastic and I know we haven't got a penny more or a penny less, but I think it's so wonderful now that Bill Kenwright's in charge, because at least we know our future is in our own hands and not in the hands of some outlaw.

With hindsight, does he think he took our adulation for granted? With a little more application could he not have satisfied Gordon Lee's "work ethic" demands while at the same time cementing even more the bond which still exists with the fans? *John Shearon, Dronfield, England*
Well, you are what you are and you either accept that or you don't. I've always felt that I was very down to earth, and it's your game, its not my game.

What does he think of Walter Smith's attempted rebuilding of Everton under such difficult circumstances? *Colin Jones, Wavertree, Liverpool*
I think he deserves Manager of the Season, to be honest with you. I thought getting the best part of four million quid for Bakayoko was a miracle to begin with, and we've never looked back since. I think he's got wonderful returns for the players that he's had to sell, and he's got such a team spirit going. Because we are fans and you lot pay your money – I'm lucky, they let me in for nothing – we have a right to have a whinge and call the Mark Pembridges and the Mitch Wards and John Collinses, but the bottom line is what Walter's achieved with what he had available is phenomenal. I look at the triangles that we've had, Barmby, Campbell and Jeffers, Joe-Max Moore and Don Hutchison, these have been the crux of how far we've come, and at the back the real revelation this season has been David Weir, he's been terrific. Walter has got this lovely 'through-the-middle' happiness that the players have latched on to, and it's created a team spirit.

Ground move. Stay or go? *Frank Hargreaves, Anfield, Liverpool*
I suppose, in an ideal world, we would like to have an 80,000-all-seater stadium with car parking for all, but realistically that's not going to happen. Unless we can move to a stadium that will take your breath away, I think we're probably better off staying where we are.

Did he ever get stick from team mates for not passing as much as he could or should have? *Rob Bland, Morecambe, England*
Very rarely, but occasionally in the heat of the moment. It's not like Rodney Marsh ever to come to my aid, or anybody's aid, for that matter, he'll have a go at anyone. But he once said of me: "Whenever his team mates are in the shit, he's the first one they look for to get them out of it because he'll have the ball and they won't."

He was the most talented player to grace English Football in the last 30 years.

Why wasn't he an automatic choice for England? *Andy Richardson, Hackney, North-East London*

Bob Latchford got picked from Everton when I was in the side, and Dave Thomas got a call-up, but I think a lot of it is down to the club manager. If they're not sending the right vibes out for you then you've not got much chance.

Realistically, I missed the boat when Brian Clough took me to Leeds, because I hadn't realised how much Don Revie and Cloughie hated each other. Alan Clarke was getting picked for the England team from Leeds reserves and I was keeping him out of the first team and I never got a smell.

I think, sometimes, you're a victim of your own circumstances or private battles, although, funnily enough, it's not something I look back on with any regret.

Why hasn't he ever battered Tommy Smith? *Les Anderson, Keighley, England*

I think an awful lot of it was tongue-in-cheek. Everybody knows what Smithy is and what he's like. He was a great servant to his club and to football, and I've never really had a grouse because we made money out of each other, if the truth be known. People wanted Tommy Smith and me at the same venue as co-speakers, and so we didn't do too badly. He slagged me off in the *Echo* and I would slag him off on 'Mac an' Tosh' on Radio City in the old days. Anyway, I would never mock the afflicted, God bless him. He's suing somebody for a course of his own injections now, isn't he?

There was a story about a golf game with Dave Mackay. Mackay used every club in the bag, but our wee Dunc just threw the ball and rolled it on the green. Any truth? *Charlie Deeney, Ottawa, Canada*

It is true, yes. We played nine holes in a place called Espinho, in Portugal, and Dave lost the game. Dave's part of the bargain was that he would go and dive in the Atlantic Ocean with his best suit on. I forget what the bet was for me, but it involved hard graft. I think I had to be his slave for a week, or something, because the money I was on was that crap and neither of us saw the funny side of me being fined. He lost and you could probably feel the tidal wave in Plymouth when he dived in.

Did he get the same sinking feeling as us fans did when on match days we'd discover that Jim Pearson was going to be wearing the number ten shirt instead of him? *Sid Martin, Sandwich, England*

It was always with great delight when Gordon Lee left me out of the team. I was gutted and gobsmacked, sick as a parrot and all the phrases of football termi-nology every time I saw the team sheet and my name wasn't on it.

What was it like playing for Anderlecht? Were you appreciated there? And why did you come back? *Julian Jackson, Singapore*

The short answer is that Dot's dad was dying of cancer, but if things had been different I would never have come back. I had a brilliant time there and I liked the way that if you did something wrong they would pat you on the back and say: "Try again," not like here where you would get a serious bollocking.

Does he know whatever happened to Ludo Coeck? *Osmo Tapio Räihälä, Helsinki, Finland*

Ah, bless him, he was killed about 12 years ago in a car crash. He was a wonderful, left-sided midfield player and a good man. I was really sad when he died.

He played alongside such world beaters as Arie Haan and Rob Rensenbrink. How did the overall quality of his new team mates at Everton differ from them? *Osmo Tapio Räihälä, Helsinki, Finland*

Trevor Ross wasn't exactly Arie Haan, but each to his own. Good teams are made up of different types of players and you have to be appreciative of what each individual has to offer to the team. You can't all be Duncan McKenzie and you can't all be Mick Lyons, but one needs the other.

Is there much call for his car-jumping and golf-ball-throwing antics these days? *Frank Hargreaves, Anfield, Liverpool*

There is. Everybody who meets me mentions it, which is wonderful in itself. I'm an after-dinner speaker now, and I literally go all over the world. The questions always crop up and people always want you to talk about it. As long as they keep asking then it will have been worthwhile jumping over everything. I don't think I could jump over a car now, though – at my age, I'm grateful to be able to jump in one.

Does he believe, as I do, that the presence of one brilliant individual can really transform a team? *Charlie Deeney, Ottawa, Canada*

I think it can. If you look at Paul Gascoigne, I know he's happy daft now, but what we don't have in the England team is that creative aspect. In Beckham you've got the best crosser of the ball in the world, and that's enough to rank him in second place in Europe? He hasn't scored for three months. I'm not knocking him, but look at Michael Owen, someone said he ran 20 yards and we're calling him a world-beater. I think we are so short in terms of somebody you could call a playmaker, an English Rivaldo. That's why one player can make a team. When Gascoigne was in full flight England always had a chance.

Ask him whether he remembers the reception he received when he scored for Chelsea against us shortly after Gordon Lee transferred him. It was the only time I've seen a home crowd cheer the opposition for taking the lead. *Ian Chaderton, Berkshire, England*

That was quite remarkable and it started earlier on in the day. We arrived at Goodison Road and there were thousands of Evertonians. I remember Brian Mears, the Chelsea chairman, saying he'd never seen anything like it in his entire life. It was like the whole of Liverpool had turned out to welcome me back.

When I scored it was mind-blowing, and I don't think anybody could quite believe it, but I had to give the lads a couple of quid each for letting me through.

What were his thoughts after having scored for Chelsea at Goodison in 1978?
Osmo Tapio Räihälä, Helsinki, Finland
It was more "thank you, God." I wasn't a natural goalscorer, but to come back and stick two fingers up to Gordon Lee was marvellous. The lads afterwards said it was so funny, he was in the dugout and when I scored he clutched his head in his hands and groaned: "Why me, why me?"

With such a colourful career both on and of the field, has he ever thought of writing a book? *Rob Bland, Morecambe, England*
I have, and a few journalists have asked me if I would be up for writing a book. It's very time-consuming, and I really don't want to be an anorak. I love going up and down the country and all over the world speaking at dinners. I did the World Cup in America, so that to me is just as good as writing a book because you're retelling your stories over and over again and eulogizing about the modern game and talking about the great characters of yesteryear. There will always be someone to write your book, but I don't think there will be many after me who can tell stories. I can't see David Beckham being an after-dinner speaker in ten years' time, somehow.

It's the morning of the European Cup-winners' Cup Final in Rotterdam Square, just outside the Big Ben alehouse (where we'd slept the night before), and you can't move for Evertonians. Everyone is waiting for Duncan and Brian Clough for a Radio City phone-in or chat show or something. Duncan is carried into the pub on everyone's shoulders. Ask him can he remember why Cloughie never turned up? *Kevin Hazard, Sumbawa, Indonesia.*
Brian Clough was primarily a guest and he did the commentary with Brian Moore for the game. I can't remember why he didn't come, but it was nothing personal. He had said a lot of wonderful things about Everton, that the team had the ability to dominate European football for the next ten years providing the contracts could be met and the players were happy to stay. Of course, that couldn't happen because Liverpool got us banned from Europe.

I got carried in there and I got into all kinds of bother when I got home because I ended up rat-arsed and on people's shoulders for the rest of the day.

What did he think of the NASL when he played for Chicago Sting? How was he received there? *Mark Kenyon, Minnesota, USA*
It was lovely and a great experience, not least for me to see what a wonderful and vast country America is. Funnily enough, I played for Tulsa Roughnecks first and Joe-Max Moore's dad owned the football team. Joe was a ball boy then, his dad made his money in the oil business. I actually got sent off in Minneapolis. It was a case of mistaken identity, I was 40 yards away from the incident, but such

was the quality of the American referees in those days, the linesman had told the referee it was me. I was later admonished. They didn't apologise; they just said further action wouldn't be taken. That's why, sometimes, I have a little bit more tolerance for the refereeing over here.

Was Andy King really as crazy about Everton as it looked? *Osmo Tapio Räihälä, Helsinki, Finland*

Yes, he was, he's another one. He's brighter than Gascoigne, but his nickname was 'Tit Head' and he used to answer to the name 'Tit'. He became manager at Mansfield and I went to speak at their dinner. He was terrified, he pulled me to one side and said: "Don't call me Tit." He loved Everton, though, he really did.

Why is it that despite many better facilities, academies, soccer schools, etc., England still can't produce enough players with the gift of creativity, but we continue to churn out Tony Adams clones with boring regularity? *Mark Wilson, Warrington, England*

I think, to be honest with you, we do churn out a fair few good kids. I don't think we've lost the art of doing it. I think one of the major problems now is that as we're getting into a position to dominate Europe nobody wants to play for England any more.

The clubs don't want the players to go anymore. Look at Dwight Yorke with Man United. They're all whinging like crazy because he's been away playing in some nonsense trophy and he's missed about six games. Every time there's an international now the players are going off left, right and centre and they come back tired and it's just a big burden. I think that players now are quite happy to pull out of big internationals, and I think it's a great shame and I think that's why, as a nation, we don't produce a good England team. I still think we produce a few good kids, but not oodles of them.

Which player of the 1984-5 Everton side does he think he could have replaced so that the team would still have marched on to win the Championship? *Osmo Tapio Räihälä, Helsinki, Finland*

Turn round and tell our friend in Helsinki that that is a very unfair question and that I refuse to answer it on the grounds that I could end up requesting political asylum in Finland.

Like many others, the reason I am a Blue is my dad. The last time he ventured into Goodison Park was 1978. He'd followed us passionately for over three decades and suddenly he stopped. The reason he stopped was that Duncan McKenzie was sold. He said the day Everton Football Club can't find a place for a player like McKenzie was time enough for him. He never went again. He died last year. When I think of Everton, I think of Duncan McKenzie. My question for Duncan is: Does he realise how much he meant to us and does he realise how much pleasure he gave? *Mark Kenyon, Minnesota, USA*

To be honest with you, I don't think I did at the time, but it's been brought home to me so many times since then. It's very humbling and very flattering to hear things like that, thank you.

What did he feel was his best-ever game (for anyone)? *Mark Kenyon, Minnesota, USA*
Every one, even the bad ones.

Altogether now: We all agree, Duncan McKenzie is magic.

Thank you very much for your time.

Derek Mountfield

Born 2 November 1962
June 1982 to June 1988
£30,000

'ANDY King hit it straight into the back of the net and he got some almighty abuse from us in the crowd – imagine it, he'd just scored Everton's fifth goal. But we were all so desperate for Bob Latchford to get his 30th that season.

When he scored a penalty in the last minute there was a mass invasion of the pitch and I was one of those who ran on. My friend got his hand on the old D behind the goal to get over and got walloped by a policeman's stick, and I was shouting: "COME ON. Get on the pitch." He couldn't because he'd crushed his fingers, but I was there, bouncing round the park, absolutely delirious. There must have been two or three thousand of us on there that day, the very same pitch as Bob Latchford and Mick Lyons, and five years later I was playing there, in front of all those people. Sometimes I found it hard to believe it was really happening to me.'

A goal-scoring centre-back, Derek Mountfield was a local lad playing for Tranmere Rovers. In the drop of a hat he crossed the Mersey for a trial with his beloved Everton, making a guest appearance in an end-of-season testimonial against Preston.

Always a man with an eye for a bargain, Howard was on the case. "I considered him to be well worth a gamble and he turned out to be a magnificent and invaluable asset to the club. I signed him for £30,000 and you would have to look carefully at the record books to find a centre-back who came near him in his goal-scoring contribution."

'Every kid wants to be a professional footballer, but I never ever thought I was good enough to make it. I didn't join Tranmere until I left school. Then out of the blue a move comes for Everton, and as a Bluenose you just can't turn it down. There can be no other team you'd rather play for than your boyhood heroes. To sign for them was a dream come true, but to actually play in the greatest and most

successful side in the history of the club means so much. Nobody can erase it from the record books or ever take it away from me.

Valiant, sure-footed, handy to have around at either end of the pitch and if that's not enough for you, impassioned Evertonian, Mr Derek Mountfield – come on down.

How did he feel when he pulled on the Everton shirt for the first time in the first team? *Osmo Tapio Räihälä, Helsinki, Finland*

I always remember as a boy queuing up for the Street End with my season ticket and my two friends. The same gate every Saturday at about half past 12. We were among the first in the ground on the Street End, singing and chanting and swaying.

With me being a Bluenose, to go on and play for them was magnificent. I remember my League debut as if it was yesterday away at Birmingham City, marking that big hulk of a man called Mick Harford. We came out quite well in the game; we only got beat 1-0, so I must have done something right. I just played the one game and it was a wonderful feeling. It took me six or seven months to get into the first team, but the Birmingham City game meant an awful lot to me.

The double feint by Gray and Sharp against Norwich in a 3-0 stroll in 1985 which allowed him to arrive unescorted at the back post to head in while kneeling, was that planned or did it just happen? *George Lee Stuart, Lismore, Australia*

I think I must have fallen over. I just happened to be in the right place at the right time on many occasions and managed to get on the end of either Kevin Sheedy's or Trevor Steven's crosses. It wasn't planned, I just made a run and Sheeds saw me and put it on a plate for me. I made a meal of it by going on to all fours just to make it look more spectacular.

How many black eyes did he get in his career? *John Staines, Adelaide, Australia*

I lost count, really, I just happened to have the type of skin that would bruise rather than cut. I had one or two rather large shiners; and the biggest will be remembered at the Luton Town game when I'd actually broken my nose and by mid-half my eye was almost closed. I got on with it and scored the winning goal, and with the state I was in it made it even sweeter.

Can you please ask Derek what it was like to play alongside the solid Kevin Ratcliffe? It must have been so reassuring to know that he'd be covered when he went up for corners. *David Chow, Manchester, England*

I think I made Kevin a great centre-half because he kept covering my mistakes. He was pure quality, he was lightening quick, he covered very well and he wasn't really interested in going forward, so that gave me a licence to attack a bit. He was a fantastic defender and a great communicator, a great captain and a brilliant leader on the pitch.

How did it feel to send thousands of Blues flying through the air after scoring the winner in the semi against Luton, and did he point out to the arse of a ref. that justice was done after Ricky Hill clearly fouled Reidy for Luton's first goal?
Mark Kenyon, Minnesota, USA

I don't remember much about Luton's goal, I just remember them scoring and us getting quite dejected. If you saw the expression on my face when the ball went in the back of the net and the way I took off like a headless chicken, as I did after I scored a goal, you can see how much it meant for me to take us to Wembley. My abiding memory is seeing the ball hit the back of the net, setting off and then Andy Gray literally grabbing me by the neck and half-choking me.

That Luton semi-final was one of the best games I saw live. At half-time did the team think that the game was slipping away from them? *Mark Kenyon, Minnesota, USA*

In a way I think we did. We'd come back from a 0-0 draw in Munich on the Wednesday night and we were a bit tired and we didn't play well the first half, but we knew that if we kept battling we'd have a chance. That was Everton's strong point in those days, we never, ever gave up. We always believed we could win the game. I remember in the dying minutes, I'd been thrown up front by Howard Kendall, I think it was a charge on Neal that got the free-kick for Sheedy, and the Luton fans had those little bowler hats on and were singing "Going to Wemberlee." I'm convinced Sheeds mis-hit the free-kick, but it went in the bottom corner and the rest is history. We knew we could win every game if we just kept trying.

With the likes of Gough playing on towards his forties, does he think that, injury apart; he would fancy "getting old" in today's Premiership? *Mark Wilson, Warrington, England*

If you look at Richard Gough, the way he's handled himself is fantastic. I'm convinced that if I'd have looked after myself a bit better and the injuries hadn't happened to me like they did, I might still be playing now, but you just don't know.

Which goal felt sweeter, the winner against Luton or the equaliser against Ipswich? *Osmo Tapio Räihälä, Helsinki, Finland*

It's really hard to say, the equaliser against Ipswich was vital, we were about three minutes away from going out of the FA Cup. How I was there I don't know, because it was actually Pat Van den Hauwe who passed the ball in from the right-hand side, so I don't know what was going on there, Pat playing right-wing, me playing up front, but the goal was vital. Everton fans always mention the 1985 semi-final against Luton, so in their mind that's the most important goal I've scored for the club, but, looking back, Ipswich might hold just as much significance for me.

How does it feel to be the greatest goal-scoring defender in history? *Martin Smith, New Jersey, USA*

In history? Wow! It's nice that somebody's said that to me. It's great to have scored so many goals and not have to rely on penalties to boost my ratio, which one or two central defenders have done in the past. I wouldn't say I was the best in history; I just got on the end of some pinpoint crosses from either flank and got my share. If I'd have scored all my chances, I'd have certainly reached three figures, but I seem to have missed more than I scored. I got 60 in my whole career and that's enough for me.

How did he feel when our first goal in the European Cup-winners' Cup Final was ruled out for the 'offside' that never was? *Osmo Tapio Räihälä, Helsinki, Finland*

I remember coming in at half-time and Howard Kendall said to me: "You shouldn't be offside in that sort of situation." and I said: "Well, I wasn't," because I knew I'd timed my run right and it was Kevin Sheedy's left foot that put the ball in the right area for me. The cameras proved that I definitely wasn't offside and we could have gone in at 1-0 instead of 0-0. But the second half just got better and better for us, so it didn't matter in the end.

Did you wind up other team's strikers by telling them you'd scored more goals than they had? *Mark Kenyon, Minnesota, USA*

No I didn't. I think looking at my goal-scoring record, I was just fortunate to be in the right place, some people say at the wrong time, at least opposition fans will. I think I scored 20-odd in my time at Everton, and every one means a lot to me. I think with being a centre-forward as a kid, I had some instinct left in me.

Can you ask Derek what Neville Southall was really like behind the scenes in the 1980s? Surely he was more sociable. *David Chow, Manchester, England*

I think anyone who knows Big Nev will know that he's a fantastic character. He's one of the people who was always cracking jokes and always taking the piss. He was also the butt-end of a lot of the jokes but gave as good as he got. On the cameras he always looked dour and a dull type of person, but I can assure you, off the field he was certainly one of the boys and one of the prime piss-takers in the club.

Did he ever ponder the possibility of changing position to attack, especially after Watson arrived? *Osmo Tapio Räihälä, Helsinki, Finland*

I did play up front a couple of times for Everton. Before Dave Watson arrived I remember scoring a goal against Spurs. I would have liked to play up front, but as the years go on you tend to adapt yourself to playing in a different position.

It was my manager in the Under-14s who moved me, I was a centre-forward until then. He decided that he'd swap me over with the centre-half, so I was suddenly at the back and I loved every minute of it.

How did he get on with Howard Kendall, and which of his qualities would he (a) want to utilise and (b) NOT want to utilise in management himself? *San Presland, New Brighton, Merseyside*

I got on well with Howard, he signed me for Everton so I've got to say thank you to him for giving me a chance. He put me in the side and he had faith and belief, and if he hadn't have given me that chance I might never have been an Everton player.

You learn from all your managers and you pick up things from everyone you work with. I especially enjoyed Everton's pre-season training schedule, it was never the hard, intensive sessions like they had at other clubs, and there was a light-hearted atmosphere. I liked the way he treated players. One or two things happened while I was there that upset me and there were a couple of things I didn't like, but I won't go into them in detail. The things I wouldn't use from his school are the same things I wouldn't use from Graham Taylor, Ron Atkinson and people like that.

Does he remember coming in at number-three for Mosslands SCS away at Henry Meols Grammar School in 1978 and hitting a six off his first ball (I've still got the scorecard to prove it), with the author of this question watching from the non-striker's end? *Simon Bradley, Meols, Wirral, Merseyside*

I remember being a big hitter at cricket, I could never be a steady pace batter because I had to go for every ball that came at me. I don't remember that game at all, but I do remember hitting a fair few sixes in my cricket days.

Ask Derek Mountfield what does he think of the money players are earning now as compared to what he earned, and how much more does he think he might earn if he were playing now? *Michael O'Connell, Galway, Republic of Ireland*

That's the million dollar question. It's an interesting fact now that there are players earning more in a week than I earned in a year when I was winning the trophies with Everton. I don't begrudge them, it's become a business not a sport now, and it's big business. The money in the game is there to be used up and if the players can get a slice of it, then good luck to them. I'm not jealous, I'm not envious, but if I'd have been ten years younger people say to me I'd be worth £10-12 million pounds now, but I maintain that if I was ten years younger I may not have been good enough to play in the First Division, because there are so many good players now from abroad that I might never have made Everton's first team.

Why did he so obviously play the best football of his career for Everton when so many other players seem to do the opposite? *Osmo Tapio Räihälä, Helsinki, Finland*

It's hard to say, I just happened to be playing for a side that 'clicked' at the right time. I was playing in a great team, I feel fortunate and privileged to have been playing in the most successful team that Everton ever had.

I was in the side when we were towards the wrong end of the table up to Christmas. I remember playing the game at Christmas against Sunderland and getting booed off the pitch, the following day going to Wolves and getting stuffed 3-0, and then we embarked on a fairly long unbeaten run culminating in the FA Cup Final victory. Not many people ever repeat success from one club to another, though. I had reasonable success at other clubs, but the only teams that I played for that won anything always wore blue. Everton, who won just about everything, and then I went to Carlisle for a season and was quite successful there, too. They wore blue, so it must be my lucky colour.

Ask the 'Golden Boot' what was the best atmosphere he ever played in? *Matt Traynor, Finchley, North London*
It has to be the European Cup-winners' Cup semi-final at home to Bayern Munich. I'll never, ever forget the atmosphere in that game. I remember we used to go to a hotel before a mid-week game. We left the hotel at something like six o'clock and we couldn't get the coach down the Gwladys Street. There were about 20,000 fans blocking the way as we arrived at about 6.15.

We came on the pitch to kick off at 7.25pm, and that was unbelievable, but when we came out for the second half the half-time roar, literally, made my hair stand on end. It was an absolutely unbelievable night, and I know for a fact that Neville Southall and Andy Gray say exactly the same thing.

Did he ever feel he was in with an England chance while they were picking the likes of Terry Fenwick or Alvin Martin? *John Shearon, Dronfield, England*
There are two things in football that are regrets for me. The first one was never getting a chance to compete in the European Cup after winning the League twice in the mid-80s. The ban was in place for both of those years, and I often wonder how Everton would have fared in the European Cup.

The other thing is never getting a full international call-up. It disappointed me, and I thought that being part of a good side and scoring the goals that I did and being reasonably successful, they might have given me a chance, but people like Terry Fenwick got called up and Alvin Martin. Even Gary Pallister got a cap, and he was playing in the Second Division at the time. It's one of those things I look back on and say that maybe the manager at the time didn't think I was good enough, but as long as I was good enough to play for Everton, that was all right with me.

In his greatest Everton team as chosen for *The Evertonian* **a few years back, Derek included Ray Wilson and Brian Labone from an era prior to his playing days, and probably prior to his earliest memories of supporting the Blues. However, he could not find a place in that fantasy team for Kendall, Ball, or Harvey. Instead, he opted for Steven, Reid, Dobson and Sheedy. Does he really**

rate these outstanding midfield players even more highly than one of the greatest midfield trios ever to play the game? *Charlie Deeney, Ottawa, Canada*

It's hard to say, I spent a lot of time with my Father talking about Everton in the past. Ray Wilson won the World Cup with England. Brian Labone was probably one of the greatest Everton centre-halves ever. The Ball, Harvey, Kendall midfield was a fantastic partnership, but I always admired Martin Dobson as a player when I was a supporter, and the midfield Everton had in the mid-80s will take some beating. It was a perfect blend, players who could cross the ball, who could fight for and win the ball. When someone asks you to pick the best ever Everton side you could probably pick about seven or eight sides in different combinations, and in the end you've got to whittle it down and try and be brutally honest with yourself. I picked that midfield because I used to admire Martin Dobson so much, and the other three were part of the fantastic partnership.

Which derby game was the best one Derek played in? *Rob Bland, Morecambe, England*

Probably the 1-0 victory at Anfield. I think it was our first win at Anfield for 13 or 14 years and Graeme Sharp scored a screaming right-foot volley from about 35 yards over Bruce Grobbelaar. We got invaded by the fans and I always remember an Everton supporter ran on the pitch dressed as Superman to try and mob Graeme Sharp. I remember seeing a picture of it in the paper and thinking: "I recognise that face." I'm not saying who it was, but it was definitely someone who I knew.

Does he still live on the Carr Lane estate in Moreton? Did he object to kids (like myself) scouring the estate to find out exactly where he lived? *Martin Smith, New Jersey, USA*

No, that's just part and parcel of being a footballer. I had people knocking on my door all the time. You feel a bit embarrassed at times when they come up and ask for your autograph, but you can't knock them back because the people who asked me were the ones who were paying my wages. The only thing I do object to is when you're trying to have a nice quiet meal with your family or your wife and it causes ructions. Ask any player and they'll tell you the same thing.

Anyone can ask me for an autograph any time they want, but I find it hard to believe it's still happening. I'd been away from Merseyside for the best part of 12 years and I've just moved back. I seem to be recognised more up here now that I've got rid of my moustache and I've got shorter hair than I was in my heyday.

How did he feel when Dave Watson signed? Did he feel it was the end for him? *Martin Smith, New Jersey, USA*

No, I didn't feel it was the end. Unfortunately, I got another knee injury in a pre-season trip to Holland and it knocked me back a bit. When Dave Watson was signed, There were quite a few injuries in the back line. Gary Stevens was out injured, Alan Harper, Pat Van den Hauwe, and we were quite short for numbers at the back. Howard told me he had to sign somebody, but he didn't know who, and he actually signed Dave Watson. He must have known deep down who it was going to be and he tried to pre warn me, but at the time I was maybe a bit too gullible to realise what he was trying to say. When Dave arrived my Everton career came to an end, but you can't knock Dave after all that he's done for the club. He's been a fantastic servant for 15 years and everything he's got, he's deserved.

I remember a picture in a match programme of Mountfield and his Grandad, who had *Pink Echo's* going back pre-war celebrating Everton's finest moments. A dyed-in-the-wool Evertonian from a Blue dynasty – he gets my vote as a good skin. *George Lee Stuart, Lismore, Australia*

I lost my Grandad about 11 years ago and I inherited all those *Pink Echo's*. The old ones are not like you get now with a condensed version of the game; you used to get a ball-by-ball, minute-by-minute detailed account of the match.

I'm a terrible hoarder – I've still got all my old shirts, tracksuits, pictures, programmes and newspaper cuttings. Every now and again, I open one of the boxes and sit there and the memories will come flooding back. My wife asks me how I remember all those games, but I can literally reel off instances from the game, from a piece of paper or a picture, and she thinks I've got a photographic memory. On top of the shirts I've got the medals, and they can't take that away from me. I sit there and I look at them and I start reminiscing about those glorious days and those happy times.

Who was the best Everton player he played with? *Rob Bland, Morecambe, England*

It's hard to say, there were so many quality players round the mid-80s. Andy Gray came and enlivened the place. Peter Reid, who really hadn't been heard of for many years after being an outstanding youngster, came to Everton and literally took over and dominated the midfield for years. Kevin Ratcliffe was an outstanding defender alongside me, and that big bin man behind me, too. If anything got past us, we knew they still wouldn't score because Big Nev would get his enormous frame in the way. It's very, very hard to pick a best player because there were just so many around me.

When he played his last game for Everton did he know it was going to be his last, and if so, how did feel about that? *Michael O'Connell, Galway, Republic of Ireland*

No, I didn't know it was going to be my last game. It was an awful wrench to leave Everton. Fans ask me why I went, but Dave Watson had come and I played about 20 games in two seasons. I felt my career was going nowhere at the time and I needed a change to get myself going again. I couldn't see myself breaking up Dave Watson and Kevin Ratcliffe, they'd become an established partnership, and I didn't like being carted round the country as the 13th man. Then it was only one sub and I was around with the squad and never getting a game. I was the occasional sub and getting in when one of the players was injured and getting pulled back out again when they were fit. After being successful at Everton it wasn't what I was looking for. I thought my career was going nowhere at the time and I was going stale. To leave was a mighty, mighty big wrench for me, but I had to do it to get my football going again. It was the hardest decision of my life. I look back and think maybe I left a bit too early. If I'd have given it another season I might just have dislodged one or two of them, but that's there to ponder. Should I have gone or should I not, but I did in the end and maybe I might live to regret it.

Wherever I've gone, there's been a warm welcome for me and there are so many people who I recognise now. They ask me about my time there and what it was like.

When I look at people like Mick Lyons and my hero, Bob Latchford, and they won nothing playing for Everton, and Mick Lyons played over 400 games for the club. Within three years of me being at the club, we'd won the FA Cup, the European Cup-winners' Cup and a League Championship. It's there in the record books and nobody can ever take that away from me. I've been a Bluenose all my life and I always will be. I'm a very proud and privileged man to be able to say that.

I don't believe there is anything left to be added.

Joe Parkinson

Born 11 November 1971
March 1994 to May 2000
£250,000

JOE Parkinson arrived in tandem with Anders Limpar, both results of Mike Walker's desperate bid for professional and Premier League survival. As fate would have it, the 22-year-old from Bournemouth only found his spiritual home at Goodison after Walker's departure and under the paternal eye of Joe Royle.

Strong, intrepid and determined in the midfield, The Pieman fitted into the Royle blueprint perfectly and was the epitome of dedication. But it's a funny old game and that niggling knee injury was beginning to take its toll.

He was young and optimistic when he travelled to Sweden to undergo treatment. After two years of painful and pioneering surgery, Joe Parkinson has finally hung up his boots at the age of 28.

Is he bitter, twisted and boring the arse off anybody who'll listen with his cries of "Why me?" Oh, no Sirree, not the Pieman – he's been appointed as the brand new Everton's Fans Liaison Officer.

> I've only just officially finished as a player, I got my P45 in May so I never actually had to leave, which is fantastic. I still get on well with the lads, I see them training a few times a week and obviously on match days, but I've had my time. I'm not bitter at all, whatever they're doing on the field, I'm right behind them and I'm just glad that I'm still involved with Everton Football Club.

Fellow Bluenoses, tug your collective forelock to the gentle giant – Joe Parkinson.

Did the club give him any idea about how his injuries would worsen if he played on, or did they just inject him and tell him to get running? *Chris Lord, Blackpool, England*

No, it was nothing like that at all; it was all down to me. I knew I'd ripped my cartilage, but I could play on it for at least another six weeks. The manager asked me to play, but he always said to me: "If you don't want to, you don't have to." I always wanted to play, but it got to the stage where I just couldn't any more and I had to stop. I kept having little operations, getting back to full fitness and playing as soon as I could, but the style of my play didn't really help. It was a unique injury in how quickly it deteriorated, it could have happened to anyone, but it just happened to be me. I've no regrets in the way everything went, and I think I did quite well in my career; I was just unfortunate the injury got worse so quickly.

In your opinion, why do Everton have so many players recovering from long-term and career-threatening injuries? *Phil Williams, Chester, North Wales*
Whether the players are a bit more honest and get stuck in more, or maybe, with them being true to their club, they play through injuries which makes them worse. I don't know what it is but it does seem to happen at Everton quite a lot.

Were you surprised when Everton came in for you initially, and at how quickly you became established in the team? *Neil Wolstenholme, Chelsea, South-West London*
The whole thing was really quick; I'd played the night before away at York. I'd come home and gone out with my family, and when I came back my manager from Bournemouth was there. The next day I signed for Everton. It was a big shock for me and I don't think I settled in quickly when I first came – I didn't realise the size of the club and what it took to be a good footballer on the big stage, but I think in the end I won everyone round and did all right.

Does he think Mike Walker would have been successful if he had been given longer at Goodison? *San Presland, New Brighton, Merseyside*
I'm not sure, but probably not. I owe a lot to Mike, he bought me and brought me to the club, but I don't think he realised how big Everton was, because I know I didn't when I first arrived. A lot of people wondered if he was going to be good enough to do the job. He had his time and it didn't work out, so we'll never know, but he was a nice fella and I'd like to thank him for bringing me to the club.

Was Mike Walker as clueless about tactics and formations as he actually seemed? *Neil Wolstenholme, Chelsea, South-West London*
I think he always was a bit strange, but I was only a young lad and I would never have questioned my manager. Maybe some of the senior players did, but I just did as I was told even though I don't think it was helping my game. Really, it all just started going right for me when Joe Royle arrived.

Did he even dream that we'd beat Tottenham so convincingly in the 1995 FA Cup semi-final when no one gave us much of a prayer (I was lying through me teeth in the car all the way to Leeds saying I thought we'd win 1-0 when I actually thought we'd get stuffed...) and was that match his finest performance in an Everton shirt? *Billy Williams, Cologne, Germany*

When we realised we'd got Tottenham at Elland Road we thought it would be a hard game because Tottenham were the fancied team, but only until we pulled up at the ground and we saw how many Evertonians were there. We ran out on the pitch and saw we had three sides of the ground. It was then that we knew that we would win, and in the end it was very easy.

Most people said to me it was my best game, but I wouldn't say so, I just stood out a bit more, that's all. There were other games where I did more work and was more benefit to the team, but it came to the semi-final and I just happened to be more noticeable. Others say it was the Cup Final when we beat Man United at Wembley. On a personal level, I always think that when I signed for Everton was a great moment for me, and another was when the club was kind enough to grant me a testimonial.

How on earth did we beat Man United in the Cup Final? This is still a mystery to me to this day. I was sat there with my face buried in my hands and my eyes closed through most of the second half. *Billy Williams, Cologne, Germany*

Well, we'd played them about a month or so before and beaten them 1-0, and we knew we had to get stuck into them and not give them the time they expected from most teams, we gave them respect, but only as players. We knew we could beat them on the day, and me and Barry (Horne) got stuck into them, and over the time we won most of the individual battles. It wasn't the prettiest of Finals, but the point of that Final was to win the Cup for the club and a medal for ourselves, and that's exactly what we did.

Did Paul Ince shake your hand after the FA Cup Final after you totally outplayed him? *James Goddard, Ipswich, England*

Yeah, he did, I was surprised too. I was told to go out and kick him, which I did – for the rest of the game he was after me, but I was just laughing at him and winding him up. The only problem I had that day was at the end of the game when I wanted his shirt and he wouldn't swap it with me. In fact, there were a lot of people walking past and no one would do it. Then Lee Sharp came along and he said he'd meet me in the bar afterwards. I wasn't holding my breath because I didn't think he would, but he came over, shook my hand, said well done and swapped shirts. Most of them were a bit stuck up, but I did shake their hands, which rubbed it in a bit.

What is his true opinion of Andrei Kanchelskis? Was he really as complete a mercenary as many Evertonians think? *Billy Williams, Cologne, Germany*

It's always hard to talk about another player and say bad things about them, but with me being out the game now I can honestly say I think he was only ever in it for the cash. I don't know if he had problems himself, but he was certainly causing problems in the dressing-room. He was a great player with enormous talent, but all he wanted was another move to get more and more money, he never wanted to play for the shirt or the club, and he let himself and the other players down.

How did he feel when he and Barry Horne out-muscled Keano and Ince in the Cup Final, was it like fulfilling a personal vendetta? *Tony Kuss, Republic of Ireland*

It was, yes. I come from Manchester and they were my team when I was a boy. I've got great respect for Keane and I think at the moment he's one of the best midfielders in the world, and that went for Paul Ince as well at the time, so for me and Barry to come out on top and get the medals was just fantastic. It was to be our day and it's as simple as that.

Did he think that the 1995 Cup-winning team had finally turned the corner after that semi against Spurs only to find that the chairman turned out to be not as far-sighted as the rest of us? *Jon Berman, West Derby, Liverpool*

When we won that Cup, we'd staved off relegation again and we all thought: 'This is it.' We thought we'd get a few more signings and it was just going to get better and better. Everything was going well, but I personally think Joe Royle was let down by a few people, namely Andrei Kanchelskis, Anders Limpar and Vinny Samways – he didn't really want to play for the club. It was the big-time players, the big-time charlies, who let the manager and the other players down, and I think it cost the manager his job in the end.

Was Amokachi any good, especially when you take into account he got your 30-yarder struck off for offside? *Phil Williams, Chester, North Wales*

Yeah, that was unlucky that. Daniel was a good player and was just coming right when we sold him. In the changing rooms he was fantastic to be around and a great character – he just took a while to settle in. I'll tell you what, he was missed when he left, and I personally think we sold him a year or two too soon.

In 1995, we were being shown around Goodison in the pre-stadium-tour days and bumped into Joe on the stairs leading to the executive areas. Ask him if he would have posed for a photograph with us if my bottle hadn't completely gone at being confronted with the hero of the semi-final, played but four days before? All I could manage was a stammered: 'All right, Joe', and he was gone. *Dave Richman, Johannesburg, South Africa*

Of course I would have. Signing autographs and things like that is all part of the job. It's great to give autographs and you've got to worry when people don't ask you for them. As long as the people are well-mannered and haven't been rude to me, it's a pleasure and I would have done if he'd have just asked.

How pissed off was he that he never got an England cap? *Pete Rowlands, Enfield, North London*

That never bothered me at all. People say that at the time of my injury I was getting touted for England for a call-up, but I got injured so I'll never find out whether it was going to happen. Quite honestly, I was just happy to play for Everton, if England was ever going to happen it would only have been a bonus.

What does he think was Peter Johnson's biggest faux pas? *San Presland, New Brighton, Merseyside*

Probably the youth academy. The thing with Peter Johnson is that when you meet him he seems all right, but the way it comes across is that he doesn't seem to know much about how to run a club like Everton. People say he always was a Liverpool fan, so whether he wanted to run the club into the ground, I don't know. Johnson never seemed to realise how big the club was and how it should have been run, and now with the club being in so much debt the academy isn't the way it should be, it's not right, you see Liverpool's and it's fantastic. Peter Johnson has caused a lot of problems and I'm glad to see him go.

Does he keep any bits of his body in a glass jar somewhere? *San Presland, New Brighton, Merseyside*

There's a jar, with parts of my cartilage in that liquid they use, in the treatment room at the club. It just looks like bits of gristle really, but next time I'm in I'm going to pick it up and bring it home with me.

In these days of obscene wages, and please emphasize obscene, do you think it's right that there are still such things as testimonials? *Frank Hargreaves, Anfield, Liverpool*

I know what you're saying, look at me, I only signed a contract five years ago and here I am getting a testimonial. The way it's worked with me and other players whose careers have been cut short, they do seem like a good way of helping the player along, especially when they've still got a young family to look after. On the other hand, when you see people like Sir Alex Ferguson, with the things he's won and the money he must have made from the game, it all seems wrong. Obviously, the money's going to help me, but I'm more honoured that the club have recognised me and said thank you, and I'm really grateful.

What's your new job like and how are you enjoying it? *Liz Wyman, Stoke on Trent, England*

I was lucky enough to be appointed by Bill Kenwright as the Everton Fans Liaison Officer. Really, I act as a stepping-stone between the supporters and the club. Fans can phone, email or write to me if they have any questions they need answering. I'm still quite new so I don't know everything just yet, but I'll certainly find out as fast as I can, call them back to tell them what they wanted to know. It's a fantastic job and I really love it. I can't believe my luck.

It's been great doing an interview with questions asked by the fans. Evertonians are something special. Since my injury, and now my retirement from football, I've had many letters and great support from fans and it helped me through my darkest days. It's another good reason I'm made up I've got a testimonial because I'll be able to go back and say goodbye to them properly.

A few people have asked me what I'd do if I could turn back the clock, and I have to say if I had the chance I wouldn't change anything, I loved my time as a player and I've got no regrets at all.

Graeme Sharp

Born 16 October 1960
April 1980 to July 1989
£120,000

"Graeme Sharp, superstar, scores from miles out past Grobbelaar."
And so he did.

But he could certainly never be billed an overnight sensation. Graeme Sharp signed as a raw 19-year-old from Dumbarton, but crippled with insecurity, homesickness and self-doubt, he spent the first two years of his contract on the reserve team bench.

> I was like a fish out of water when I came down from Scotland, and I was well aware of it. I knew I was being paid all that money, but when I got into the dressing-room, even with the younger lads, I felt I was out of my depth. I thought they were better than me and I really shouldn't have been there, so much so that it was embarrassing at times.

Endless months of character building on the training ground followed, and under the tender guidance of Colin Harvey the ugly duckling was transformed into the most beautiful swan of all.

Still proudly holding on to the highest goalscoring record this side of the war and capped a dozen times for Scotland: Graeme Sharp; pundit, match commentator and newspaper columnist, walk this way, your public awaits.

His debut was Brighton away – he looked like the game was passing him by, it was all too fast, too skilful. How long did he feel he took to get up to Division One standard? *Steve Kirkwood, Brentford, West London*
I played in the Brighton game and then at Nottingham Forest, but I knew myself that I was absolutely miles away from being a first-team player. For the first two years I was very homesick, then, in the last year of my original contract, I realised it was shit or bust and I had to get my finger out. I made sure I didn't go home as often to Glasgow; for the first two years, I was home every weekend, I was getting the train home after reserve games and coming back down on the Sunday night.

I started getting things together with a lot of help from Colin Harvey. At the time, I knew the only way I was going to get a chance would be through a lot of injuries. When my opportunity finally came along, I took it and things went on from there.

The goal you scored against Watford in the 1984 Cup Final. I saw you trap the ball and shoot, but didn't see the ball go in off the post as we were all up celebrating the goal before it had actually gone in. Did you feel that once you'd hit it you knew it was going in – even if it did hit the post on the way? Did you ever get a better buzz out of scoring a goal than that one? *Sid Martin, Sandwich, England*

Probably not, it was the fact it was my first goal and the Cup Final, which made it so memorable. You don't have a lot of time, so when I controlled it and shot I just hoped it would go in. It was a good enough connection; it was a good enough strike and maybe a bit fortunate to go in off the post. On another day, it could have come off the post and back into play, but it didn't.

It was a fantastic feeling, especially with all your family down there watching you. I know it's an old cliché, but you did dream of that when you were a young boy, especially up in Scotland when we used to get the English Cup Final live, so it was a joy just to actually be there, but to score was brilliant.

We'd been to the Milk Cup Final the same year and lost out to Liverpool after the replay, so I think it was more important for the club to get to winning ways, and that was the first trophy as a team that we had won. I'll always remember the goal, but at the time it was more important for the team because we realised then that we could go on to greater things.

When you joined us from Dumbarton did you have any idols you looked up to? *Ari Sigurgeisson, Hafnarfjordur, Iceland*

In the Everton dressing-room when I came in there were a lot of household names, Asa Hartford, Brian Kidd, but the one with the most attention was Bob Latchford, and Bob was there when I joined at first.

In Scotland, you always have your favourite Scottish team, but you also have your favourite English team. Mine at the time was Aston Villa, and he won't have this, but Andy Gray was my favourite player. I remember when Andy first came into the club and I told him he was my favourite player when I was a young boy, and he said: "Sod off, you cheeky monkey, how old do you think I am?" But he was the one, and because he was Scottish and had come down from Dundee United, he was my idol.

Ask him why in hell's name he didn't wait a few minutes until he scored that volley at Anfield, because I was in the bloody bog and missed it. *Lol Scragg, Arbroath, Scotland*

That's the one goal everybody remembers me for – except Lol – and I wish I had a pound for everybody who's asked me about it. I think everyone remembers it because it was against Liverpool and it was special in the fact that we hadn't won there for so long. It was always nice scoring against them, it was great to see the joy on the faces of the Evertonians and the glum faces on the Reds. Tell Lol I'm sorry about that, but for just one person to miss it isn't bad odds.

When was he first aware of his heading ability? Was it just something he found he could do or was it something he had to practise day in and day out? Could he teach it to others? *David Catton, Sheffield, England*

That's a difficult one. It's something that I didn't necessarily practice all the time and when I was younger it certainly wasn't a skill. I wasn't bad in the air, but I didn't go to any extremes to practice it or to practice jumping.

The consensus of opinion when I first came to Everton was that I wasn't physically strong enough or aggressive enough. I worked very hard on that; Colin Harvey worked hard on that as well. I don't know why, but when Andy Gray came to the club, certain things rubbed off on to my play. I got into the habit of jumping early into centre-backs and gaining fouls. Heading wasn't something that I especially trained in, I think it just came as part and parcel of training every day and becoming a professional footballer.

Does he reckon that the delirious Evertonian in the big coat who ran on to the pitch after his wonder goal at Anfield is second in the Evertonian pitch-invaders folklore only to the late Eddie Cavanagh? The image of him celebrating that goal will always stay with me. *Colin Jones, Mossley Hill, Liverpool*

I remember it well. I was coming back on the train from the West Ham game the other week with some of the supporters and they were mentioning it, so I think he definitely comes into folklore now. Eddie will never be forgotten. Unfortunately, he's sadly departed now, but the fact that it was captured on the television immortalised it, and it always makes fantastic viewing. But certainly, when I think of my goal, I always remember the bespectacled gentleman running on with the duffel coat, and I'd say he's certainly second to Eddie Cavanagh.

As Graeme used to live next door to Ronnie Whelan, how did they discuss the achievements of their respective teams, especially around the time of any derby game? In other words, did he give Ronnie a decent wind-up on Sunday, 21 October 1984, or were the curtains drawn all day in the Whelan household? *Osmo Tapio Räihälä, Helsinki, Finland*

To be honest, I didn't see a lot of him. We did live next door in Southport, but I don't now. If we were in the drive at the same time we'd let on to each other or if I saw him in the pub. We weren't really close neighbours; I certainly wasn't going round for afternoon drinks or to borrow a cup of sugar, or anything like that.

Who was the best player you ever played with at Everton (not necessarily striking partner)? *Mark Staniford, Woolton, Liverpool*

If you look throughout the side it would be hard to pick one out. Kevin Sheedy was outstanding, Peter Reid, Trevor Steven and Paul Bracewell in their own way, as well. It's easier for me to pick out the best striker I played with and I've had a lot of those, I had 15 partners.

For goalscoring it would have to be Gary Lineker. We scored a lot of goals in the season we worked together, but unfortunately we didn't win anything. But as a footballer and being on the same wavelength, Adrian Heath and myself just seemed to hit it off. We didn't have to practise in the training ground because everything came automatically. I think as a partner and a player he was the one I most enjoyed playing alongside up front.

Is it true you battered Tony Cottee after the Cup Final? *Frank Hargreaves, Anfield, Liverpool*

No, I never came to blows with anybody. I was very disappointed if my memory serves me well, and I thought that some people on the day didn't give enough, to be perfectly honest. Whether Tony Cottee came into that category, I can't honestly remember, but I do know I was gutted on the day and afterwards I wasn't the easiest person to live with.

Did your constant whinging at referees ever get them to change their minds about one single decision? *Mark Staniford, Woolton, Liverpool*

Yes. People say that I whinged, and it's true. I think as a football team when we were successful we had a few whingers, to be honest. Howard Kendall always said when decisions go against you or if a player gets fouled, then get round the referee and the next time he comes to make a decision he might just be swayed. So yes, I was constantly on the referee's back, I wouldn't say all the time, but most of the time.

Once you'd let your feelings be known, I think you did get away with the occasional challenge, so it was all part of the game. I know they're trying to outlaw it now, but that was then and I certainly thought there were benefits to doing it and that's why we continued to do it. Now, they say it's a bad example to kids, but I think when you're playing in a very volatile atmosphere, passion tends to take over a bit.

Ask him if he would have enjoyed playing in those Lycra cycling shorts that seem so popular. *San Presland, New Brighton, Merseyside*

I actually did wear them. When I was at Everton they were just coming out. I had a hernia problem, so I was one of the first to wear them, but they weren't like the ones you see just now. I have worn some of those on the training pitch, but looking at me now I don't think we'd get a pair big enough to fit me.

Having dealt successfully with a number of thug centre-backs during his career, does Graeme think that today's defenders are nothing like as hard as the ones in the 1980s? *Phil Pellow. Waterloo, Liverpool*

I think the game has definitely changed; there were some very hard opponents in the 1980s. Nowadays, I think it's all different. With the tackle from behind being banned, the forwards certainly get off far more lightly than we did then.

I think the laws have helped the attacking players because when I was playing, there were some hard battles fought out there but that was also one of the things you looked forward to. Andy Gray and myself liked putting ourselves up against the likes of Graham Roberts, Kenny Burns and Larry Lloyd. There are definitely not as many hard men now as there was in my day.

How did he get on with Lineker on a personal level? *Vince Balfe, Wicklow, Republic of Ireland*

It was a tall order to come in to replace a legend like Andy Gray, so it was always going to be difficult for him. Andy left in unfortunate circumstances and everybody was shocked when he went. Our football did change to accommodate Links, but as a fella he was fine. He wasn't the greatest of socialisers, but he did come out for a drink on his way back to Southport. He was smashing and I had no problems whatsoever with him.

The 84-85 side could take care of itself physically, but was it ever discussed prior to games who were the opposition hard men. And who was the hardest number five he played against? *Steve Kirkwood, Brentford, West London*

They all had their own reputation and you were well aware of who they were. Andy Gray and I used to love a physical battle. If it became physical, we could mix it with them, there wasn't a problem there. Graham Roberts and the boy Miller were the so-called hard men at Tottenham and we enjoyed playing in those games. First and foremost we went out to play football, but if the game turned out that way, then we certainly could look after ourselves.

Why doesn't the club employ him at the very least as a heading coach? *Colin Berry, Wavertree, Liverpool*

I read Alan Hansen's book the other day – I shouldn't be saying that, should I? Anyway, he said I should be involved in some capacity, maybe in a striking role. To be fair, there are jobs all round the place, goal-keeping coach, defensive coach. It's surprising we don't have an attacking coach, but maybe it will come to fruition. I think I could certainly teach them a thing or two about heading.

What does he think of *Speke From the Harbour* (fanzine)? Because we often give him freebies outside the ground and I just wondered if he actually read it or just took it so as not to offend us... *Mark Staniford, Woolton, Liverpool*

I do like it and I do read it, before the game and then at half-time. I think it's got some very interesting articles and points of view, and everybody is entitled to a point of view. They're very loyal fans and committed to Everton Football Club, it's enjoyable reading, sometimes more enjoyable than others, but always very readable.

When you were playing how did you react to fellow (ex-) professionals sitting in judgement on your performances as part of the ever-growing media circus,

and does what you felt then affect how you do your radio job now? *Mark Wilson, Warrington, England*

In all honesty, it wasn't as high profile then as it is now. Everything's analysed now. When I was playing it wasn't really ex-professionals who were criticising, it was more the media. You did get upset with certain sections of the media who gave you stick and you always thought: "What does he know? He hasn't even played football before." But regarding my job, what I say is my opinion; it's how I see the game and the situation. I've come in for a bit of stick over the John Collins situation, that John is better than people make him out to be. I think it's a bit easier to take if criticism is coming from someone who has played the game and has got a general idea of how it works.

Can you ask Sharpie if, in his opinion, his old mate Andy Gray could have performed the miracles that Walter Smith has produced had he accepted the job at Goodison Park? *Steve Jensen, Wamberal, Australia*

We'll never know, but I'm sure he would have given it a good go. He was a volatile character, players would certainly have known what was required of them and if they weren't willing to do it they would be out the door. Very similar to Walter, he'd have a code of discipline. Andy, through no fault of his own, turned the move down, or it didn't materialise. He had a little bit of history with Ron Atkinson at Aston Villa as assistant manager and it would have been his first step into management with Everton, and it was a big job to take.

Walter had handled a big club before in Glasgow Rangers. I know the circumstances were different, but at least he had experience. Andy would have come into this job as a raw novice. It worked for Peter Reid, but it might not have. It was a shame because I'd have liked to have seen it happen, but I think we've got a man in charge now, doing a very good job.

Ask him if he's still in touch with Ratters and Big Nev? *Colin Berry, Wavertree, Liverpool*

Yeah, I see Kevin regularly, I play golf with him, and our wives are close as well. Nev we don't see too much, he travels to Bradford and all over the place. But Kevin, I do keep in touch with.

When he managed Oldham, he presumably learned some of the realities of life as a football manager. Has this experience put him off management, or does he see his media career as a stopgap before he has another go somewhere else? *Nick Williams, Warrington, England*

It was a let-down with the Oldham thing and I certainly got my eyes opened. It was my first job, so you're in a learning process, but I had people around me I could learn from.

Colin Harvey was a great help, but things didn't work out for me because Oldham Football Club was cost-cutting, they'd had their time in the Premiership, they were happy and they no longer wanted to get back in there. I got a lot of hassle and I was bringing it home, I wasn't really getting any help or support from behind the scenes at Oldham and it was time for me to walk away.

I certainly don't envy the likes of Kevin Ratcliffe, Ian Atkins and Steve McMahon going into jobs where there's no money and they're scrimping and scraping. I'd love to get back into football but I'd have to seriously look where I was going if I ever get the opportunity. I miss the day-to-day basis of football, but as to being a manager at a small club again, I don't know if I could put up with the hassle.

How many different ways has he seen his name spelled? *Ken Myers, California, USA*

Everton spelt my name wrong the first time I played. It didn't really affect me; it was my father who used to go mad. It's happened on many occasions and it happens at posh establishments where they're supposed to know your name, but they still spell it wrong. The most annoying thing is when they spell my first name AND my second name wrong, Sharp with an E and Graeme with an H but I think the one that rankles most is Sharp with an E – I believe that's the English way to spell it, but mine's the proper Scottish way!

Would you like to be the manager at Everton one day? *Colin Berry, Wavertree, Liverpool*

I'd love to back there in any capacity, to be honest. Does that sound like I'm touting for a job? I was there 13 years and thoroughly enjoyed every minute of it. I've still got a big affinity with and passion for the club and I've seen them week in, week out with my job on the radio. I'd go back even as a ball boy, but only time will tell if that happens.

Looking back, did you suspect when you travelled down to Goodison to sign for us that you'd still be saying hello to us all strolling along Goodison Road on match days almost 20 years on? *Neil Wolstenholme, Chelsea, South-West London*

No, definitely not, but that's just how I've settled here. I played for 13 seasons at Everton, but I had my family down here and my kids were born down here, although my wife's from Scotland. There was talk of us moving back up to Scotland when my career was finished, but fortunately we decided to stay put. Personally, I've spent more time down here now than I did in Glasgow, so you can call me an adoptive Scouser if you want.

Ask if he wished he'd have left earlier, perhaps to play abroad? *Colin Berry, Wavertree, Liverpool*

I had the opportunity to move a couple of times, but I was happy at Everton. When my departure did eventually come about, it was in a bitter way and I was disappointed in that. Looking back, I think if I had moved abroad I would have been financially better off, but I was happy to stay at Everton and I wouldn't have left a day earlier than I had to.

My father's generation rave about Alex Young but I have seen Latchford, Gray, Heath, Ferguson and Campbell *et al* **in the space of 25 plus years watching**

Everton and you are without doubt the greatest centre-forward I have ever seen in the royal blue shirt. You had it all – skill, vision, bravery and the ability to take the chances. If you'd played for a more media-friendly team you'd be a national institution. *Neil Wolstenholme, Chelsea, South-West London*

That's a lovely thing for somebody to say about me, I feel immensely proud and flattered. I love Everton Football Club and all that goes with it, and I still say to this day that you'll never find more loyal and dedicated fans anywhere else in the land.

There's nothing more to be said other than, Graeme Sharp, it was a pleasure to wander down nostalgia street in your delightful company. Thank you for your time.

Kevin Sheedy

Born 21 October 1959
August 1982 to March 1992
£100,000

Time ticks by slowly in the reserve team especially for the hungry and incredibly talented. Kevin Sheedy was virtually unknown on Merseyside despite his four years on the wrong side of Stanley Park, when he was head hunted by Howard Kendall.

And imagine, if you dare, what might have happened without the deadliest of left feet, the king of the cross and most consistent penalty taker of all. One thing is for certain, the history of Everton Football Club would be written much differently.

And as calls go – this one was pretty damn close.

Kendall swooped.

> I met Kevin and spoke to him about signing for Everton but his personal demands were too high. I took the team to Israel for an end of season trip, and while I was there, Harry Cook who was then the chief scout phoned me and said he'd agreed to lower his price. I was a bit miffed and wasn't sure that I even wanted him anymore, but I decided it was an unsuitable time to be stubborn. I told Harry to wait for half a day, then phone him and tell him he was in.

Game, set and match.

Fellow Bluenoses, allow me to introduce you to the genteel and softly spoken master of the dead ball, Mr Kevin Sheedy.

In the dark days before the 1984 Oxford game did he think we were ever going to come good? *Clive Blackmore, Washington DC, USA*

You always believe in your team. When I was at Liverpool I was in digs in Anfield so I used to go and watch the Everton first team playing midweek whenever I could. I saw all the good young players they had, Graeme Sharp had just broken into the team and Adrian Heath had recently signed, so I knew when I was going there that it was going to be a young team and it would just be a matter of time. After I'd seen what the players could do in training I knew it would come right eventually.

Is Sheeds aware of just how much undiluted pleasure he has given Bluenoses over the years as, we once again, watch a re-run of him giving the fingers to the Kop? *Phil Pellow, Waterloo, Liverpool*

It's difficult to explain how I felt at the time, I mean a free-kick goes into the top corner and I think it was just a reflex emotional reaction. I usually just put one finger up signalling a goal, but, it being the Kop end, two fingers just automatically went up. Maybe it was frustration at the four years I spent there not making the first team very often.

The follow-on to that was that Adrian Heath and I got hauled up in front of the FA because somebody had seen it on the telly. It was hilarious, really, I was like Ted Rogers trying to go from two fingers to one finger and trying to explain it wasn't a V-sign. The week before, Mark Falco had been fined £2000 for a similar type of gesture, and in those days that was a lot of money. So I went down there convinced I was going to end up forking out a couple of grand, but, fortunately, because of my good record, they let me off with it.

Tell him I was in the Kop, and he gave the fingers to me too. *Billy Williams, Cologne, Germany*

Well, there was both Liverpool and Evertonians in there, I knew that, but I decided it was the Kop after all, so I just had to do it.

I used to watch Sheeds at Hereford before he went to Anfield. How big a leap was that in terms of quality, fitness and hardness? *Steve Kirkwood, Brentford, West London*

Hereford was a good training ground for me, I'd been with them in the Fourth, Third and Second Divisions. I knew Liverpool were interested in me and I got a 'phone call asking me to go and speak to them. On the way up, I didn't want to sign for them because you have to serve your time in the Reserves and I didn't want to do that. I thought that I was good enough to play, maybe not for such a big a club as Liverpool but I wanted to go to a bigger club than Hereford and straight into the first team. I'd watched Liverpool that summer when they'd won the European Cup at Wembley and then I got the 'phone call to go up. Once you get there, you see the place and the history and I ended up signing. I got some good and bad things out of it, it was a good learning process and it certainly toughened me up.

When he was finding those immense passes, which forward gave him the best options, i.e. the best movement up front? I reckon it must have been Inchy, but others say Lineker or Graeme Sharp. *Phil Pellow, Waterloo, Liverpool*

Without question Adrian Heath, we seemed to have a good understanding. I knew exactly where he wanted the ball, he'd come short and I knew he wanted it long and he would spin off and vice versa, he'd go long and spin off short and I'd deliver the ball to him. I think out of all the strikers I played with, we certainly had the best understanding.

When he was at Hereford he had really poor posture. Did Liverpool or Everton work on him on that aspect? *Steve Kirkwood, Brentford, West London*

I was OK when I was at Hereford, it was just when I went to Liverpool I had a problem with my back. I don't know whether I was still growing or what, I never really got to the bottom of the problem but I was out for nearly 12 months on and off with it. It didn't really help my career at Liverpool, because I think they really thought there wasn't a lot wrong with me and I should just get on with it. It wasn't the case, I was desperate to succeed at Liverpool and that didn't help my purpose at all, in fact it really set me back. Once I moved to Everton that cleared up and that was how it worked out.

Which team was better; 84-85, 1986-87 or maybe the unlucky 85-86 side? *David Chow, Manchester, England*

I'd have to say that with the players we had on a regular basis, the 84-5 side was the best. We won the League, the Cup-winners' Cup and were one game away from doing the unique treble.

When he put the first free-kick past Ipswich, Kevin Ratcliffe seemed to have a go at him. Did he, and if so, why? *Jim Conboy, Southport, Merseyside*

It was Peter Reid, actually. When a free-kick is given the goalkeeper starts lining the wall up and shouting instructions and he's not ready to make a save. Peter Reid was telling me not to take it because the ref wasn't ready, but needless to say I took no notice of him and bent it into the corner, so he turned round and said: "I told you so." Well maybe not quite those words, but that was the general gist of it...

But what he didn't realise is that when I'd done that, the goalie knew I could put it in that corner. He moved too far to cover that part of the goal and left a big hole on the other side. Peter has a very limited knowledge of free-kicks and he should always leave it to the experts.

Do you get hacked off with all this rubbish talked about Beckham when you were the original? The kick you had to retake after scoring and then promptly putting it in the other corner – Beckham could never do that now could he? *Mike Royden, South Wirral, England*

I think to give credit to David Beckham; he can score from longer range than I could have. I was probably 20 to 25 yards maximum but I think you have to look at the quality he can deliver from 30 yards plus, he's probably got more power but he's a good a specialist as I was. Zola is excellent, too, but I think he's more of a similar distance to myself, around the edge of the box and 20 to 23 yards out, and he bends them in. Beckham has that same power and accuracy only over 25 and 30 yards. It takes a lot more skill to be able to do that.

How scary was it having Pat Van den Hauwe running up behind you?' *Phil Pellow, Waterloo, Merseyside*

In a French maid's outfit? *Colm Kavannagh, Co Wicklow, Republic of Ireland*

A French maid's outfit? Well, I wouldn't know about that, but to have Pat behind me was great. He was a no-nonsense player, a good, strong tackler who won the ball. I always said to him: "When you get it, Pat, just give it to me, don't try to play it whatever you do. Just get it, win it and give it to me, I'll do the rest."

Was he really injured after scoring a header from 18 yards out during the 5-0 rout of Manchester United or was he just pissing himself laughing like the rest of us? *Jim Conboy, Southport, Merseyside*
Kevin Moran is a good friend of mine and we played for Ireland together, so there was nothing malicious in it, but he was playing at right-back and was well known for butting people in the head and spilling blood. The cross came over and I've gone up for the header and he has, too, from behind me, but he's managed to head the back of my head. That's what generated the power for the header and that's why it ended up in the top corner. If he'd have left me alone I think it would have comfortably rolled back to the goalkeeper. I didn't know where the ball had gone or what had happened because I went down a bit dazed.

I got a cut on my head and had to go off and have seven stitches, but I came back on and managed to score another goal. After the game I had to have the stitches taken out and put back in again because they'd been done in a rush. But thinking about it now, it was worth it just to score two goals. So the answer is that the header was never within my powers and Kevin helped me very much on that instance, everybody knew I wasn't a good header of the ball.

Pat Van den Hauwe. Scary? *Phil Pellow, Waterloo, Liverpool*
Different, I would say. I think his bark was worse than his bite but he was a good player.

When I saw him in the Weld Blundell (public house) after we'd put six past Arsenal, why exactly was he carrying his football boots with him? *Richard Marland, Waterloo, Liverpool*
Possibly I was going away with Ireland on international duty, that would be the only time I'd do that – I didn't normally walk around pubs with my football boots. When you go away, you have to take your boots and your pads with you, so maybe that was one of those times – or at least I hope it was.

What did you say to the referee to get two yellows and hence a red card, away to Chelsea in that League Cup match? *Andy Clarke, Billericay, England*
We should have had an offside decision, but the referee never gave it and about six players prior to me had slaughtered him for being a cheat. By the time I got to him and said exactly the same, he'd just had enough of it – I think I was the final straw. I only said what everybody else had said, but that was me off. I'd scored a free-kick just before, too, and we were playing really well, but we were down to ten men and I think we ended up with a 2-2 draw.

Was he gutted when he heard there was a film called *My Left Foot* and he wasn't in it? *Colm Kavannagh, Co Wicklow, Republic of Ireland*

Yes, I was, but Daniel Day Lewis did a good job anyway.

What do you consider your most important goal for Everton? Was it the equaliser against Luton in the semi-final, or maybe the third against Rapid? *David Tickner, Bowring Park, Liverpool*

The Cup-winners' Cup goal made it 3-1 and if we hadn't have scored that we probably would have hung on to 2-1. But if I hadn't have scored at the semi final then we wouldn't have got through to Wembley so out of the two of them, I would say the semi final was definitely the most important one.

What was it about Astroturf that always seemed to cause Everton to wish they weren't there and play really badly? I appreciate that falling on it could cause very nasty and painful graze-type injuries but that was true for all teams who played on it. *David Catton, Sheffield, England*

As a footballer you need to be 100 per cent right in the head before you go on to the pitch, but I think once you knew you were playing on that awful Astroturf, it was so foreign to what football's all about – it was like playing five-a-side football in the gym. The banks of the ball were different and you could end up with bad burns if you were making sliding tackles and a lot of players did get those. The teams that had the Astroturf played and trained on them every day, whereas we just played on them twice a year when it was QPR and Oldham, so it was something you didn't look forward to as a footballer and how they were ever allowed in the first place, I'll never know.

Does he feel he gets enough credit for the number of chances he created for us in the mid-1980s? Sheeds supplied around 70 per cent of our goals... *David Chow, Manchester, England*

That's for other people to say, I'm just pleased with the contribution I made to the team. A lot of the goals were down to crosses and different parts of my game but I was just happy to involved in what was a very good Everton team.

Did Jack Charlton's 'put them under pressure' philosophy frustrate you when playing for Ireland? I felt we rarely got to see Sheeds at his best in the green shirt. *John Reynolds, Co Wicklow, Republic of Ireland*

It was different because all international teams played a set way. When Ireland burst on to the scene, we played a bit like Wimbledon but with a lot more quality and a lot better players. When we played the ball forward, we played to areas where our strikers were the first to get the ball. We certainly missed out midfield a lot and that's why Liam Brady couldn't have played in Jack Charlton's team – he's a ball player similar to myself, but whereas I played on the left side he played in the middle, so he was never going to fit into Jack's side. I was so fortunate to be part of a good Ireland team that played in Europe and got to the World Cup quarter-finals, so I can't ever knock the way we played because we were successful.

What was the feeling like to burst through the English defence in Palermo to equalise during the 1990 World Cup Finals? *Colm Kavannagh, Co Wicklow, Republic of Ireland*

From a personal point of view that's the highlight of my career. I think every player dreams of playing in the European Championships and the World Cup; it's the highest you can go. There was the big build-up with the England game. It's important when you play in the World Cup qualifying games that you don't lose the first game, so with going 1-0 down early on there was a lot of pressure on us. It wasn't the best of games, but fortunately I got the break and intercepted a pass by Steve McMahon.

Steve had come on as substitute and sometimes it takes a few minutes to get the pace of the game. He just tried to play a square ball across to Gary Stevens, but I intercepted it. He got a lot of stick at the time over that, but to be fair to him he just got caught. I hit a good shot past Peter Shilton and that got us the draw that enabled us to continue and eventually qualify for the next stages.

Playing in the World Cup is fantastic. We finished the end of the season and then went to Malta to prepare. From the word go, everyone's geared up for it and you just can't wait for the first game. It's absolutely magic.

Was his goal against England at Italia '90 his personal favourite, and if not, which goal was? *Tony Kuss, Republic of Ireland*

The penalty against Romania was good, too, that's about as good as it gets.

The penalty shoot-out against Romania in Genoa – what was his heart condition like as he stood up to take his penalty? That day still brings a tear to my eye, with all its memories. *Colm Kavannagh, Co Wicklow, Republic of Ireland*

After the game we were talking about who was going to take what and I said: "I'll take the first one and we'll get off to a good start," so I stepped up for it.

Goalkeepers have got to make a move, they've got to dive, so I just thought I'd keep it down the middle and hope he does. You have to go by your judgement more than anything, and I thought: 'I'll just hit it as hard as I can – straight down the middle'. It was a 50-50 chance, but he dived to his left so the pressure was off me personally and it got us off to a good start.

It's important that you keep a check on your emotions; David O'Leary took the fifth penalty, and I think Jack Charlton stole my lines on this one because as David was going to take his penalty and with him not being a goalscorer I said to him: "Just pick your spot and don't change your mind whatever the goalkeeper does, then hit it as hard as you can and if you do it well, you'll score." Fortunately, he kept his mind and his head. That's the secret; just never change your mind. I missed one in my career and it was when I changed my mind at the last minute.

Ask him does he remember the name of the poor Romanian who missed their vital last penalty kick, and the name of their 'keeper? *Colm Kavannagh, Co Wicklow, Republic of Ireland*

It doesn't spring to mind, nobody remembers the people who finish second, do they? I think when you miss a penalty; your body language shows that you're not confident. Remember Gareth Southgate taking his penalty against Germany? I was on holiday with my friend, Ian Snodin, and as he walked up to it I said: "He's gonna miss this." His body language said that he didn't fancy it, and it was the same with the Romanian, it was just the way he walked up, you could tell.

How did he feel after Phil Neal nobbled him in the Milk Cup Final and forced him to miss the rest of the season? *Kenny Fogarty, Amsterdam, Holland*

That probably led to the biggest disappointment of my career. I got injured a couple of weeks before I played in the FA Cup quarter-final against Notts County and I hadn't trained for a week because I'd done my ankle ligaments.

Howard wanted me to play, I wanted to play, but I couldn't twist and turn. At half-time I told Howard that all I could do was run in straight lines, so he said: "Well, just run in straight lines then." I took a free-kick and Andy Gray scored a header, which was about two inches off the floor, and we got through.

I didn't train again for about two weeks, and then it was the Milk Cup Final against Liverpool. It was my decision whether to play or not, and I knew I was only about 60 percent fit. Howard asked whether I wanted to play or not, but once you get to Wembley you just can't say no.

The ball broke on the edge of the box and Phil Neal put a tackle in on me. At the time I didn't realise what I'd done, but I'd actually ruptured my ankle ligaments. I played the first half and 20 minutes of the second when I had to come off – I couldn't move. I didn't feel much pain at first, but I woke up in the middle of the night and my ankle was on fire. I went to see the specialist the next day and he told me I'd snapped my ligaments. I had an operation and that was me out for the season and I missed the big one, the FA Cup Final.

Looking back, I made the wrong decision to play in the Milk Cup Final because I missed out on winning an FA Cup Final. I'd probably do the same again, though; because once you get there you don't want to miss it.

Could you ask Sheeds what he thought, if anything, of Tricky Trev's decision to leave when Liverpool got us banned from Europe? *Gagandeep Sethi, Minnesota, USA*

It was a lack of foresight by the club and the manager. When Colin Harvey took over, Trevor was the best right-sided player in the country, but they didn't approach him with a new contract, they thought they'd be clever and let his contract more or less run out and then go to him. Of course, it was far too late because Trevor had got fixed up somewhere else and that's why he left Everton. I think if they'd have gone to him earlier with a long-term contract and offered him the right money he'd have stayed. Everton lost a very good player needlessly.

Sheeds was still at his peak in 1987 when Howard left, and was a cultured type of player who could have fitted well into, say, Italian football. With his medal bag full and the European ban in place, was he tempted to move? *John Reynolds, Co Wicklow, Republic of Ireland*

I always wanted to go and play abroad; I just didn't get the chance. Maybe it was the way I played, I mean, I wasn't the quickest player, I lacked a yard of pace for the Italian game, which was probably the reason why I was never asked to go there. I certainly would have liked to have gone and tried my skills over there, but the opportunity just never came my way.

Does he ever wish he was born other than Irish and had had a more successful international career? *Mike Hazard, Calgary, Canada*

I would say I've been as successful as you can be, I have 47 caps and I played in the World Cup quarter-finals. When I was a young lad I had the option to play for Ireland or Wales. My dad is Irish and I was born in Wales, so I had to choose between them, and I chose Ireland. It was a difficult decision, but I felt Ireland from a football point of view was the best one. I played Under-18s, Under-21s and all the way through; it was only later on that others came in from Scotland and whatever. They chose Ireland and there was a lot of stick flying about that there were non-Irish playing for Ireland, but there was John Barnes and Tony Dorigo, they played for England, so it's what suits. I played seven or eight years before anyone else came on the scene with Jack Charlton, so it was a good choice for me. I always felt I'd made the right decision and I still feel I made the right decision.

Did he ever spit at anybody during a match? *Phil Pellow, Waterloo, Liverpool*

No, I never spat at anybody, no, no, no. That's disgusting and probably as low as you can stoop as a footballer. People punch you and kick you, and it's part of the game, but I think if somebody spits in your face then it's probably worse than being elbowed in the face.

How does it feel to have been involved with all three Merseyside teams? *David Chow, Manchester, England*

From a footballing point of view it's brilliant because with this game you usually have to move around quite a lot and apart from my 15 months up at Newcastle I've been in the same area, I had a spell at Blackpool but as you say, from a family point of view I've not had to move at all which has been very good news. I suppose it is unusual to be connected for them all, though, Red, White and Blue.

Was he sick watching Steaua Bucharest lift the European Cup via a penalty shoot-out in the season when we should have been competing for it, and does he reckon we would have won it if it weren't for the ban? *Colm Kavannagh, Co Wicklow, Republic of Ireland*

It's a hypothetical question, but I would say yes, we would have had a very good chance. At the time and over two legs they'd have had to be a bloody good side to beat us. We turned out against Bayern Munich and that should have been the Final of the Cup-winners' Cup. Rapid Vienna was a bit of an anticlimax, even though we still had to go and win the game.

We had a squad of players who would have given the best in Europe a good game. That would probably be the one regret, that the ban stopped us from competing. We'll never know, but at that time and with the team we had, we certainly would have come very close.

Which did he think was his best goal from a free-kick? *Darryl Ng, Southampton, England*

Probably that one against Liverpool. No matter which goalkeeper was in there he wouldn't have saved that, it was right in the top corner, and if there was one place on earth you wanted to do that it was at Anfield. The two free-kicks against Ipswich in the FA Cup, where I put it in one side then the other, I think would be the ones most Evertonians remember. It's difficult for me to choose between those two.

Did he get stick from any of the players for having played for the other lot? *Mike Kidd, Pietermaritzburg, South Africa*

No, when I first went from Liverpool to Everton I think the fans thought: "Well, if he's not good enough for them why should he be good enough for us?" which is fair comment. Fortunately, the first few games I did very well for Everton, and I scored in my second game against Tottenham. I think if I'd have started poorly I would have had a lot more pressure on myself, but it was all done and put to bed early on.

Have you ever scored a goal with your right foot? *Ari Sigurgeisson, Hafnarfjordur, Iceland*

I think I scored about five or six goals with my right foot throughout my career, but they were probably two-yard tap-ins. I'm so predominantly left-footed that I always tried to move on to it, but when players were closing me down I couldn't always manage it. If I had the time I would go on to my left foot, but the funny thing about it is that right-footed players don't often score with their left foot because they're so poor with it, but nobody ever seems to notice.

How did he feel when every time we got a free-kick around the box people chanted his name, and does he know that even after he left this used to happen from time to time? *Colin Berry, Wavertree, Liverpool*

Well, you earn a reputation for doing certain things and whenever I got a free-kick, they expected me to do something with it. To hear your name just fills you with confidence. I never ever took a free-kick and didn't think it was going to go in.

I remember one game when he screwed up a cross and the fans groaned. He

just stood there staring into the Gwladys Street end – what was going through his mind? *Matt Traynor, Finchley, North London*

I remember that very well, but that's football supporters. When you're doing well you're the best player in the world and everyone's patting you on the back, then when you're not doing much good, they turn. You can go from hero to villain very suddenly. That was when I was going through a bad period and I wanted to leave the club. It can affect your game when the crowd turns on you, it just depends on your strength of mind. I always knew I could do something to turn it around, I knew I could score a goal; I could score a free-kick or make a vital pass. You always had confidence in your ability and you know that no matter how bad a game you're having you're not going to hide from situations. When you've got confidence you overcome the crowd. You're not always appreciated until you're gone.

How did he get on with Colin Harvey? After he left, he went up to Newcastle United, how did he like it there? *Keith Giles, Perth, Australia*

I didn't really get on with Colin, I have to say he wasn't my type of manager. I don't think he could handle the transition from coach to manager and it was very difficult for him.

As for Newcastle, it was a great move, I only wish I'd have done it sooner. I'd have loved to play for Newcastle like I did for Everton in the prime of my career; the supporters up there were fantastic. I went there in March when Kevin Keegan had just taken over. We played Tranmere the one time and there were 7,000 locked out and that was in a relegation game. Fortunately, we stayed up in the last game of the season and the following season we won promotion, so I had some great moments and happy memories from up there. I wish I could have stayed a bit longer, but that's football.

After the passage of years, can you tell what happened in the 'bonding' meal in the Chinese in Southport, PLEASE? *David Tickner, Bowring Park, Liverpool*

No comment!

How is he and what's he doing now? *Mike Hazard, Calgary, Canada*

I'm very well indeed. I've got a great job and I enjoy it enormously. I'm assistant manager to John Aldridge at Tranmere Rovers. I came here as reserve and first team coach five seasons ago. Before that, I was at Blackburn coaching the youth team for a season. I'd like at some stage to go into management and have a go, but I'm not in a rush. I think it's best to get the experience and then, when the right opportunity comes, I'd be prepared to go on into management. If I had the right experience, the ultimate would be to go back to Everton, but there are a lot of teams in the League so I'll keep an open mind.

Kevin Sheedy, once again, thanks very much for everything.

Neville Southall

Born 16 September 1958
July 1981 to March 1998
£150,000

THE proprietor of the Llandudno hotel was an Evertonian and it was on his recommendation Howard Kendall travelled to Winsford to check out the gifted, local lad, Neville Southall. The word was that not only could he play centre-half, he was also pretty nifty between the sticks.

> **I liked what I saw, but I was at Blackburn at the time and I already had John Butcher and Jim Arnold on the books, so I couldn't make a move. Bury nipped in and signed him for about six or seven grand.**

A year later, recently installed as the manager at Everton – Howard Kendall got his man.

Uncompromising, outspoken and dedicated, Big Nev went on to make an astonishing 750 senior appearances for Everton, 93 for Wales and in 1985 was voted Player of the Year – an astonishing achievement for a goalie. In turn he gained the status of immortality.

Fellow Bluenoses take my hand and stroll down Memory Lane with the Big Man himself, Neville Southall.

How old was he before he decided that his best position was in goal? *David Chow, Manchester, England*

I think other people made that decision for me; I certainly didn't consciously make it. We played in counties at that time and the first year I was in goal and the second time around, centre-half. In actual fact, I played in goal on a Saturday and out on a Sunday until I was 21 really, right up until I joined Bury.

Could you please ask the venerable Mr Southall which goalkeepers he admired as a youth? There was certainly no shortage of excellent 'keepers playing in the First Division during the 60s and 70s. *Charlie Deeney, Ottawa, Canada*

Pat Jennings was my favourite because he never seemed to do very much, he was nice and cool and he didn't do anything he didn't have to – which is always a good sign.

During those Glory Days he worked with some class acts, but who was the best he ever played with, and why? *Gagandeep Sethi, Minnesota, USA*

It's a toss up between Trevor Steven and Kevin Ratcliffe. Kevin was the best sweeper ever and I always knew I wouldn't have to do much because he was so quick. Trevor was absolutely fantastic in every game and he never had a bad day. The lads would have loved him to have a bad game, but he just never did. I saw him at Goodison again this season and he looked exactly the same, but he seemed to have more hair.

Did he ever think he was on his way out of Everton when he was sent on-loan to Port Vale? *David Chow, Manchester, England*

Yes, and Port Vale tried to buy me but Howard wouldn't let me go. I'd have been happy to go to Port Vale at that time too because I was enjoying myself and I got my confidence back. John McGracken and John Rudge were brilliant with me and with them getting promotion, I got a medal from the supporters. That was one of the first medals I ever won when I was at Everton. We went to Vale Park and played a friendly the next year, which had been part of the loan deal, and it was great to go back. I most certainly did think I was on my way out though and when I had to go back to Everton, I had to prove myself again which is all part of growing up I suppose.

There's you, a teetotaller, and there's Howie who likes a drink… How the hell did you both coexist so successfully for so long? *Michael Kenrick, Washington, USA*

I think what people like to do in the privacy of their own home is up to them. Howard's drinking never, ever bothered me. He liked a drink – so what? Half the squad liked a drink in those days. It's taboo now, but then it was expected of footballers. I had great deal of respect for Howard and he had respect for me, that's why we were successful.

Did it really annoy him that because he was at Everton and played for Wales, he never really received the recognition as the best in the world? *Colin Berry, Wavertree, Liverpool*

I was quite happy playing where I was, I worked with some great players both at Everton and in Wales. I didn't really bother about what people had to say about me and if I'd taken all the criticism on board after my first couple of seasons at Everton, I probably would never have put on another pair of football boots again.

Ask him if he recalls a save against Southampton – 0-0 dying seconds, Le Tissier cross – header far post Nev saves and almost knocks himself out on the post – shown once on *Match of the Day* and despite being the best save ever in the history of ever – nobody ever recalls it. *Colin Berry, Wavertree, Liverpool*

I don't really remember it either. It's nice for somebody to say it was the best save ever but they're probably slightly biased in that department. I don't tend to remember most of the saves I've made, it's just the mistakes I recall with great clarity.

Which player made his hands sting the most? *Steve Kirkwood, Brentford, West London*

None of them, really. To me, there were always two types of strikers – the ones who'd come and smash you and try to blast it past you, and then there were the ones who were crafty. Rushie was crafty, Ian Wright was crafty, but there weren't many others about.

Did you ever felt like punching the stuffing out of Ian Rush after derby matches? *Neil Wolstenholme, Chelsea, South-West London*

You've got to hand it to him – he's the greatest. We've been mates for years and years since the Wales days. You've just got to give him credit, he's the best striker I ever played with or played against. All right, he scored a lot of goals against Everton, but Les Ferdinand scored a lot of goals, too. Some players score against certain clubs, and he was just one of them.

Could you ask Nev how did he feel immediately after he had handled the ball outside the box at Hillsborough in 1993 – he had been sent of at QPR only weeks earlier for a similar thing? *Osmo Tapio Räihälä, Helsinki, Finland*

The first thing that came into my head was "Oh Shit!" I didn't make a conscious decision; it was just a reflex reaction to stop the ball because that's what I did every day of my life and I trained for that reason. Colin said I should have let it in but there's no way I can stop my natural reaction.

Was the Bayern Munich at Goodison the greatest moment? *Colm Kavannagh, Co Wicklow, Republic of Ireland*

Yes, it was, it was brilliant, I've never seen the ground so packed. On the days I've come back I wished those great times back again. It's hard to be a Blue sometimes. I think after Harvey, Ball and Kendall there wasn't a team to touch them until we came along – and there hasn't been a team to touch us since. But it comes in cycles, so I'm just hoping that the next run is due very, very soon and I can be part of the crowd at matches like the Bayern Munich game.

The image of Neville, leaning against the upright at half-time against Leeds is one that sticks in the memory, what was that all about? *John Staines, Adelaide, Australia*

Lots of people thought it was because I'd put a transfer request in, but it was nothing to do with that. I'd actually done it once before against Wimbledon at Plough Lane; I'd come out early and nobody took a blind bit of notice. This time, I think we were losing 3-0 and I was absolutely shocking.

I got to the dressing-room and there was all sorts of arguments going on so I thought: "Well, I can't clear my head in here," and I just went out and sat at the posts, and to be fair I didn't think anything of it.

I still don't think it was the wrong thing to do, people just interpreted it that way. I'd do it again, even now if I thought that it would help me.

Did it get on your nerves not being able to blow the whistle on the goings-on behind the scenes at the club? It seemed like it in various interviews. *Frank Hargreaves, Anfield, Liverpool*

You should endeavour to tell the truth, but on some of those occasions, it would have done the club more harm than good.

What I would say is that I've had respect for every manager who's ever been there and all the players. There are things that I wouldn't have done, but I expect that happens at every football club in the land and I'm not the sort to tell tales. What goes on in the four walls of the dressing-room should stay there, I think.

Were you impressed when we met the morning of the game against KR in 1995? *Ari Sigurgeisson, Hafnarfjordur, Iceland*

I remember Iceland, I think we won 3-2. Matt Jackson got cramp halfway through the game, so we were lucky to get any sort of result that night.

Did he ever play better than his performance in the 1995 Cup Final when he beat Manchester United almost single-handed (literally, with one awesome moment going backwards for a lob)? *Neil Wolstenholme, Chelsea, South-West London*

Yes, I played miles better in lots of games but because of the occasion it always seems that you've played better in Cup Finals even if you only made two saves. Overall, I didn't have to do that much I probably made two or three saves and that was it. In other games I've been seriously busy from the first minute to the last and played better, but it's the timing of the game and the actual occasion itself.

If he was given the choice of all the players he played at Everton with, what is his all time best team? *Phil Williams, Chester, North Wales*

Gary Stevens, Dave Watson, Kevin Ratcliffe, John Bailey. Midfield would be Trevor, Reidy, Brace and Sheeds and up front would be Graeme Sharp and Andy Gray.

"Wales, Wales Number One!" Did it make him cringe? *Steve Kirkwood, Brentford, West London*

No, not at all, I've certainly heard worse. I'd rather be Wales' number one than Liechtenstein's number one.

How does he feel about Ryan Giggs not playing any friendlies for Wales? *Phil Pellow, Waterloo, Liverpool*

I don't blame Ryan in a way. If he's genuinely injured, I think he should stay away but there should have been a compromise early on in his career where people realised how successful Man United were going to be. How many games can you ask the lad to play in? I don't mind him not playing the friendlies if he turns up to the qualifiers, I think that's a sensible precaution really, the fitter he is, the fresher he is, the better he's going to play in the qualifiers. He knows what he's doing in the Wales team and it might sound unfair on the lad who plays instead of him but he's a world class player and you've got to make room for Ryan. If he's available, you've got to play him, it's a matter of common sense.

What is the one abiding memory you have of Everton and, in particular, Everton under the reign of the Johnson-Finch Circus? *Frank Hargreaves, Anfield, Liverpool*

I don't have any abiding memories of them. I think the club's gone nowhere and we've spent an awful lot of money. But saying that, Peter Johnson actually put his money where his mouth is when the club probably would have gone under – there's good and bad in everybody.

I would have liked to see the academy and that was my one regret. If they'd have got that off the ground, he could have left us with something worthwhile.

Why is there seemingly a scarcity of top class goalies from Britain and Ireland these days? Is it maybe a symptom of the general penchant of managers for overseas players, or has the standard in the UK and Ireland deteriorated that much? *Charlie Deeney, Ottawa, Canada*

The standard has gone down and the ones that are there are so expensive. There are much cheaper versions abroad, so most managers are going abroad to buy a goalkeeper and most of the young kids aren't getting a look in. Teams in the Premier League especially are going out and buying quality from abroad for the half the price of the British lads over here. Its showing itself in the fact that there are now only three English goalkeepers who are young, Richard Wright, Nicky Weaver and Nigel Martyn – and even he's getting on a bit now.

Did you feel like Big Bird in that yellow monstrosity at Wembley in the 1995 FA Cup Final? *Colm Kavannagh, Co Wicklow, Republic of Ireland*

I think that was my worst kit, but it's one kit I didn't have any control over, most of the others I'd had a say in. So yeah, I suppose I did, but we won, so who cares?

Why didn't he go the party after the 1995 Final, the real reason? *Pete Rowlands, Enfield, North London*

Once you've been to one party you've been to them all – they're just piss-ups really. With me not being a drinker, I had no part in that. I'd done my job and we'd won the Cup so I decided I'd go home with my wife and my daughter, which I did. We'd hired a car and I seem to remember that we watched a ridiculous cartoon on the car video all the way home.

What was it that brought on his transfer request? Was it Colin Harvey or the team he hated? *Colin Berry, Wavertree, Liverpool*

I don't hate anybody and I get on great with Colin, in fact, I think we probably get on better than a lot of people.

I just didn't rate the team and I couldn't see us going anywhere, so I thought it was round about the right time to ask for a transfer. I never had any offers to play abroad and I probably wouldn't have gone abroad unless it was Germany. I had a couple of offers from other clubs, but I think one time Howard came back and another Colin wanted too much money for me. I was quite happy, although sometimes it's easier to move on than it is to stay.

How pissed off was he when he had to purchase his tickets for the Newcastle FA Cup tie? *Lol Scragg, Arbroath, Scotland*

I thought it was an absolute disgrace. I didn't see why I should have to pay out after 18 years' service to the club. They said: "You're not playing, so you have to pay for it." Apparently, the FA in their wisdom say there are only a certain amount of comps that the club can give out at a time, or at least that's what they told me.

Do you think that the specialised football training of goalkeepers nowadays is having an adverse effect on their kicking ability? I remember the goalkeepers of a few years ago liked to play up front in testimonials and they could play football and kick the ball well. *John Walton, Dubai, United Arab Emirates*

We spend a lot of time on footwork believe it or not but it comes down to balance. If you look at footballers in general, the worse their balance is, the worse they are at kicking. All the ones with good balance like the lad over at Liverpool Sander Westerveld; he's got great balance so he's a good kicker. If you've got the right balance and the right body shape then you'll be good. These days you spend most of the time catching instead of kicking and it's a big and important part of the game now and we spend a lot of time at Huddersfield, Bradford and York, trying to make sure that their feet are right.

You've just played what is likely to be your last match ever in the Premiership for Bradford against Leeds. Were you disappointed that your last game wasn't for or against Everton? *Darryl Ng, Southampton, England*

Yes, I am it would have been nice to be against Everton at Goodison but you can't pick when somebody gets injured. Who knows if it's going to be my last game anyway – you should never say never in football but odds are it will be my last game in the Premiership. Everything comes to an end but it was really just helping somebody out and I would do it again tomorrow if I thought they needed me.

What did he make of the reaction to his appearance for Bradford City against Leeds, at the age of 41? Comments like 'Neville Scoff-all' were totally uncalled for, given he was helping out his club in an injury crisis. *Matt Traynor, Finchley, North London*

Most people think I've been in 'full time' football all this time but I haven't trained properly since I left Stoke, the season I left Everton. I've been part time everywhere and most of my time is spent in my car. I've not trained properly for two and a half years and I thought I did OK taking that into consideration. I don't think many other people have come out of retirement played a game and gone back into retirement and got so much stick. I was a bit disappointed with the press I got because I thought I did all right in the game.

What's it like having several players there older than the manager?. Do McCall, Beagrie and himself ever talk about the 'old times'? *Keith Giles, Perth, Australia*

It's nice having experience in any camp and we do talk about the 'good old days'. Peter Beagrie, if you know him, is the biggest fibber in the world, his stories get bigger and better every time you speak to him, even if you were there and know the stories, you can hardly recognise them by the time he's finished. I've known Dean for almost 20 years with being at Wales, so Bradford is a good club for me.

I'd like to know how Neville rates Paul Jewell as a manager – I admire Bradford's plucky spirit, particularly with so many ex-Evertonians in their team (well, they have a few). *Keith Giles, Perth, Australia*

Paul's going to be a good manager – its funny having a manager younger than myself, I think I'm about seven years older than him. He's doing a good job there, obviously he has limited resources and it's nice that there's two or three ex-Evertonians there that makes a good backbone for the team – there was nearly another one with Dean Saunders too.

What, in his opinion, was his best ever game? *David Chow, Manchester, England*

My best games for Wales were probably ones where we got beat 3-1 at home or 7-1 away because I had an absolutely ridiculous amount of work to do. My best game for Everton was probably one of the games we played against Coventry when we drew 0-0 it was one of the last games of the season before the Cup Final in 1995. I thought I made the best save I've ever made in that game but nobody seems to remember it so maybe that was just me being silly.

Now that he's been to other clubs who does he feel will be the next 'Neville Southall'? *Phil Williams, Chester, North Wales*

Looking round the young ones, I'm hoping Nicky Weaver might develop into a good goalkeeper, he's all right now but he's still a bit raw. I can't see many more coming through in this country in the next three or four years unless we have a big push on goalkeepers. There's a lad at York, actually, who's not bad, he's only 17.

Did he feel a bit disappointed when Mark Hughes was named the new Wales manager, and not himself? *David Chow, Manchester, England*

Only on a personal level, I was obviously disappointed that I didn't get the job but that's life. I don't make decisions, other people make them and I would like to see Mark take Wales through to the World Cup finals and everybody in Wales will benefit from that. It's what's best for the country and if people think Mark is better suited to the job then I'm not going to argue with that.

I'd like to know whether Nev thinks he will ever return to Everton in some coaching capacity. *Neil Wolstenholme, Chelsea, South-West London*

It's up to them. Howard offered me the job as goalkeeping coach, but I wasn't quite ready for that then, I still wanted to play a little bit, so I turned it down. I'd like to go back there one day as manager, not as a coach. The manager's job would suit me fine.

Does he think that because he has always been a bit outspoken and moody, chairmen would be wary of trying him as a manager? *Colin Berry, Wavertree, Liverpool*

I don't believe in lying, so if that means being outspoken, then, yes, I am. I'm just honest, I'd rather be up front with people and I don't like playing politics, I say what I mean.

I know what I want and I know how I'm going to get there. It's only a question of time before somebody gives me a chance.

What does he think about our current stoppers? No offence intended to them, but I don't think any of them is even good enough to clean Big Nev's boots... *David Chow, Manchester, England*

Well it would be handy to get somebody to clean my boots because I have to do it myself these days.

I spoke to Thomas the other day; he's a bit frustrated obviously he needs to play before Euro 2000. He's a good goalkeeper and always has been. Paul Gerrard has come on in leaps and bounds with playing regularly and I think he's showing England form at the moment. Simo's going to be good but he needs a lot of games and to get some experience behind him. It's a strange situation when you've got three goalkeepers who are good enough to play in the Premier League sadly only one can play at a time and the problem lies in keeping the other two happy.

Who had the hardest shot in the game? *Ciaran McConville, Dublin, Republic of Ireland*

I wouldn't know now but I thought Sheeds was pretty powerful when I was there. I never used to worry about the hardest shot; the harder they hit it the easier it was to deflect. It was the ones who placed it that I didn't like because it was always a lot harder to get to them, a bit more craft and less brawn.

Will you ask Big Nev why our two goalies seem stuck to their lines and won't even come for a cross within the six-yard box. Surely it must give a big confidence boost to the defence with a dominant 'keeper behind them. The only time Gerrard came off his line against Newcastle, he dithered so much he was easily lobbed. Surely Chris Woods must coach them in the lost art of coming for, and catching crosses. *David Tickner, Bowring Park, Liverpool*

It's a two-fold thing, I think they do come for what they can get and the quality into the box is a lot better now, it's improved every year. It's hard because if somebody's whacking the ball in from the sideline at 70mph, then you've only got a split second. But I thought they'd done well, when I first saw Thomas play I thought he was magnificent at coming off his line, I haven't seen an awful lot of them playing recently but I can't see that he would have changed that much.

Does he think the media have gone to far in their coverage of players now? On the one hand they criticise the wages players get, but are only to happy to carry lifestyle articles on the Beckhams this and the Beckhams that. *Matt Traynor, Finchley, North London*

I think they have gone too far but I think a lot of player's court it and use it to their advantage too. At times and they have gone a little bit far in digging the rubbish up because they've got so many sports channels now and they've got to fill them somehow. A lot of it is complete and utter nonsense but at the same time, its not all one way. The players are as bad as the press at times.

With the number of specialist coaches working with'keepers these days, I would expect that the standard of goalkeeping in the Premiership would go up, but my feeling is the opposite – certainly since Nev left EFC, there has been no one near to his standard at the Club, and looking at the British 'keepers around, there are very few you would say are top class. Does he agree? What's the answer? *Phil Pellow, Waterloo, Liverpool*

I'm hoping some club is actually going to take on ten young goalkeepers and make a separate academy – that's the way to go. Spending time just coaching the goalkeepers day in and day out.

I don't think they get stretched physically or mentally now; they just do their little bit because in general, the kids now have a worse work ethic than ever before. It's the age of computers and it's all far too easy for them to get a lot of money too quickly. We need to bring back the pride in what we're doing and that goes for outfield players too. But I think if you could get an academy going where you've got ten goalkeepers and if two of them come through, you can sell the rest and you've made your money back for the academy.

Has he ever scored a goal against the opposition while in goal? *Ciaran McConville, Dublin, Republic of Ireland*

Only if you count a 'Four Members' penalty where I beat Bob Boulder from the spot, but we still went out because John Ebbrell missed his, but then again he shouldn't have taken it because he was only about bloody 15 at the time. I hit the post once when I played for Bury – it bounced over Jerry Peyton, who came on later to Everton, then it hit the post and went wide.

Does he get a bit cheesed off about young kids on £7,000 a week treating the game like a part-time hobby, instead of knuckling down and working at it? How can managers and coaches get these kids to sort their attitude? *Phil Pellow, Waterloo, Liverpool*

I think with the scarcity of good players, clubs just pay what they have to for them. A lot of the kids are on real good money and it's all too soon. You can't blame the kids, but they don't really understand what money is and they don't have money values.

When I started playing there was at least three other goalkeepers who were desperate for my place, now it doesn't matter because on £8,000 a week or even £50,000 a week – you can't hurt them, the only way you can hurt them is by playing the 'A' team. If Brian Clough was starting out now – he wouldn't have got a job.

Are his relationships more stable since he shaved his muzzie off? *Les Anderson, Keighley, England*

I haven't shaved my muzzie off.

Would he like to enter the annual Evertonia Gnome-Throwing Competition? *Simon Burke, Toxteth, Liverpool*

Yeah, I will, but only if the gnome can be Tony Cottee.

Is he thinking of going for the full UEFA badge? *Phil Pellow, Waterloo, Liverpool*

I'm going to try and do the A, B and C in the summer. It looks as if you're going to have a full badge to be a manager in the future, so I'll need them. I know more than schoolteachers and I'm a bit disappointed that a lot of schoolteachers are running football because they've never played and they don't know the ins and outs of it.

Who is the current best overall last-line-of-defence? *Charlie Deeney, Ottawa, Canada*

It's hard to say but I would say Nigel Martyn on his current form. The lad from Coventry, Hedmann and Paul Gerrard – the way they're performing now, they're all better than David Seaman.

I read somewhere once that the big feller always wore boots two sizes too small; his explanation was that it stopped the air getting in so he could kick better. *John Quinn, Tewkesbury, England*

That's not true but I did wear two different types of boots. If it was decent and firm, I wore thicker leather but if it was really muddy then I wore a cheap pair of plastic boots if I could get them, although Mitre didn't like me wearing them and actually stopped making them eventually. The plastic boots made it easy because they were a lot lighter and they didn't get me bogged down in the mud.

The same article mentioned that after away international matches he used to tour the poorer suburbs and give his kit away. *John Quinn, Tewkesbury, England*

That's not true either; I'm going to end up looking like David Pleat at this rate – being kind to the poor. I've given a lot of my kit away but last time I gave my

Alan Ball: "You play for your country and you're immensely proud, and 1966 was a fantastic time for England, but winning the championship with Everton and the Liverpool derby games...they were absolutely fantastic days and it's difficult to describe what it meant for me."

Paul Bracewell: "I knew Howard from my days at Stoke and I took him on his word that I was joining a good side. I met up with him again, just before the FA Cup Final, we agreed everything verbally and I signed a blank contract."

Martin Dobson: "I came from Burnley, a small-town team, which was very friendly and a family club. Everton is a big-city club with 40,000-odd people watching every week, and I must admit that I found it tough at the start."

Everton at the beginning of 1978-79. Back row (left to right): Wright, Lyons, Smallman, Ross, Jones, Latchford. Middle: Steve Burtenshaw (coach), Pejic, Telfer, Higgins, Wood, Lawson, Kenyon, Pearson, Jim McGregor (physiotherapist). Front: McKenzie, Darracott, Thomas, Gordon Lee (manager), Dobson, Nulty, King.

Andy Gray and Graeme Sharp celebrate Gray's controversial goal in the 1984 FA Cup Final. Says Andy: "I didn't touch the goalkeeper, and I defy anyone to look at the video of the match and say where they saw any contact… I just got lucky and I stuck my head in there."

Adrian Heath signs for Howard Kendall in January 1982. Says Adrian: "I wasn't surprised, because Howard played with me at Stoke. He told me if he got a big job he would come and get me. I didn't know where that would be, but when he went to Everton I kept my fingers crossed…"

Howard Kendall: "When they knocked on the door of my house, my father immediately asked: 'Is it Liverpool?' They told him it was across the park."

Brian Labone: "Harry Catterick is supposed to have called me the 'Last of the Corinthians' but to me he used to say: 'Brian look on the bright side, if you'd have been a racehorse, they would have shot you!'"

Everton's 1966 FA Cup winning team. Back row (left to right): Harris, Labone, West, Gabriel, Wright, Tommy Eggleston (trainer). Front: Scott, Trebilcock, Young, Harry Catterick (manager), Harvey, Temple, Wilson.

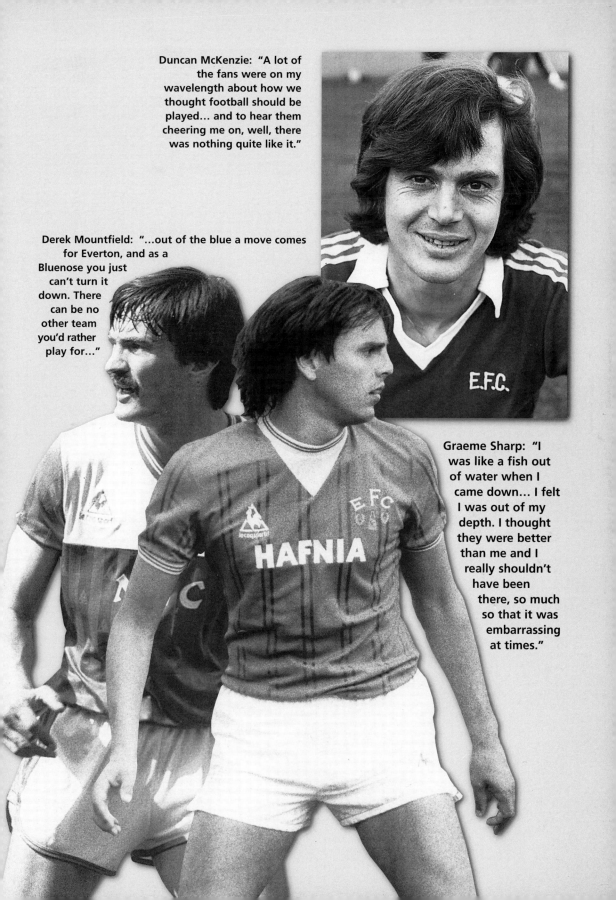

Duncan McKenzie: "A lot of the fans were on my wavelength about how we thought football should be played... and to hear them cheering me on, well, there was nothing quite like it."

Derek Mountfield: "...out of the blue a move comes for Everton, and as a Bluenose you just can't turn it down. There can be no other team you'd rather play for..."

Graeme Sharp: "I was like a fish out of water when I came down... I felt I was out of my depth. I thought they were better than me and I really shouldn't have been there, so much so that it was embarrassing at times."

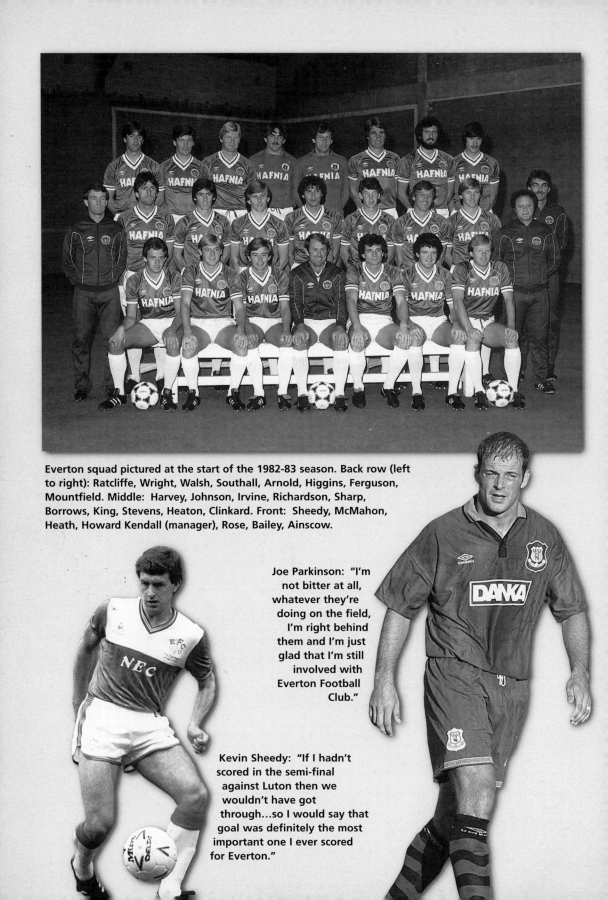

Everton squad pictured at the start of the 1982-83 season. Back row (left to right): Ratcliffe, Wright, Walsh, Southall, Arnold, Higgins, Ferguson, Mountfield. Middle: Harvey, Johnson, Irvine, Richardson, Sharp, Borrows, King, Stevens, Heaton, Clinkard. Front: Sheedy, McMahon, Heath, Howard Kendall (manager), Rose, Bailey, Ainscow.

Joe Parkinson: "I'm not bitter at all, whatever they're doing on the field, I'm right behind them and I'm just glad that I'm still involved with Everton Football Club."

Kevin Sheedy: "If I hadn't scored in the semi-final against Luton then we wouldn't have got through...so I would say that goal was definitely the most important one I ever scored for Everton."

Neville Southall receives the 1985 Footballer of the Year Award from Howard Kendall. Says Neville: "If I'd taken all the criticism on board after my first couple of seasons at Everton, I probably would never have put on another pair of football boots."

Alex Young: "When I came to Everton I'd obviously heard about Dixie Dean and the other great stars who'd worn the number-nine shirt, but the enormity only hits you when you've been there for a while."

Gary Stevens: "Goals were always an extra part of my game...with the quality and type of football Everton played, I was often in a position where I could have a pop, and fortunately I was lucky enough to score a few."

Umbro kit away was when we used to train at a prison in Usk so I dropped it off at there last time. When you're Welsh, the only thing you ever get is the kit.

It also said that when he played home internationals he used to take his own sandwiches into the hotels and changing rooms. *John Quinn, Tewkesbury, England*

I never took sandwiches to any game. I don't know who's being writing this but that's just rubbish. It must be Billy Liar on the phone. It's not Beagrie is it?

Will he be the new manager when Walt goes off to manage Scotland? *San Presland, New Brighton, Merseyside*

I would love to be manager at Everton. I'm hoping Craig Brown will still be in a job, and to be fair, I'd like to leave Walter where he is. Walter's done a remarkable job at Everton, he's had a limited budget and he wasn't obviously fully aware of the situation behind the scenes when he took over. He's a good manager and I feel that things have taken a turn for the better at Everton now.

Every day when he wakes up does he thank the Lord he's Welsh? *Jason Palmer, Merthyr Tydfil, Wales*

I just thank God I'm still alive, especially considering the amount of miles I drive and the state the roads are in. But I do like being Welsh.

I would thank him for being such a great servant of the club, for sticking with Everton when I am sure he could have gone anywhere else in the world for much more money and for the great memories he has left us with of a truly outstanding 'keeper. *Mike Coville, New York, USA*

Wherever you go in the world, there's always an Evertonian who comes over to say hello. It amazes me, especially considering that the time in-between the success has been really bad, they're a bunch of magic people. I often wondered what the hell they were doing there, like when we were playing the Super Cup at Spurs in the snow – and there were our fans. I thought: 'What are these people doing? We've got to be here, but they've got a choice.' They're remarkable people, really, and I can't think of any fans who come anywhere near them.

If you could do it all again what would you change? *John Walton, Dubai, United Arab Emirates*

There's no point in looking back – you've got to look for tomorrow. I had a really good career at Everton, I fought off a lot of competition and stayed Number 1 for a long time and I'm proud of that fact.

If I had my time over again, I'd do it all the same but just a little bit more – that's all.

Big Nev, thanks very much for your time.

Gary Stevens

Born 27 March 1963
March 1981 to July 1988
Apprentice

IMAGINE a defender with skill, courage, pace and phenomenal stamina. That would be Gary Stevens. Unruffled and elegant, the natural athlete ghosted over the park, as cool as you damn well like.

The young and dashing apprentice from Barrow began his football career on the left wing, but in a manoeuvre cleverly choreographed by Colin Harvey he eventually found his niche both on Goodison Park and in the nation's hearts at right back. He was capped 46 times.

Fellow Bluenoses, allow me to introduce you to the man described by Howard Kendall as one of the best trainers and finest athletes he's ever worked with, and who sported the number 2 shirt with such aplomb, Gary Stevens.

Which was the sweetest goal he scored for Everton? And let me help in counting, there were 12 of them. *Osmo Tapio Räihälä, Helsinki, Finland*

I remember one in particular against Arsenal. I don't even know why I shot from where I did – it actually gets farther back each time I tell this story, but I'll be honest this time – It was about 35 yards. A half-volley which hit the bar and then Pat Jennings on the back of the head and went in. That was quite early on in my career and I hadn't realised I could even kick the ball that far.

What does he think was the weakest part of his game? *Clive Blackmore, Washington DC, USA*

Probably my technical ability. They always used to say I was a tremendous athlete, which I took on board, and I tried to work harder on the technical side of it, my touch and my control, but I knew I had my limitations there.

The first time I saw Gary he was playing left wing for the youth team and had a stinker. I never thought I was watching the future England right back. What happened? *San Presland, New Brighton, Merseyside*

I seemed to get further and further back, from left wing to right midfield and right back, and I didn't know where it was going to stop because I never really fancied myself in goal. It was all down to Colin Harvey, it's something I can always pat him on the back for and I can never thank him enough.

I once shook hands with Trevor Steven after the 1985 Final outside the main doors at Wembley and then with Gary Stevens as he came out immediately after him.

I was very disturbed by Tricky's handshake – very limp, wet, and fishy. Gary's was nice and firm and very manly, in keeping with his Adonis athleticism. Did Gary ever have any serious doubts about Tricky and did this affect their friend-ship? *Mike Royden, South Wirral, England*

Trevor must have been feeling weak after a hard game. I have to say I've never had any problems with Trevor's grip.

Where does his coolness come from? In the 1980s he always seemed so relaxed that the harder they came at his feet the broader he seemed to smile. *Osmo Tapio Räihälä, Helsinki, Finland*

I don't know about that. I think it's the old swan adage – he looks very cool, calm and collected on the surface but under the water his legs are going 15 to the dozen. I was a bit like that, but it relieves a lot of the pressure when you've got quality players around you who can give you the time and you have respect and confidence in their ability. You know they can mop up any of your mistakes, and that really helps.

What was it like playing behind Tricky Trevor and how was it with Nev seeing as he never (or hardly ever) socialised with his team-mates? *Joe Hannah, Sydney, Australia*

Well, I don't know about not socialising. Neville reserved his off-the-field persona for the players and people who know him. I think he seemed rather aloof as far as the press went because he was a little bit shy when the micro-phones came out. He's a very funny chap and he did mix. As for Trevor, it was a pleasure to play behind all of our midfield and our front two. Trevor worked very hard in front of me so I was never afraid to go beyond him, and I knew he would always be there. He felt the same and trusted me, too. The whole team was like that, though, to be honest. That was why we were so successful.

Does he still collect stamps? *Osmo Tapio Räihälä, Helsinki, Finland*

Yes and no. I've still got them, but I've also got a two-and-a-half-year old daughter, so they don't see the light of day too often.

Was he as amazed as the rest of us when he scored that long-distance goal against Liverpool? *John Staines, Adelaide, Australia*

The one in the bottom corner, the left peg deflection? I wasn't amazed, I was a one-a-season type of bloke, so I was about due one. But it's always nice to score at Anfield and even nicer to score the winner against the old enemy.

Did he fall out with Colin Harvey? And what was it over? *Ciaran McConville, Dublin, Republic of Ireland*

We had words just before I left and it was over something typically football-orientated. I won't go too much into it, but the only thing I will say is that of everybody in football, Colin is the person I respect most. I was very disappointed at the time, but we've made up and shaken hands since. I'm particularly glad we sorted it out because if it wasn't for him I wouldn't have had the career that I did. Of everybody I've met in football, he's the chap I look up to and respect the most.

Can you think of any Everton full-back in the last 30 years who is worth cleaning your boots? *Marko Poutiainen, Oulu, Finland*

John Bailey and Pat Van den Hauwe were very good friends of mine and both quality left-backs. Brian Borrows, too, he's still playing and he's a fantastic guy. It was down to him or me, really, and it may have even been a toss of a coin that decided which one stayed and who left. I've got a tremendous respect for all of those players.

I wonder if anybody can tell me where Pat Van den Hauwe is now. I roomed with him for a long time and really liked him. His public image was a façade and totally different to how he really was.

Being a full-back, what was it like to score? Did you go mental, celebrating? And did you always have a £10 on yourself for first goal just in case? *Ste Daley, Speke, Liverpool*

I would never have a bet on myself. Sixty games a year and I was bound to score in one of them, so I'd have been wasting an awful lot of money. At a certain point, I didn't know how to celebrate. I saw a lot of goals scored in front of me – I managed to score a couple of nice ones, but I was a fish out of water in the celebration stakes.

Goals were always an extra part of my game. My job was to defend, but with the quality and type of football we played, I was often in a position where I could have a pop, and fortunately I was lucky enough to score a few.

You are my all-time favourite Everton player. How do you rate your partnership on the right with Trevor Steven? You two did it for Everton and England, and later at Rangers. Did playing together make it easier for the two of you? *Yusuf Kay, Singapore*

We were very close friends, and we still are and that always helps. I've got a tremendous respect for him, both football-wise and as a man, he's probably one of the nicest people you would ever meet. He was also one of the most technically gifted players around, a hard worker, and he helped me out enormously.

Was Psycho really? *Clive Blackmore, Washington DC, USA*

He had a way of looking at people that frightened them, but I shared rooms with him for a considerable number of years and he was a pussycat.

Which second-string player in the 1980s Everton did he think would become a big name, yet didn't? *Osmo Tapio Räihälä, Helsinki, Finland*

I don't know if you remember him, but there was a lad called Robbie Wakenshaw who came on and scored against Man United. I thought he had a lot of talent. Unfortunately, with the likes of Sharpie and Inchy and Andy Gray up front at that time he never got a look in. I don't even know where he went or what happened to him.

Can you ask Gary Stevens how he rates the right backs currently plying their trade in the English League, and especially Gary Neville (whom I think is over-rated). *Mike Kidd, Pietermaritzburg, South Africa.*

Have we got to talk about Man United now? The quality of the Premiership has probably peaked. I'm sure Everton would be competing with the likes of Man United, but the influx of foreigners brings its problems. There are some quality players knocking around. As for Gary Neville, he does a great job for Man United and I can't knock him. He's playing at the biggest club in England at the moment so he must be all right.

I saw him play as centre-back at Ipswich, when we were shorn of cover, and he didn't look comfortable at all. He's a tall guy, hadn't he played at centre-back before in his career? *Steve Kirkwood, Brentford, West London*

I filled in quite a few times, actually. In fact, at the end of my career at Tranmere I enjoyed playing as a three there. It's quite difficult when you're just thrown in as a full-back, you're used to seeing a certain picture in front of you, and as a centre-half it's slightly different. You're also up against some big marauding centre-forwards who like to give you a few bruises, rather than the small wingers, but once you adapt it's an enjoyable position to play.

Does he think Gary Lineker still remembers he once played for us? *Osmo Tapio Räihälä, Helsinki, Finland*

I'm sure he does remember the five minutes he was there. It was obviously sandwiched between two League Championships, but we got him a good move and earned him a few bob, didn't we? He must remember us.

Actually, Gary, Trevor and I used to mix a lot. We used to watch and play a lot of snooker, then he disappeared off to Barcelona and that was it, I don't think they play much snooker in Barcelona.

Ask him to give me one, just one, good reason why I shouldn't shoot him dead on sight for committing THAT back pass error. *Billy Williams, Cologne, Germany*

I'd better think about that. I'm a nice guy and I've got three kids...?

In the Luton semi-final Gary made what must be the best, most crucial ever block-tackle on Ricky Hill, right in front of the goal. He just seemed to come from nowhere. Now I believe a man can fly. Was he really Superman in disguise? *San Presland, New Brighton, Merseyside*

You'd be better asking my wife that question!

Last-ditch tackles are all part of the job but I remember that incident quite clearly because it kept us in the game. There was another incident in that game where I allowed Kevin Sheedy to take a free-kick, and he pulled things out the fire for us.

How does he rate the recent right backs at Everton, especially Earl Barrett and Matt Jackson? *Osmo Tapio Räihälä, Helsinki, Finland*

It's difficult for me to say, really, because when I moved up to Scotland I missed an awful lot of week in, week out football.

I do believe Earl Barrett got a lot of stick, but people who I've spoken to thought quite highly of him. It's a difficult position to play these days; you're almost playing as a wingback. I think the job description has totally changed since my time.

He scored the winner at Anfield late on in the Littlewoods Cup. Was this his most satisfying goal? *Steve Kirkwood, Brentford, West London*

Howard Kendall's idea was to try and copy what Liverpool were doing in his training sessions and off the park, and it worked. Eventually, we usurped them and it was particularly nice to score there. Many a time, we were on the receiving end of a drubbing at Anfield, so to go there and win was special, but to go there and score was fantastic, I'll never forget it.

A part of you is portrayed on an Argentinian stamp? Do you have any idea what the stamp is about? *Marko Poutiainen, Oulu, Finland*

That's very intriguing, but I had no idea.

Oh, I bet you it's the 'Hand of God' incident, and I'll be in the background as I always am. I was perhaps the closest player to him, other than Peter Shilton, and I was the only one on the pitch who didn't see the handball, other than the referee of course. If you watch the video again, apart from seeing me forlornly looking on, you can see it takes me about 30 seconds to realise that everybody else is slapping their hands, I thought: "What the hell is everybody on about?" So I just joined in.

It's bound to be something like that, me chasing back or putting my head in my hands saying: "Oh, no, not another one."

How did it feel scoring the winner at Anfield, particularly as we'd missed so many easier chances? Did he give the front lads a bit of stick? *San Presland, New Brighton, Merseyside*

Yes, I showed then how to do it. I'm trying to remember who's backside I had a bit of help from – it's a fair chance it was Jan Molby's, wasn't it? They missed a few chances, but when push came to shove, you could always rely on Derek Mountfield or myself to score.

Was he surprised that he wound up playing for Tranmere? Did he join them mainly as a chance to get back closer to Everton and to all of us for

whom that 80s side are gods? *Neil Wolstenholme, Chelsea, South-West London*

It's always nice to come back to Merseyside, that's definite. My wife and most of her family are from here, and it was like a homecoming, really, for me. I've settled down now, and I don't think I'll be moving too far away from Merseyside for the rest of my life.

What was the lowest point of his career? *Colin Berry, Wavertree, Liverpool*

Probably the Cup Final against Liverpool. We came back and there was a joint tour of the city, and I think I spent most of it downstairs on the bus. Even though we'd been beaten the lads soaked up the atmosphere, but I spent most of the journey downstairs looking at my feet.

'Three Gary Stevens…', there's only three…' I think there were three high-profile Gary Stevens' playing at the same time. Did he encounter any misunderstandings because of this? *San Presland, New Brighton, Merseyside*

The one thing that stands out in my memory was one of the games in Mexico in 1986 against Paraguay. Gary Stevens of Spurs came on as sub and I think he came on to the right side of midfield. Trevor was outside of him and I was behind Trevor, so the commentator had a few problems – Stevens to Steven to Stevens, but I think that was the only time we were confused.

Is it true that his record long jump is well over seven metres? Did he ever think seriously of going into athletics instead of football? *Osmo Tapio Räihälä, Helsinki, Finland*

Wow! Somebody knows me well! That was a long time ago, Barrow Grammar School. I think I still hold the record.

No, I didn't consider athletics. As soon as I left school I went to be with Everton and I didn't look back. I suppose if it hadn't worked out there, maybe I would have looked to something else, but it was never a serious consideration.

Is a he still best mates with Trevor Steven? *Martin Smith, New Jersey, USA*

I am, actually. I tried to get hold of him this morning to sort out an Everton dinner later this week. I'm hoping he'll come down and we can wreak havoc in Liverpool again.

Had he anything to do with Trevor Steven joining Rangers? *Ciaran McConville, Dublin, Republic of Ireland*

No, definitely not. I wasn't there at the beginning of his decision to leave, but when Trevor phoned me and asked about Rangers, I told him it was a fantastic club. I'm not sure whether that counts as attracting him away from Everton, or not. I don't think so; I was just being honest with him. At the time, Trevor had decided to go and he was talking about Man United and all sorts of other clubs, so Rangers doesn't seem such a bad alternative when you look at it like that.

What on earth was Colin Harvey thinking when he sold you at the height of your career? *Marko Poutiainen, Oulu, Finland*

I wasn't playing particularly well at the time and I needed a change. I sometimes think I should have played through it, but you make these decisions and have to live with them. I've been fairly loyal in my career, I've only played for three teams, you see some who've played for 13 or even 23 sides. There's no doubt that I enjoyed myself at Everton, but I moved on. I'm back on Merseyside now and have enjoyed my career thoroughly.

Ask him if his computer is working okay these days. *Les Anderson, Keighley, England*

Who asked that? Oh, I'm scared now; remember what happened to Gary Glitter!

Would he (and Trevor) have stayed had it not been for the Euro ban? *Matt Traynor, Finchley, North London*

That's a difficult question, really. It certainly would have kept an interest there. We all thought we had a chance of doing well in Europe. It's got to be the pinnacle of any club footballer's dreams, so when we didn't get a chance to play it was obviously very disappointing. Whether it affected who stayed and who left, I don't know, I'm afraid I can't answer that one.

Did you think when you left for Rangers that the Everton team would never ever again reach the heights it had done in the mid-80s? *Darryl Ng, Southampton, England*

That wasn't part of it. I expected Everton to carry on where they left off, to thrive on their success. Success usually breeds success. They got through to a few FA Cup Finals, but the success they had in the mid-80s has never been topped.

I think Walter is looking to improve that record, and as an old Everton player and a guy that looks at the results week in and week out, I hope that they can.

What does he think of Walter Smith? *Martin Smith, New Jersey, USA*

I really enjoyed working under Walter. He knows a tremendous amount about football.

When he first came to Everton, I was asked this same question many times. I said then, and I still think now, that he will continue to do well. Even with the hiccup of them selling Duncan Ferguson behind his back, he's managed to keep his chin up and speak very well of the players. He handles the press very professionally and I think he is, and will continue to be, a great manager.

Did he feel that the success in Glasgow was tempered by the lack of competitiveness of the Scottish Premier League? *Matt Traynor, Finchley, North London*

Yes, certainly, there's no doubt about that. It is difficult to continue to moderate yourself when the fans are expecting a 5-0 or 6-0 win every week and it's a Cup Final for every side that you play against. It's also difficult because the other clubs raise their game, but the opposition is weaker.

There are only two or three sides that could ever compete with Rangers: obviously, Celtic and maybe one other. Each season seemed to throw up a slightly stronger Aberdeen or Dundee United, whereas down in England you were looking at the first 15 teams in the Premier League, or the First Division as it was then, being very strong and competitive.

What's he up to these days? Seeing Reidy, Rats, Sheeds, Inchy *et al* doing well on the manager/assistant manager fronts, does he think that he could do that? *Julian Jackson, Singapore*

I'm at Bolton Wanderers Academy looking after the young lads, which is a tremendous experience for me. I'm also a mature student at Salford University doing a degree in physiotherapy. I've done several courses in sports injury management, but I need these letters after my name so that I can work in the highest echelons of football from a physiotherapy point of view.

Would you ask Gary why there (almost) never seemed to be the sort of rifts between the players and the clubs over various things in his prime time at Everton as there are now? *Osmo Tapio Räihälä, Helsinki, Finland*

Money breeds a bit of contempt and nowadays it's difficult for managers to force any player to do anything with the amount of money they're on.

In the olden days – *Bloody hell – the olden days!* – we were happy to play, and if you were told you weren't playing, you just knuckled down and made sure you were on the team sheet the next week. You wanted to get on with it, but now it seems the attitude has changed slightly and I think money has a lot of answering to do, the amount of money they earn now is vulgar in some respects.

I'm sure there were rifts in certain places, but part of Everton's success was that we gelled so well and worked for each other. If that's not the secret of a good side it's certainly an aspect of what all good sides need.

Did he ever dream of returning to Everton in the 90s, or was he happy enough to win the League in Scotland and get beaten in Europe? *Osmo Tapio Räihälä, Helsinki, Finland*

It's a difficult one. Of course, I would have liked to play in the Premiership but it didn't work out that way. I got a couple of bad injuries and but for those, I would have been looking towards the end of my Rangers career to move back down here.

I did come back and went to Tranmere, but I think there were question marks around my fitness at the time. Looking back, there was a period of two years where I had several injuries, really. I managed to save them all up. I didn't get too many, but they all seemed to come at once, but I'd have loved to return because I loved playing in blue.

He once said it's a pity he was born in 1963 and not in 1973 as the wages are so much better nowadays than in the 1980s. Surely he's not saying he's not got

the dosh – Rangers must have paid him relatively well? *Osmo Tapio Räihälä, Helsinki, Finland*

No, I'm saying that I didn't have the luxury of thinking: "What sort of car will I buy this week," which is probably the only worry these boys have got nowadays although I'm sure that people playing ten years before me would say exactly the same.

I had a tremendous career and earned a good wage and a few bonuses, but I think when you look at some of the players and they're on ten times the money you were on, you can't help thinking 'if only' from time to time, but there you go.

Did you enjoy yourself more with Rangers than with Everton? Bearing in mind that our bad spell didn't start till quite some time after you had left. *Darryl Ng, Southampton, England*

I probably did, but I put it down to the fact that I was a more confident person. I was older and more settled. I remembered things a little bit more clearly when I was at Rangers, so from that point of view I did, but the days and nights that I remember more were at Everton.

Who would he go out for a drink (or whatever) with from the Everton stars of the 1980s? *Osmo Tapio Räihälä, Helsinki, Finland*

I'd go out with most of them except Reidy, because he drinks too much. Then there's Trevor's limp handshake, and now as we've spoken about it I might give him a miss too.

I enjoy going out with Trev, he's a bit of a smoothie and you can tell him that if you speak to him. Paul Bracewell, Peter Reid, Inchy, Sharpie, we all got on well. In fact, I'd give anything to go for a drink with them all, right now.

Gary Stevens, it was delightful to speak with you, all the very best for your exams and your future.

Alex Young

Born 3 February 1937
November 1960 to August 1968
£42,000

Talk to anybody 'of a certain age' and their eyes will mist over as they recount how he enchanted them. They'll tell you he was cut from a different cloth than your run-of-the-mill centre-forward, right down to his beguiling smile, halo of flaxen curls, and slight frame. And how they would roar as they witnessed him outwitting the toughest of the lot with his cunning and sublime skills. They'll remind you that he was our Golden Vision.

Injured a couple of days earlier playing for the British Army up in Aberdeen, Alex Young hobbled into Bellefield in November 1960 with torn ligaments and wearing a back splint – his price tag read £42,000, the record fee for a Scottish player. It was three months before he pulled on the sacred number-nine shirt. But those same people will sigh, and tell you it was worth the wait, and that they were the lucky ones.

Fellow Bluenoses, I swell with pride as I bring you the most dignified, unassuming and gracious man of all, Alex Young

When he started playing, did he find that he had the 'touch' or did it come through a lot of training? *David Tickner, Bowring Park, Liverpool*
I was about seven when I became really interested in football, and after a short time after I found I could control the ball quite easily.

I was born in a place called Loanhead, and there weren't a lot of cars around then. We only had a tennis ball, but I would go off with two or three other boys and try and score goals through the gates of people's houses. If I did practice it wasn't deliberate, I just used to play with a ball all the time and it seemed to come quite naturally to me. It was only when I got older that I used to try and copy special players.

Who were his greatest influences? *Phil Pellow, Waterloo, Liverpool*
When I was a young lad in Scotland you didn't get many games on telly, but now and again we saw guys like Stan Matthews playing. Tom Finney was a tremendous influence on me, he could play on the left wing, the right wing and through the middle, he was a fabulous footballer. I played with Dave Mackay at

Hearts before he was transferred to Tottenham, and to play on the same side as him was something special.

Surely he was aware of the Everton tradition of centre-forwards in the mould of Dixie Dean, Tommy Lawton and Dave Hickson, so what on earth was a namby-pamby big girl's blouse like him doing in an Everton number-nine shirt, for God's sake? *Billy Williams, Cologne, Germany*

When I came to Everton I'd obviously heard about Dixie Dean and the other great stars who'd worn the number-nine shirt, but the enormity only hits you when you've been there for a while.

I wouldn't say I was a big girl's blouse. I had to struggle all the way through when I was a kid. I was from a working-class area and I had to look after myself, and maybe I wasn't as big as Dixie or Tommy Lawton or Dave Hickson, but I had to battle just the same.

What was Catterick like to play for, as his public persona never suggested he would naturally embrace flair yet his teams were packed with it? *Neil Wolstenholme, Chelsea, South-West London*

What was he like to play for? Hellish. Before Harry Catterick even arrived at Everton the top sports writer for the *Liverpool Echo* at that time, Leslie Edwards, warned me to beware. He said Harry Catterick was after my blood because he didn't like the way that I played, and that was before I'd ever met the man.

It never changed all the time I was there. It was a constant battle all the time I played for him. He couldn't encourage me to play because if he said anything I didn't believe him. He had some good sides, but I don't think he liked to go a great deal for flair players. I think he preferred other types.

Alex was never the most powerfully built man and was not very tall. He was, however, terrific in the air with the ability to hang. Was this an instinctive attribute or was it hours of practice and training? *Pete Rowlands, Enfield, North London*

It wasn't practice and training, it was something that I had even as a kid. I was about 13 when I started to realise that I could jump high and I could hang a bit. I would always take one or two steps before I jumped and tried to give myself a couple of yards when I knew the ball was coming into a certain area.

Ask him if he remembers signing a brilliant painting of a donkey with a number seven-shirt on, the most treasured possession of a young (and now old) Everton fan. *Paul Tollet, Oxford, England*

I can't remember it but I would have been delighted to sign a picture of a donkey. Who was the donkey meant to be – the number-seven? Hopefully, that was our lucky mascot and not a player.

And what did he weigh? 10st 10lbs wet through, yet he competed against (and destroyed) some relatively massive centre-halves. He drove Harry Catterick mad

because he could play a complete game and never get his shorts dirty. He never lost his balance and went to ground – the big guys just couldn't get near enough to tackle him. His only weakness was those blistered feet – do they still trouble him? *David Catton, Sheffield, England*

Not as much now, because I'm not running up and down a football pitch all day, but even before I came to Everton I used to be bothered with blistered feet, it was the bane of my life.

I performed well when there was a little bit of give in the pitch and I could get the studs into the ground, but when I was on top of the pitch, even before half-time my feet were raw with red blood blisters.

Before games, I used to turn up about an hour ahead of the rest of the team and get my feet bandaged up like a mummy. Then I had to pull my boots on and inside my stockings was a half-inch of foam rubber, taped on with 2" tape to try and take the soreness out of my feet.

If I'm going to make excuses, lots of times I drifted out of games because I was absolutely shattered with blistered feet.

Was Roy Vernon the greatest ever penalty-taker? Did they just naturally gel together as a partnership, or was there a lot of work on the training ground to develop that understanding? *Phil Pellow, Waterloo, Liverpool*

Roy Vernon was the best penalty-taker I've ever seen and even to see him practising was brilliant. After training he would take about ten against Gordon West or any goalie that wanted to go in. He always scored ten out of ten, and in all the time that he played at Everton I can't remember him missing one penalty.

The partnership just happened. He was a brilliant runner off the ball and fantastically fast, which suited me down to the ground. He couldn't head the ball, or anything, and he couldn't even kick the ball with his left foot, which was amazing, really. Roy played number-ten, he was all right-footed, but a fantastic footballer and when he played in the middle of the park he'd make surging runs right through the middle.

He used to say to me it takes two to make a pass, not just the guy who passes it but the guy who picks it up and runs with it, and Roy was fantastic at that. There was nothing, really, that we worked on, it was just a natural thing that sometimes happens between certain players. Roy and I just clicked.

When you signed for Everton I lived in London and the London press were regularly touting you as 'London's next soccer import', with Spurs the glamour team being most frequently mentioned. Was there any serious likelihood of your signing for Spurs? *Dave Morris, Glasgow, Scotland*

I think that's the connection with Dave Mackay. I remember once or twice I innocently went down to Tottenham to see Davey because I was doing National Service in London, but there was never any talk from managers, and I certainly didn't realise that the press was writing about it.

Evertonians worship him, but why do other football fans look blank when we

mention his name? Why didn't he win more Scottish caps? Why wasn't his genius universally recognised? *John Reynolds, Co Wicklow, Republic of Ireland*

I think it's because lots of times I didn't play as well as I should have. I should have been better, like a lad with his school report card; I did all right but I could have tried harder.

At that time there was no Scottish team manager. A committee picked the team and the majority had a West of Scotland bias. There was a divide between the West and East of Scotland, and when it came down to a vote, sometimes the West of Scotland players would get it.

I got eight caps for Scotland and, of course, I should have got more than that, but it was my fault that I never played to true form. I'm a relatively shy kind of guy and it takes me a while to get used to the surroundings I'm in and I couldn't do my best until I felt adjusted. For Scotland, you didn't get time to adjust, you were just thrown in the team and that was it.

Did he ever meet the late Eddie Cavanagh of 1966 FA Cup Final "...and he's lost his jacket, he's lost his jacket," fame? And what was the consensus of opinion among the Everton players that day regarding Eddie's pitch-invading antics – hooligan or over-enthusiastic supporter? *San Presland, New Brighton, Merseyside*

He didn't do anybody any harm. He was so happy he just wanted to run. We all know how that feels – sometimes you just need to run.

They all knew him and liked him enormously; he could be a very funny guy. He used to come and talk to lots of the players, Brian Labone and Brian Harris in particular. He was a real character and a real Scouser and a tremendous Everton supporter. He died just lately and I heard there was a huge turnout at his funeral. He will be sadly missed.

Which winger, from either side of the pitch, was the best he played alongside? *Phil Pellow, Waterloo, Liverpool*

There were some good wingers in those days. Derek Temple, John Morrissey and Alex Scott – all three of them were good wingers. John Morrissey had a bit of a slow start when he came from Liverpool, he didn't really come in until the last three or four years of his career. I played a short while with him and then I came out of the team in 1968. At that time John Morrissey was just as much an influence on the side as Bally, and that's saying something. He was a really special left-winger and as good as anyone in the First Division. Temple had sheer pace and they were great to play with.

Does he realise how many sons were named after him? I named my own son Ian Alexander and Ian named his son Andrew Alexander, and so the tradition goes on. *Mike Coville, New York, USA*

I'm absolutely flattered. I didn't know that and I feel very proud and honoured. I hope all of those boys grow up to be fine and decent men. Thank you very much.

What was his best or weirdest derby match memory? *San Presland, New Brighton, Merseyside*

I remember one terrible derby match at Anfield, it was 1964-65 and for the first time ever they beat us 5-0. Before the game, we were about sixth in the League and I think they were top.

The week before the game Harry Catterick must have panicked a bit and we were put on heavy weight training; squat thrusts like you see the weightlifters do in the Olympic Games. We were doing all these squats and thrusts and pushing iron with our legs and everybody was shattered.

Derek Temple at that time was the left-winger and he called off – I think he had a sore back from lifting the weights – and Johnny Morrissey came in. John hadn't been involved that week in the heavy training and he was the only player in the Everton team that day who could run with the Liverpool team that day and wasn't a yard short of pace.

It was 5-0 at half-time and it finished 5-0 and that was the weirdest game I've ever played. We never did the heavy weights after that.

Would he like to play in today's game with the much greater protection forwards are afforded by referees? *John Reynolds, Co Wicklow, Republic of Ireland*

There's supposed to be no tackling from behind now. Defenders do it some-times, but they get penalised. When I played in the 1950s and the '60s defenders could kick right through. I used to come off at half-time and both of my heels would be bleeding. They would put their studs down the back of your legs, and they were allowed to do that then.

The game's a lot easier now, and if the ball is played to your feet in the box defenders are frightened to tackle because a tackle from behind is going to be a penalty. It would be great to have played now with the extra protection. It would have helped a lot of the skilful players I knew in those days.

With his delicate feet, did he ever try any 'old wives' tale' remedies for his blis-ters? *San Presland, New Brighton, Merseyside*

I used to get all kinds of letters come to me suggesting things to do. One, I remember said I should pee on my feet. Others said I should try methylated spirits, and salt water – I tried everything, even the ancient cures. I used to get hundreds of letters, all wishing me well and there was none of them I didn't try because at that time I would have done anything.

How much did he used to get paid? It was 40 years ago now, so it wouldn't be breaking any confidences. *John Quinn, Tewkesbury, England*

When I was with the Hearts I was getting £20 a week plus £3 for a win. That was the maximum, no bonuses, nothing.

I went to Everton and after about two weeks, I was getting eight quid with £3 to stay over for the weekend in digs with an Everton player called Micky Lill.

I was transferred in November, and until the following July, I was on £8 and the rest of the players were getting £20, but there was nothing I could do about it because that was the rule in England if you were doing National Service.

Ask him if the height he could jump was ever measured, especially for the goal he nodded home at the Gwladys St end to clinch the title against Spurs in 1962-63? My dad reckons he was about three miles into orbit, or maybe that was my dad after the goal... *Ste Daley, Speke, Liverpool*

I never used to jump off two feet. I used to give myself one or two paces and then jump, and everybody knows that a running jump will get you higher than a standing one.

That day it was a wee bit of timing. Maybe I got the jump and run, but the ball just seemed to rise. The goalie came off his line and I just headed it over him and high into the net. That more or less put us in front and we were never headed after that.

I was obviously delighted because Tottenham were the big danger to us in the League that year. The season before they had done the Double, and it was the first time it had ever been achieved in England.

Ron Yeats – pussycat or yard dog? *Phil Pellow, Waterloo, Liverpool*

He's not a pussycat. Ron was a formidable centre-half, a big powerful guy and tremendous in the air. We used to be bosom pals, but it sort of changed a bit after one or two of his attitudes on the park after the game. He wasn't like the Ron I knew when I was in the army and he played for Dundee United, he suddenly changed into a different sort of guy, but he was never, ever a pussycat.

Did Roy Vernon really used to have a crafty smoke in the shower after training? *John Quinn, Tewkesbury, England*

He did. It's incredible, but he was the only person I ever knew who could smoke in the shower. Sometimes, when we were leaving the dressing-room, he would have a secret ciggie and flick it out halfway down the tunnel – obviously, none of the officials saw him, but he would put it in the pocket of his trousers until he came back in again. He was an awful guy for smoking the fags, and they were the ones with no tips in too.

Did he think it was a penalty in the Final against Wednesday and did he and the team believe we were dead and buried at 2-0 down? *John Quinn, Tewkesbury, England*

It was a sure-fire penalty. The goalkeeper pulled my instep. I'd taken the ball past the goalie and it was going to be a narrow thing for me to get to the ball and then just roll it into an empty net, but on my last step he pulled my foot away. There was no use appealing; the referee had made his decision.

Immediately you go 2-0 down in a game you feel dead and buried, but fortunately we got one back relatively quickly, and when we got one we knew we were going to get more. I think we may have been the only team who's been 2–0 down and gone on and won it.

Overlooking for the moment the blatant 'non-penalty' award in the 1966 Cup Final, what did he think of the referees at the time compared with today? *San Presland, New Brighton, Merseyside*

The referee in the Cup Final seemed to be running behind the play all the time, and right through the game he gave us a bit of a hard time – in fact, if he gave us anything at all, it was grudgingly. I think they're fitter and more athletic these days than they were back then.

I would like to know whether he thought Catterick was right to drop him in favour of Joe Royle against Blackpool. *Mike Coville, New York, USA*

Joe is one of the nicest guys I've ever met in football. He was a young lad then, and maybe they put him in too quickly, but I came back in again and we won the Cup that year. I felt sorry for Joe in that game, but he proved his worth in the side and he went on to be a terrific centre-forward at Everton. He played differently to me, but we were always friendly and I was never jealous of Joe or angry with him.

A certain Alan Ball scored for Blackpool on that same sad day (we lost 2-1). If you were with the team, did you see anything special about him back then, or did you ever think he was special? *Tommy Davis, Texas, USA*

I wasn't there that day. I was back at Goodison with the Reserves, so I didn't see the game. I hadn't seen much of Alan then because I think Blackpool were in the Second Division. I saw plenty of him when he came to Everton, though. He was a terrific player, a dear friend, a great signing for Everton and a pleasure to play alongside.

One more link to that day that will live in infamy with many older Blues was the incident with Harry Catterick being 'assaulted'. To me, it looked like a harmless scuffle, with HC slipping on the ice. Did Alex see it and what did he think? *Tommy Davis, Texas, USA*

Whoever said that has got it 100 per cent right. I wasn't there, but I've spoken to a few of the players who were. One of them was Brian Labone, who quite liked Harry Catterick. He said nobody touched him; he slipped and fell on the ground then got himself up. Catterick said hooligans assaulted him and he said the next week he would bring what he called the hooligans' team, which meant Gordon West and Jimmy Gabriel and myself were back in the side.

We went about 18 games undefeated and we won the Cup that year. The story from all the players that were there said that nobody assaulted Harry Catterick, he slipped and fell. Maybe somebody jostled him, but it wasn't any real assault.

Did he feel his Goodison career was over when Fred Pickering scored a hat-trick on his debut? *John Quinn, Tewkesbury, England*

Yes. I didn't know Fred was coming, obviously, but the week before we'd played at Tottenham. We won 4-2 and I scored two, so I was quite pleased with that, and then along came Fred. I met him and really liked him, and when he left the club I was still there.

I was disappointed that Harry didn't say anything to me. He just put the team sheet up and I was put in the reserve side at Nottingham Forest. That was the thing that upset me the most – the silence. I was suddenly in the reserve side and he never even said a word.

What was his best goal, and why? *Mike Coville, New York, USA*

One of the goals I enjoyed the most was a home game not long before I left and we were kicking away from the Gwladys Street end. We were playing West Ham, Bobby Moore was in the team and they were a good side.

We were on top in this game and I was playing wide right, number-seven. Everton suddenly got the ball in the middle of their half and pushed right up to the half way line. It was chipped over the back four, right over Bobby Moore's head. It was a similar type goal that David Beckham scores now. The goalie had come out, so I hit it high and to see the ball rolling into an empty net made it one of the goals I enjoyed most. Oh, yes, I liked that one!

Which team does he support? I have always wondered. *John Quinn, Tewkesbury, England*

My father's team was Motherwell, so when I was a little lad it was Motherwell for me, too. I didn't much care for the Hearts, but after a wee while I became acclimatised to the team and I began to like them. Then I arrived at Everton. I knew that Everton was the team for me, and to this day Everton is the team I follow and support and it's always the first result I look for.

Over the seasons, who has caught his eye at Goodison? *Pete Rowlands, Enfield, North London*

I admire players who have grit and determination in the way they play. Dave Watson is one, and so is Neville Southall – who wouldn't want to go and see him? I like to watch skilful football. We've not really had a great deal of skilful players, in the last few years to be honest but I want to see them winning and I always give players the benefit of the doubt.

Howard's 80s side – 83-4-5 – was the best Everton side of the whole lot. They played attractive football and they had quite a few players I enjoyed watching. Kevin Sheedy I really liked, he had a magical left foot, and Andy Gray, of course, did a terrific job.

It was a magnificent team and so unlucky. They were going to rule Europe and win all the trophies, but we were banned after the Heysel disaster and the team broke up. Players went different ways and it was a very sad episode.

What did he think of the 'Tony Kay Affair'? *San Presland, New Brighton, Merseyside*

I was very sad about Tony. He was a terrific player when he came to Everton and I really felt sorry for him. He swears that he never took any bribes, he told me that and I believe him.

The week before he had been talking to a guy in a club and told him that we sometimes struggled at Ipswich because they were a very good side. Everybody knew at that time that Ipswich were one of the hardest teams to play, especially on their home ground. Tony got nine out of ten in *The People* that day for his performance, he played his heart out and after the game he went back to the nightclub in Sheffield.

This guy gave him 50 quid and said to him: "Thanks for the information, Tony." Tony was about 18 or 20 then, so it was a lot of money to him and he took it. It wasn't as a bribe; he thought it was a present. That's what Tony Kay told me, and I believe him.

What tips would he now give to someone like Cadamarteri, who is a genuine player, on how to beat a defender? Is this teachable? *Ian Bonnar, Plaistow, East London*

It's hard for me to give advice to young Danny. In the last few games he's come on as substitute and he looks as if he's playing a bit better wide right. He seems to be very effective and he turned the game in one I saw on television.

Players are all different and lots of Danny's game is based on pace. I couldn't tell him how to control or how to beat a man. I think he would just have to practise things. He has one of the main things needed, nowadays, and that is his genuine pace. He just has to really, really practise his short passes and close control and he'll become a good player.

Does he know where George Thomson is these days? *Phil Pellow, Waterloo, Liverpool*

I wish I did know where he is, he owes me some money!

I've not seen him since about 1971, which is almost 30 years. I've heard he's down in Liverpool occasionally, and I've heard he's in Blackpool and sometimes in Edinburgh, but I've not seen George. We were transferred at the same time and he was a good friend of mine, but where he is now I honestly don't know.

Who would win in the following fights? *Frank Hargreaves, Anfield, Liverpool*
Brian Labone against Ron Yeats:

In a football fight or a scrap? I don't know. Yeatsey was a fantastically strong guy and Brian was a gentleman and a nice guy. I was with Yeatsey for a year and a half in the army, but before that he used to work in a slaughterhouse up in Aberdeen. He used to kill the bulls by hitting them on the head with something – enough said.

Alex Young against Roger Hunt:

We were different sorts of players altogether. Roger Hunt was excellent. He had good pace and was really strong, stocky, powerful and a formidable player. Lots of people never noticed it, but Roger Hunt was a terrific striker of the ball and Ian St John really rated him.

Alex Young against Ian St John:

The same sort of thing, similar heights, but Ian was a bit more powerfully built and he would rough and tumble a bit more than me. It's no use if your 5ft 8ins and 10st 10lbs going roughing it about with guys who are 6ft 2ins and 14st – it doesn't make sense. You try to beat them with skill and a bit of pace.

Ian and I had relatively similar heading styles and he was very good in the air, too. He was good on the floor and had great control, but one of the things that Ian had over me was confidence. I had to surf for confidence sometimes for games, and how I felt affected my game. Ian was the type of lad who oozed confidence and nothing seemed to bother him. Even when he appeared on television it was no bother to him, but I could never have done that.

I was fortunate to witness what must have been one of your last games, and that was a semi-final appearance against Leeds at Old Trafford. You came on as a sub and mesmerized us all with a run down the wing, and then you just trapped the ball against the corner-flag so that, I think it was Paul Reaney, couldn't get the ball back into play. Johnny Morrissey used to try the same trick, so I am sure you must have taught it to him, but the question is: Did you feel that you finished too early and that you could have played on a bit longer, or was it an injury-enforced retirement? *Tony Field, Rotterdam, Holland*

That wasn't my last game against Leeds. My last one was at Goodison against Coventry. I think we beat them 4-1 and I had a good outing, but I didn't know that it was going to be my last game. The following week I was taken into the manager's office and they told me I wasn't going to be played that week, but I was going to be coming back into the team because I'd done well on the Saturday. But it was the last game I played.

From about 26 or 27 I had a knee injury, trouble with my ligaments, but there was another thing that people don't know and I've never really said much about it. It must have been happening for years before, but from about 24 I gradually became deaf. The last three or four years especially, I couldn't hear much at all. When you're playing football the players are shouting all the time: "Watch your back, man on, give us the ball," and I couldn't hear those shouts. I was looking around a lot over my shoulder and that curbed it a bit, but the main thing was my knee injury, maybe deafness and the fact that I was forced out.

I remember coming home from the Cup Final in 1984 and sitting down to watch the full three hours of *Grandstand* – breakfast with the lads, Wembley Way and the big build-up. There was a fine piece with Eddie Cavanagh recounting '66, but then it all changed, went a little moody and a little blond-haired girl was asked: "What does your Daddy do?"
"Play football," came the reply.
Then, interspersed with her confirmation that she was the daughter of the 'Vision', was the most haunting music and a man who seemed to be moving alone between Subbuteo players fixed to the pitch. It was enough to bring a tear to a glass eye. How is your daughter, and send her our regards. *Frank Hargreaves, Anfield, Liverpool*

Jane has grown into a very pretty woman. She's slim, still looks good and is in excellent health. We live about half a mile apart and she has three daughters of her own now, Charlotte, Becky and Abi.

I've got a copy of *The Golden Vision* and it does me good to see it once in a while. I didn't know it had even been made at the time, so it was a complete surprise to me, but my daughter came across well and I was so pleased with it.

Which game stands out in his memory when he reminisces about his career?
Mike Coville, New York, USA

The game against Tottenham, which was magnificent, and to score a goal which more or less let us go on to win the League was fantastic, but I think maybe clinching the League championship, one of the last games of the season. We won the League by a load of points, but against Fulham we clinched the title – that was a fantastic day. There was an unbelievable crowd at Goodison that day, there must have been 60,000 at the game and there was the usual tremendous atmosphere.

The games I loved most of all were at Everton. I played my best football then. I played some good games when I was at Hearts when I was 23, but between 23 and 26 I was in my prime at Everton. But things happen, and when I should have done better some things went wrong and my knee injury curbed my career.

According to my records, he scored the winner in the FA Cup Final against Newcastle on 21 April 1906, but I've never seen a description of the goal. Could he take me through it step by step? *Billy Williams, Cologne, Germany*

I didn't know there was another Alex Young until I got there. It's a strange coincidence because it's not a common name. I heard some of the older guys talking about Sandy Young, but I didn't meet him and I haven't even seen any pictures of him, but it's certainly strange.

Did – or does – he ever hold any management aspirations? *Iain Cooke, Basel, Switzerland.* **Why stop there? He's only 63, surely he could still pull his boots on for us?** *Ken Myers, California, USA*

I had to finish when I was 31 with the knee injury. That was still quite young and I was shattered about it. I felt I might have been able to do it quite well in management, and I had a little shot of it in Northern Ireland, but I found after a while that it wasn't really for me. I decided to try something outside football and I started a new company, and when you do something else the years just fly by and your days for management are past.

Does he still have a furniture shop in Stockbridge in Edinburgh? If so, where is it? I tried to find it when I lived there and never could. *Mark Kenyon, Minnesota, USA*

Lots of people think I've got a furniture shop, but I was always a wholesaler in soft furnishings and I supply lots of things to the soft-furnishings market, like curtain poles, tracks, tapes and hooks and accessories for the upholstery and carpet trade. It's not called after my name, it's called Richard Wylie Ltd. It's reasonably well known in Edinburgh as a wholesaler in Scotland and certain parts of England, but hardly anybody knows that I started the business, I'm the major shareholder and I still work there.

Does he think that with the money players can earn today they can never have the same kind of bond with the fans that he had? *Ian Bonnar, Plaistow, East London*

Maybe not. I think there is some kind of bond, but I think the fans are thinking these guys are making 25 grand a week whereas lots of the times I played at Everton, especially when I first started, the fans were making more money than me.

I think there was more of a bond then when the supporters realised the players weren't getting a lot of money. That way they were playing for a living and trying their best for the team, and maybe there was a feeling that they weren't money-grabbing.

Even though the players are getting plenty of money now, they're still trying their best and playing some great football, but I think the bond isn't there as it was before.

During his career (many) players were underpaid and exploited. Now they're paid massive salaries with the power to hold clubs to ransom. Have things gone too far? *John Reynolds, Co Wicklow, Republic of Ireland*

I think it has, yes. I think the better and more skilled players now can hold a gun to the head of their clubs. I think this Bosman ruling is helping the elite at the top of the Leagues and pushing the others further down. All the money is going up to the few who are getting unrealistic sums of money and the Bosman ruling was the turning-point.

Is there anyone in the game today whom he admires for their style and talent, or does he think that the increased athleticism and speed of the game is making it harder for unusual talents to shine? *Neil Wolstenholme, Chelsea, South-West London*

The one I think of right away is Harry Kewell at Leeds; he's got a special talent. David Beckham is a terrific player, as is Andy Cole.

I think, bit-by-bit, the players are becoming more athletic. They've got a good diet now. I was brought up during the war when there wasn't a lot of food about. I think they're gradually getting stronger, more competitive and faster, and their training methods are improving. The game is stepping forward all the time. It's very tough to maintain the levels of fitness needed nowadays, but they're on so much money I don't think they care about that.

Would he like to reiterate his stance on the magic of Goodison Park just so I can hear it again? It kept me going in the GFE dark days. *Frank Hargreaves, Anfield, Liverpool*

Goodison Park, to me, just seems to be a magical place, like when you go into certain houses where the great ghosts have been. There was something there that made the back of my neck tingle when I ran on to the pitch for Everton, even when the place was empty.

It's still the same whenever I visit. That tingle is still there – you can feel the vibes from the fans. I loved playing at home, and that's why the majority of the games when I really turned it on were at Goodison Park. I could feel the good-will coming from the fans.

I felt it again in February when I was down for the Millennium Presentation. I won an award and my wife, Nancy, came on the park with me and she said it made her millennium. It was the greatest thrill she's ever had, going on the pitch with a 35,000 or 40,000 crowd and everybody wishing us well.

For me it's a magical place and the best place I've ever played football, and I'll never, ever forget it.

Could he put his boots back on just one more time so that I could say I saw him play? *Mark Kenyon, Minnesota, USA*
I would dearly love to do that, but, unfortunately, the ravages of time have taken their toll. I don't think I would dare to try. It would be lovely to be able to turn the clock back, though.

Did he realise just how much of an icon he had become while at Everton? Does he realise that he still is? *Pete Rowlands, Enfield, North London*
It has dawned on me now, and I thank everybody for that. To be remembered after such a long time – I'm gobsmacked, sometimes. I visit Goodison about three or four times a year and I stay with friends. My pal is Mike Pender, who's the lead singer in The Searchers. We've known each other for about 35 years and our wives are great friends, too.

There's something about Liverpool that I love, and I really appreciate that they've been so kind to remember me. They accepted me right from the very start and I'll never forget that. I always love going down to Goodison. I feel as if I'm going back home again.

How much does he think he would be worth on today's transfer market? *Ian Bonnar, Plaistow, East London*
I've honestly got no idea. It would be nice if I was worth a million and I could get ten per cent of that if they sold me. I'd be quite happy with that.

I think we could manage that!
Alex Young, a gentleman of the highest order, thank you.

Index

Adams, Tony 117
Adamson, Jimmy 47
Alcock, Paul 111
Aldridge, John 150
Amokachi 131
Anderlecht 106, 114
Arnold, Jim 151
Arsenal 26, 32, 34, 65, 72, 96, 103, 144, 162
Aston Villa 22, 57, 60, 66, 107, 134, 138
Athletic Bilbao 84
Atkins, Ian 139
Atkinson, Ron 123, 138
Bailey, John 54, 154, 164
Bakayoko 113
Ball, Alan 5, 13, 15, 17, 19, 21-22, 25, 28-33, 35, 78-79, 82, 109, 177
Ball, Michael 93
Banks, Gordon 101
Barcelona 60, 83, 165
Barmby, Nick 74, 113
Barnes, John 148
Barnwell, John 48, 107
Barrett, Earl 166
Barrow 162, 167
Bayern Munich 24, 42, 55, 124, 149, 153
Beagrie, Peter 157, 161
Beckham, David 116, 143, 178, 182
Belfitt, Rod 17
Bell, Colin 80
Bellefield 171
Bennett, Harry 33
Best, George 37-38, 82
Bilic, Slaven 88
Bingham, Billy 106
Birmingham City 82, 120
Bishop, Pedro 60
Blackburn Rovers 98

Blackpool 20, 24, 28-29, 31, 99, 128, 148, 177, 179
Blake, Nathan 66
Bolton Wanderers 50, 82, 169
Bolton Wanderers Academy 169
Bonetti, Peter 102
Borrows, Brian 164
Boulder, Bob 159
Bournemouth 128-129
Bracewell, Paul 5, 37-39, 41, 136, 170
Bradford City 27, 64, 138, 156-157
Brady, Liam 145
Brighton & Hove Albion 133
Britton, Cliff 16
Brown, Bill 27
Brown, Craig 161
Burnley 43, 47-51, 74, 79, 82, 90, 92, 95, 98, 160
Burns, Kenny 58, 137
Bury 151, 159
Busby Babes 21
Butcher, John 151
Cadamarteri, Danny 23, 179
Callaghan, Ian 100, 102
Cambridge City 91
Cardiff City 108, 111
Carlisle United 124
Carter, Philip 61, 92
Case, Jimmy 48
Catterick, Harry 28, 32-34, 79, 96-97, 99, 105, 172, 175, 177
Cavanagh, Eddie 135, 174, 180
Celtic 169
Charlton, Bobby 18
Charlton, Jack 35, 100, 145-146, 148
Chedgzoy, Sam 16
Chelsea 15, 25-26, 32, 45, 65, 107, 110, 115-116, 144
Chicago Sting 116
Claridge, Steve 112

Clarke, Alan 109, 114
Clough, Brian 112, 114, 116, 160
Coeck, Ludo 115
Cole, Andy 182
Collins, Bobby 25
Collins, John 138
Cook, Harry 141
Coton, Tony 92
Cottee, Tony 73, 136, 160
Coventry City 26, 108
Cox, Arthur 41
Cresswell, Warney 16
Crystal Palace 60, 85
Dalglish, Kenny 94
Darracott, Terry 56, 89
Davies, Roger 79
Davies, Wynne 96
Davis, Dai 44
Dawson, Alex 81
Dean, Dixie 16, 78, 172
Derby County 79, 82
Dobson, Martin 5, 43, 45-47, 49, 51, 125
Dorigo, Tony 148
Dublin, Dion 90-91
Dumbarton 133-134
Dundee United 55, 67-68, 134, 169, 176
Dunford, Michael 9
Ebbrell, John 93, 159
Edinburgh 179, 181-182
Edwards, Leslie 172
European Championships 146
European Cup 13, 18, 21, 54, 71, 84-85,
    116, 122, 124, 127, 142, 148
Evertonian, The 81, 124, 135
FA Cup 14, 19-22, 24-26, 34, 37, 50, 54-
    56, 63, 68, 70, 72, 78-79, 85, 89, 108,
    110-111, 121, 124, 127, 129-130, 134,
    147, 149, 155-156, 168, 174, 181
Falco, Mark 142
Farrelly, Gareth 75
Fazakerley, Derek 41
Fenwick, Terry 124
Ferdinand, Les 153
Ferguson, Sir Alex 91, 132
Ferguson, Duncan 67-68, 168

Finney, Tom 171
Football Echo 23
Fulham 33-34, 41, 181
Gabriel, Jimmy 17, 79, 85, 98, 177
Gallagher, Kirsty 64
Gascoigne, Paul 115
Guardian, The 25
Genoa 146
Gerrard, Paul 103, 158, 160
Giggs, Ryan 154
Giles, Johnny 81
Gillingham 63
Ginola, David 111
Glasgow Rangers 67-68, 76, 95, 138,
    164, 167-170
Gough, Richard 50, 76, 121
Gowling, Alan 108
Gray, Andy 5, 13, 19, 21, 52-55, 57, 59-
    61, 63, 65, 67, 69-71, 86, 88-89, 91,
    93, 121, 124, 126, 134-135, 137-138,
    147, 154, 165, 178
Grobbelaar, Bruce 125
Gullit, Ruud 60
Haan, Arie 115
Hamilton, Bryan 50
Hansen, Alan 57, 137
Harford, Mick 120
Harper, Alan 40, 126
Harris, Brian 97-98, 174
Hartford, Asa 134
Harvey, Colin 14, 36, 79, 81, 88, 92,
    133-135, 138, 147, 150, 155, 162-
    163, 168
Heath, Adrian 5, 27, 69, 71, 73, 75, 77,
    136, 141-142
Hickson, Dave 16, 21, 96, 172
Higgins, Mark 71
Hill, Gordon 110
Hill, Jimmy 57
Hill, Ricky 121, 165
Hinchcliffe, Andy 93
Hoddle, Glenn 84
Horne, Barry 130-131
Huddersfield Town 156
Hughes, David 49

Hughes, Emlyn 13
Hughes, Mark 76, 157
Hunt, Roger 29, 179
Hunter, Norman 81
Hurst, Geoff 31
Hurst, John 80-81
Husband, Jimmy 25
Hutchison, Don 39, 113
Ince, Paul 130-131
Ipswich Town 121-122, 143, 149, 165, 179
Jackson, Matt 154, 166
James, Leighton 48
Jennings, Pat 151, 162
Jewell, Paul 157
Johnson, Peter 27, 61-63, 65, 91-92, 132, 155
Jones, Davey 46
Jones, Tommy G. 97
Kanchelskis, Andrei 23, 130-131
Kay, Tony 23, 30, 97-98, 178-179
Keane, Roy 98
Keegan, Kevin 47, 150
Keflavik FC 25
Kendall, Howard 5, 7, 9, 27, 52, 63, 69, 75, 78-81, 83, 85, 87, 89, 91, 93, 95, 121-123, 136, 141, 151, 162, 166
Kenny, Billy Jnr 93
Kenwright, Bill 61, 63, 92, 113, 132
Kenyon, Roger 101
Keown, Martin 90
Kewell, Harry 182
Keys, Richard 61
Kidd, Brian 134
King, Andy 15, 26, 46, 108, 117, 119
Kirkwood, Danny 20
Knowles, Peter 17, 98
Knox, Archie 67
Labone, Brian 5, 17, 85, 96-97, 99, 101, 103, 105, 124-125, 174, 177, 179
Latchford, Bob 13, 15, 23, 25, 45, 82, 107-109, 114, 119, 127, 134
Law, Denis 109
Lawton, Tommy 16, 172
Le Tissier, Matt 152

Lee, Gordon 44, 46-47, 49, 106-108, 110-116
Leeds United 81
Leicester City 57
Lever, Peter 49, 80
Lill, Micky 175
Limpar, Anders 128, 131
Lineker, Gary 17, 41, 59-60, 70, 72, 87-88, 136, 165
Littlewoods Cup 166
Liverpool Echo 82, 97, 172
Lloyd, Clive 49
Lloyd, David 49
Lloyd, Larry 58, 137
Luton Town 120
Lynex, Steve 57
Lyons, Mick 17, 19, 26, 108, 115, 119, 127
Macari, Lou 48, 110
McCall, Stuart 17, 73
McCann, Gavin 85
McClean, Jim 55
McGracken, John 152
McIlvenny, Hugh 108
Mackay, Dave 30, 112, 114, 171, 173
McKenzie, Duncan 5, 14, 18, 44, 47, 106-109, 111, 113, 115, 117-118
McMahon, Steve 139, 146
Manchester City 58, 75, 84
Manchester United 42, 56, 65, 80, 91, 144, 154
Marsh, Dr David 91-92
Marsh, Rodney 80, 113
Martin, Alvin 124
Martyn, Nigel 155, 160
Marwood, Brian 69, 71
Matthews, Sir Stanley 171
Mears, Brian 115
Mercer, Joe 16, 50, 78
Milk Cup Final 59, 134, 147
Milne, Gordon 79
Milne, Jimmy 79
Molby, Jan 166
Moore, Bobby 80, 178
Moore, Brian 116
Moran, Kevin 144

Morrissey, Johnny 13, 32-34, 98, 174-175, 180
Motherwell 178
Mountfield, Derek 5, 71-72, 88, 119-121, 123, 125, 127, 166
Myrhe, Tommy 103
Neal, Phil 147
Neville, Gary 165
Nevin, Paddy 86
Newcastle United 96, 150
Newell, Mike 90
Newton, Keith 102
Noon, Keith 47
Nottingham Forest 18, 42, 112, 133, 178
Notts County 53, 89, 147
Nulty, Geoff 48, 108
Observer, The 108
Oldham Athletic 138
Oster, John 75
Owen, Michael 115
Paige, Jimmy 94
Palermo 146
Parkinson, Joe 5, 128-129, 131
Parkes, Phil 47
Pearson, Jim 114
Pejic, Mick 111
Pele 81
Pembridge, Mark 18
Pender, Mike 183
Peyton, Jerry 159
Pickering, Fred 33, 177
Pink Echo 126
Pleat, David 160
Pointon, Neil 92
Port Vale 46, 152
Portsmouth 72
QPR 16, 47, 57, 145, 153
Question of Sport 60
Rae, Alex 76
Ramsey, Alf 35, 50, 80, 100-101, 104
Rapid Vienna 55, 86, 102, 149
Ratcliffe, Kevin 22, 85, 87, 102, 120, 126, 139, 143, 152, 154
Ready Steady Cook 27
Reaney, Paul 107, 180

Reid, Mike 111
Reid, Peter 37, 53, 58, 67, 70-71, 75, 85, 88-89, 126, 136, 138, 143, 170
Rensenbrink, Rob 115
Revie, Don 28-29, 31, 50, 81, 111, 114
Richardson, Kevin 40
Rijkard, Frank 60
Rioch, Bruce 106, 108
Roberts, Graham 137
Robson, Bobby 70
Robson, Bryan 67, 93
Robson, Ken 100
Rogers, Ted 142
Ross, Trevor 46, 115
Royle, Joe 19, 33, 88, 99, 108, 113, 128-129, 131, 177
Rudge, John 152
Rush, Ian 153
Samways, Vinny 131
St John, Ian 179
Saunders, Dean 157
Schmeichel, Peter 64
Scholes, Paul 32
Scott, Alex 33, 174
Seaman, David 160
Shankly, Bill 78
Sharp, Graeme 15, 21, 53, 56, 58, 68-69, 88, 125, 133, 135, 137, 139-142, 154
Sharp, Lee 130
Sheedy, Kevin 5, 21, 24, 39, 72-73, 87, 120, 122, 135, 141, 143, 145, 147, 149-150, 166, 178
Sheffield United 84, 90-91, 93
Sheffield University EFC Supporters Club 15
Sheffield Wednesday 38, 60, 69-70, 90, 105
Shepardson, Harold 104
Shilton, Peter 45, 111, 146, 166
Shrewsbury Town 85
Simmons, Jack 49
Singapore Evertonians Supporters Club 19
Sinstadt, Gerald 14

Smith, Denis 108
Smith, Tommy 29, 111, 114
Smith, Walter 77, 113, 138, 168
Snodin, Ian 40, 147
Souness, Graeme 67
Southall, Neville 5, 9, 13, 15, 17, 24, 41,
    63, 73, 82, 122, 124, 151, 153, 155,
    157, 159, 161, 178
Southampton 19, 33, 37, 72, 79, 81, 152
Speed, Gary 74, 94
Sporting Triangles 60
Starr, Freddie 52-53, 58
Steaua Bucharest 148
Steven, Trevor 25, 38, 40, 48, 54, 69, 72,
    76, 86-87, 120, 136, 152, 163-164,
    167
Stevens, Gary 5, 41, 71, 76, 86, 89, 126,
    146, 154, 162-163, 165, 167, 169-170
Stoke City 15, 19, 45, 49, 69, 94
Stuart, Graham 26
Styles, Archie 82
Sunderland 22, 40, 71, 76, 82, 85-86,
    124
Super Cup 161
Supporters Club of South Africa 24
Swales, Peter 84
Swindon Town 46
Taylor, Graham 84, 123
Temple, Derek 23, 98, 174-175
Thomas, Clive 17, 43, 110-111
Thomas, Dave 46, 48, 114
Thomas, Michael 19
Thompson, Peter 79
Thompson, Phil 13
Thomson, George 179
Tranmere Rovers 119, 150
Tulsa Roughnecks 116
UEFA Cup 71, 87
Unsworth, Dave 112
Van den Hauwe, Pat 69, 87, 121, 126,
    143-144, 164
Venables, Terry 83
Vernon, Roy 33, 173, 176
Wakenshaw, Robbie 165
Walker, Mike 128-129

Watson, Dave 58, 63, 85, 122, 125-126,
    154, 178
Watson, Gordon 97
Weaver, Nicky 155, 157
Weir, David 113
Wembley 20-21, 34, 50, 54, 70, 80, 83,
    87, 89, 121, 130, 142, 145, 147, 155,
    163, 180
West, Gordon 20-21, 31-32, 97, 103-104,
    173, 177
West Bromwich Albion 93
West Ham United 25, 87, 94, 135, 178
Whelan, Ronnie 135
Whitehurst, Billy 42
Williams, Robin 17
Williamson, Brian 107
Wilson, Davey 79
Wilson, Ray 124-125
Wood, George 103
World Cup Finals 96, 146, 148, 157
Wright, Bernie 17
Wright, Ian 153
Wright, Richard 155
Wright, Tommy 54
Yeats, Ron 176, 179
Yorke, Dwight 117
Young, Alex 5, 21, 23-24, 30, 33, 78, 85,
    99, 139, 171, 173, 175, 177, 179, 181,
    183